James B. Angell

From the Author,

Dec. 25. 1856

ESSAY

ON

LANGUAGE,

AND

Other Papers,

BY

ROWLAND G. HAZARD.

EDITED BY E. P. PEABODY.

BOSTON:
PHILLIPS, SAMPSON AND COMPANY.
1857.

Stereotyped by
HOBART & ROBBINS,
New England Type and Stereotype Foundery,
BOSTON.

EDITOR'S PREFACE.

The collection of Mr. Hazard's writings, now offered to the public, has been made at the earnest instance of his friends. Most of these papers, called forth by occasions, have been rather printed than published, heretofore. They were the productions not even of the leisure of their author; for he has had no leisure — having been always entirely engaged with a very extensive manufacturing and mercantile business.

It is of the Essay on Language, which begins the collection, that the late William E. Channing, D.D., speaks in the following paragraph of his lecture on Self-culture: "I have known a man of vigorous intellect, who had enjoyed few advantages of early education, and whose mind was almost engrossed by the details of an extensive business, but who composed a book, of much original thought, in steamboats and on horseback, while visiting distant customers."

The editor of these papers remembers Dr. Channing's reading of this essay, when it was first published; and his efforts to discover the anonymous author, whose want of literary experience, evinced in the composition of it, was an interesting contrast, he thought, with his extraordinary powers of delicate observation and analysis, in a region only to be penetrated at all by the gifted of intellect and the pure in heart. And when he discovered Mr. Hazard, he rejoiced in him, as the representative of a class of men peculiar, perhaps, to America, and which he hoped would increase in numbers, who are to convince the world that the practical and intellectual developments of the mind are not incompatible, but may even aid each other.

Mr. Hazard, therefore, concludes to leave this maiden essay of his philosophic muse in the undress of its youth; for it is dear to him, not only as his first attempt at composition, but because it did possess a charm, that gained for him the acquaintance of that distinguished man, who (as the editor knows), having sought and found him for its sake, cherished him, to the end of his life, as one of the most valued of his intellectual friends.

The Essay on the Philosophical Character of Channing was written in answer to an appeal, from the family of the latter, to furnish an analysis for the use of his biographer. The request was founded on their observation of the fact that Mr. Hazard always drew him out, in conversation upon philosophical subjects, more than any other person; and the essay, when written, was soon after printed, also at their suggestion.

The occasions of the other essays, which were all lectures, show the value which the citizens of Rhode Island set upon Mr. Hazard's opinions, on all subjects, from the Pan-Idea of Judge Durfee, to the practical duties of governments and individuals. Mr. Hazard's absorption in business, though felt by his friends to be rather a waste of rare powers, intrinsically enhances the value of whatever he does get time to express.

For, while soaring into the empyrean of thought, his essays are not the idle flights of a visionary, but the insights of a practical mind, at work on themes which the practical too often think to be out of their sphere. They show that it is not intrinsically incompatible with doing the work of this world, to inhabit as a home the higher world of principle and eternal law; but that the former may even be done more successfully, while the latter is made manifest in "thoughts that breathe, and words that burn."

We hope, in another year, to publish a volume, on subjects more obviously — though not more really — practical, than the papers which make up this volume.

CONTENTS.

LANGUAGE.

The importance of language is at once obvious to every individual, and yet perhaps few are aware of the full extent of the advantages which we derive from it: advantages coëxtensive with knowledge, coëqual with the improvement of mankind. Language is the means by which soul acts and reacts on soul. By it the heavenly spark of thought, emanating from the solitary mind, inspires each kindred breast, wakes the slumbering fire and lights the torch of truth, which is reflected from a thousand other minds, with fresh accessions, until its light pervades the whole atmosphere, dissipates the darkness of prejudice, infuses itself into popular impressions, and gives distinctness to the views and opinions of the public. It not only enables every individual to avail himself of the intellectual labors of all others, but it furnishes him with one mode of thinking for himself, and of condensing into general propositions the mental acquirements, which, if left in particulars, would soon become too numerous for memory to retain, or so burdensome as greatly to retard his further progress. It is one of the distinguishing characteristics of man, and it appears not improbable that to this endowment we owe a large portion of the accumulation of knowledge, power of reasoning, and greater susceptibility of improvement, which exalts our species above the brute creation.

It has enabled man to form the social compact, and it is a form of words, that, by protecting him from injury, and guaranteeing to him the undisturbed enjoyment of the possessions, the comforts, and pleasures of life, obviates the necessity of a constant savage watchfulness, permitting him, with feelings of security, to abstract himself from the narrow concerns of organic existence, and range in the beautiful and illimitable fields of thought. It has thus enabled the contemplative mind to unite the opportunities of improvement and the stimulus to exertion which are found in the charms of society, with the tranquillity of solitude and seclusion. It has given mankind the power of retaining all that the past has acquired, and of circulating it combined with all that the present can bestow; thus adding discovery to discovery; improvement to improvement; refinement to refinement; continually vivifying existence with fresh cultivation; keeping alive the germ of infinity in the soul; elevating and ennobling its conceptions; and fostering and encouraging the tendency to illimitable expansion in all the powers of the mind.

But it is needless to expatiate on the importance of language, it being so obviously and so essentially connected with all that ennobles our race.

We proceed, then, to the consideration of some of the various forms which it assumes, among which we regard poetry as properly occupying the first place in point of time, as well as of interest. Various attempts have been made to define this form of language. Of these, the notice of one of the most prominent will be sufficient, as the others, so far as we know them, are at least equally defective.

Aristotle says that "poetry is an imitative art." The high idea which we entertain of the critical accuracy of this great philosopher induces us to suppose that he may have intended to imply, by this assertion, that the poetic art is, in this respect, similar to many others, rather than that it is thus contradistinguished from them. The magic of a great name has, however, wrought its charm, and imposed this statement upon us as a definition. A late writer imagines he has perfected it, and that poetry may properly be defined an imitative *and creative art*. Even with this addition, poetry is hardly distinguished from many merely mechanical operations; and if by poetry is meant the *production* of the poet, the definition is wholly inapplicable.

The difficulty of determining the precise boundary between poetry and prose, and of ascertaining their distinguishing characteristics, probably arises from the fact, that, as usually exhibited, most, or perhaps all of the attributes of each, are found blended with those of the other, varying only in degree. It is in this variation, then, that we must seek the materials for a definition.

We use the term language as applicable to every method of imparting ideas, and by the term *signs* we mean to embrace not only words, but every other representative of ideas.

A language of *words*, that is, of sounds which we produce by the organs of speech, or symbols which we commit to paper, has been adopted, as the usual and best means of communicating our thoughts. If we carefully observe the operation of the mind in this process of communication, we shall find that there is an incipient stage of our thoughts before they are connected with words. In this state thoughts might be called ideas, or images. The latter, however, is not without its objections in this application, and the word idea, though it may be strictly applicable, is yet so vaguely associated with thoughts which have already assumed the form of words, that we deem it necessary to apply another term, more clearly to designate our mental perceptions in this incipient state, and keep them distinct as objects of thought from the words with which they are ultimately united. We will, then, call them *ideals* or *primitive perceptions*, by which terms we mean to signify impressions of things, and all the images, sensations, and emotions of the mind, which are really independent of words, and, having a separate and prior existence, induce us to put them into language, in order to impart our knowledge of them to others, as well as to enable us to compare them with each other in our own mind. One person sees a landscape, and the impression it makes on his mind is an ideal. The emotions associated with it are also ideals, or primitive perceptions. He seeks corresponding terms, and describes the scenery to another, whose mind also receives an ideal of it, together with such associated emotions as the circumstances excite, and these are also ideals; for, though in him the *effect* of language, they are still as distinguishable from the terms, or signs, as any other effect from its cause.

The communication of our thoughts, then, is effected by each one associating the same sounds or signs with the same ideals, so that the right use of them will produce the same primitive perceptions, in the mind of the hearer, as exist in that of the speaker. In the outset, therefore, we observe that ideals and their signs are separate objects of thought, and it is in the different degrees in which they are respectively made the objects of attention, that we may reasonably expect to find the elements of the changes and modifications of which language is susceptible.

The first and most obvious use of language is to express simple facts,—to tell our wants and narrate the occurrences which observation has collected. This we shall call the *language of narration.* The use of it requires no effort of imagination, or of the reasoning powers, on the part of either the speaker or hearer, but simply an exercise of the memory in recalling events, and producing the proper associations between the sounds and their concomitants. Departing from this simplicity on the one hand, by dismissing, as far as practicable, the ideals, and directing the attention exclusively to the terms, we arrive at a mode which we shall call the *language of abstraction.*

If, on the other hand, the terms are so managed that the attention is directed principally to the ideals they call up, or when, instead of the immediate connection between words and ideals, the associations between the ideals themselves are the objects of attention, we arrive at a mode, the very reverse of the former, which may be denominated the language of ideality, or primitive perceptions, and which we apprehend constitutes the most important characteristic of poetry. We may bring to our mental vision a number of these ideals, and, without using any terms, observe their relations to each other, and this we would call a *process of ideality*, or *poetic mode of mind*, and it is evidently contradistinguished from the abstract, or prosaic mode, in which we examine those relations through the medium of substituted terms. It can exist in perfect purity only in thought. Any written or articulate language can be but an approximation to it, which, however, may be again purified in the mind of the recipient, by his dismissing the terms, and retaining the ideals. Poetry, depending on this prominence of the primitive perceptions, must present, or at least use for illustration, such as we perceive clearly, or feel strongly, and hence its intimate and essential connection with imagery and with passion. The art of the poet is exercised in inventing and combining, so as to present the *subjects* of his poem with such vivid coloring and striking arrangement that they shall command the undivided attention of the reader. But actual occurrences may occasionally present similar combinations, and objects of equal interest. There may be poetry in circumstances; and, in describing them, narration and ideality are blended in one common language. But, even in this case, the prose writer uses only the immediate connection between words and ideals, while the poet avails himself of the associations between the ideals themselves, and, by this means, reaches those recesses of thought and feeling to which terms have not been extended, and secures that volatile essence of sentiment, which, rising by its purity above the gross atmosphere of terms, can only be approached by this delicate process. He uses language to induce an ideal, not in itself important, but valued for the associations it brings with it. With a cabalistic word, he summons the half-recognized ghosts of departed feelings, and with the incantation of terms invokes a host of spirits from the world of fancy. And though we do not recollect the words, and cannot repeat the terms in that order which alone gives them magic power, yet the spectral or fairy forms, the impressions, the emotions, in short, the ideals they created, may be as distinctly retained as the remembrance of any external object which we have seen without learning its name.

The power which poetry thus possesses of extending itself beyond the limits of precise terms, and of reaching remote ideals, through the medium of those which are within the immediate grasp of words, is its most important and peculiar attribute. It is this which fits it for the communication of discoveries made in advance of the age. It is the receptacle of truths in their most evanescent forms,—the depository from which abstraction is continually drawing the materials for the improvement of concrete science. When knowledge is advancing, the process of condensing keeps pace with it. Truths, first suggested in the strains of the poet, imperceptibly assume the garb of prose, and become matters of demonstration. This mode, however, is confined to the immediate action of intellect upon real or imaginary existences; for, when we have prepared a set of terms, or signs, and use them to the exclusion of ideals, the processes of ideality of course cease to avail us, and we are then aided in our progress only by the language of abstraction. There are cases in which this language becomes so pure that we pursue it without being conscious of any ideals. Mathematical analysis furnishes the best specimens of this mode, and, without now attempting any explanation, we will merely state the fact, that, in this science, the mathematician, considering only the terms, and guided wholly by the relations which he discovers among them, makes his way through trains of syllogisms, reaching from the most simple and obvious premises to the most remote and abstruse conclusions, without any ideal arresting or for a moment diverting his attention. No image, no emotion obtrudes itself upon his thoughts, and he seems to be dealing with nothing but words, or with signs in a still more condensed form. Not even the thought of any particular quantity is suffered to intrude itself among the signs, from which he is laboring to deduce a formula, applicable alike to all quantities. His ideals, if such they may be called, are the first perceptions of new relations so immediately assuming the form of words, that he is not conscious that they had any prior existence. All general propositions must be expressed in this language, and, the progress of knowledge being from particulars to generals, little advancement can be made without it. We accordingly find it, in a greater or less degree of perfection, in every science.

Next to mathematics, some portions of metaphysics and ethics probably furnish the best specimens of this mode. When treating of abstract principles, of which it is at once difficult and useless to form any definite images,— which neither present any visible form, nor excite emotion,— the attention is more easily diverted from the ideals, and directed exclusively to the terms. But when, even in these subjects, we approach the consideration of mind as it presents itself to our observation, or of moral principles as applicable to the actual concerns of life, the inefficiency of terms becomes apparent, and the difficulty of progressing with our thoughts, restricted within such narrow limits as they impose, becomes insurmountable. Still, so far as they go, terms greatly assist us. They condense a subject; for a single term representing certain abstract qualities or properties may include all the individuals of a species. Or they divide them into greater or smaller divisions, as the number of abstract qualities expressed by the term is lessened or increased. (See table on next page.) In such statements as, "That which is a necessary existence must always have existed; space is a necessary existence; therefore, space must always have existed," the first calls up no ideal; it tells us of no event; its truth or falsity is to be determined only by the relations of the terms in which it is expressed, and is therefore purely in the language of abstraction. The last, being a conclusion growing out of the consideration of the *terms* of the other two, is of the same character.

This is a tiny, and we fear but a faint illustration of the influence of this form of language in the process of thought, and of the power which it imparts. With this guide, the man of abstraction fearlessly traverses the wide ocean of speculation, in search of rich discoveries in distant climes where hidden mines of knowledge seldom fail to reward his enterprise and toil.

With a view of contrasting this language with that of ideality, let us examine another illustration. If we say "That mirror is *in* this room — this room is *in* this house — therefore that mirror is *in* this house" — the repetition of the word *in* in each step assures us of the correctness of the inference. But if we say "That mirror is *in* this room — this room is *a part of* this house — therefore that mirror is *a part of* this house," the change in terms immediately warns us that our conclusion is not a necessary consequence

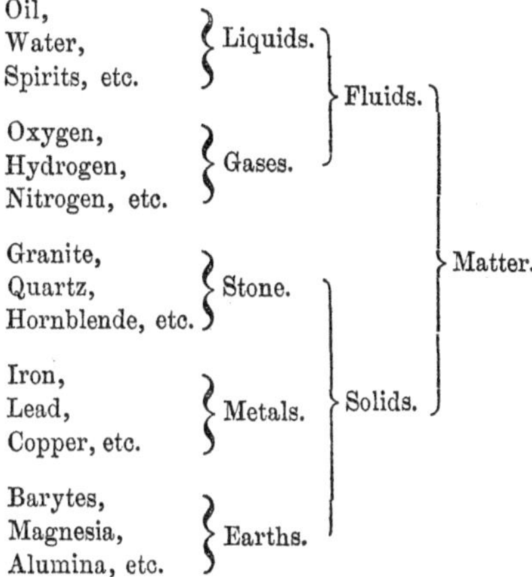

of our premises; and the effect is, in both instances, the same, if for mirror, room, and house, we substitute unknown terms, which call up no ideals in the mind. This shows us that, to connect the different parts of a discourse in the language of abstraction, we must retain the exact terms of the successive propositions which compose it; while, in the language of ideality, the terms are disregarded, and the ideals they have suggested are alone retained by the memory. The first mode fills the mind with a concatenation of terms; the other presents to its vision a collection of images, or inspires it with emotion. This shows us a distinction which every reader may bring to the test of his own consciousness, and, if it be correct, he will invariably find that, whatever the merits of a poem may be, when any portion of it requires him to preserve the connection by a recurrence to the terms instead of the ideals, there is a cessation or revulsion of all poetic feeling. By the modes of narration or abstraction, we are merely made to *know* the facts which are stated or proved; the mode of ideality causes us to *perceive* and *feel* as if the occurrences were passing before us.

In metrical works of a philosophical or narrative character, the poetry, except where the circumstances are in their nature and combination poetic, will all be found in the imagery with which the abstract truths or historical events are illustrated and adorned.

The modes of abstraction and ideality being thus directly opposed to each other, and separated by the intermediate language of narration, are easily distinguished from each other. But they are often blended so as to produce an agreeable variety. The orator, especially, may combine them with advantage, and particularly when his object is at once to convince and to persuade. We are often persuaded to approve a means, by having some desirable result depicted to us in vivid colors. But to be convinced, requires that we should not only perceive a good, but be assured that no equal or paramount evil will arise from the same cause. This requires that the whole ground should be examined; and, for this purpose, generic terms, embracing large portions of it at once, are very convenient, and are more readily known to embrace the whole, as, in recounting the countries of a grand division, we should more quickly perceive an omission, than if we attempted it in smaller districts. This, we suppose, illustrates one important difference between persuasion and conviction, and shows the fitness of the language of abstraction to the one, and that of ideality to the other. The orator should bear in mind this distinction, and, when he wishes to persuade, draw largely from the materials of ideality, and, when his object is to demonstrate and place his positions beyond the reach of refutation, use them sparingly and with caution. The scintillations of his fancy should then be employed only to illumine the depths and recesses of his reasoning. If he make them the prominent objects of his discourse, we suspect him of attempting to deceive our understanding; our vanity is offended; we feel that he is only amusing or beguiling us with pictures, when he professes to be offering us substantial argument.

Still, ideality is the grand essential of eloquence. It warms the heart, and gives an impulse like that which arises from the realities which it depicts, for it makes them present to our minds' sight, and corresponding effects are produced upon us. On the other hand, the degree of attention required in retaining the parts of an abstract argument, and observing the relations between them, and the labor necessary to follow it in its intricate paths, fatigue and perplex the mind not well disciplined to the task. In the form of ideality, the circumstances which constitute the groundwork of the verbal argument, are so arranged, that their connection with the result may be perceived without any conscious effort. When the orator has succeeded in bringing the subject home to the perception of his hearers, the effect on them approaches to that of actually observing what he depicts, and produces in them similar emotions and impulses. He, therefore, who would long command the attention, and sway the feelings of an audience, must enliven his discourse with an infusion of ideality.

While abstraction penetrates with a single concentrated beam, ideality illuminates and dazzles with a multiplying reflector, and if a ray diverge from its destined course, she interposes another ideal, which reflects it to its proper point.

It will be observed that the view thus far taken of poetry is independent of its usual accompaniments, metre and rhyme. We consider them, not as essential attributes, but as decorations, which it may or may not assume.

The artificial arrangement of feet in poetic composition produces a pleasing alternation of effort and repose, to the organs both of speaking and hearing; and, as the lines all contain an equal number of feet, similarly arranged, a rule is furnished which enables the reader to proceed by the force of habit or mere imitation, thus leaving the attention to be more exclusively exerted on the ideals. The emphatic words being manifest, make the sense clear, and give point, precision, and force to expression, which might otherwise require to be much amplified to prevent ambiguity. The attention is left still more at liberty, because each line embraces a distinct division of the sense; and this effect is again increased, when these divisions are marked by terminations similar in sound. The last of the rhyming words, carrying the attention back to the first, presents more of the subject at once, and knits the whole more closely together. Another happy effect of this similarity of arrangement and terminations arises from association. It is an interest analogous to that which we feel in a stranger, who happens to resemble a friend, and which is so often excited before we are conscious of the cause. One line enchants us, and another, though it breathes not its spirit and is destitute of its intrinsic charm, imparts a pleasure like that we enjoy in the first hasty glance of a portrait, where the hand of art has given such expression to the features of one we love, that, in the first moment of rapture, we perceive not, we think not, that "soul is wanting there."

There is another advantage of thus limiting the mode of expression by rhyme. It checks the impetuosity of the poet, and, by compelling him to dwell longer on the subject, makes his views of it more varied and complete. It also obliges him to resort to a multiplicity of terms and phrases, which will suggest many new relations and greatly extend the range of his thought. To these two causes he is probably indebted for the perfection of many of his finest ideas; for some of his most beautiful analogies; and for other of those little delicacies of expression and sentiment, which give an exquisite finish to his creations. We will omit the consideration of some minor points; those already suggested being sufficient to show the more important advantages of metre and rhyme in poetic composition. It may, however, happen, that these advantages are sometimes counterbalanced by the restrictions they impose. It is possible there may be instances in which the artless grace, the native vivacity of freedom, may lend more touching charms, and imbue unrhymed poetry with more thrilling beauty, than all this artificial decoration and refinement can bestow.

To support this conjecture, we will offer, as a partial illustration, the first portion of Burke's apostrophe to the Queen of France:

"It is now sixteen or seventeen years since I first saw the Queen of France, then the dauphiness, at Versailles, and, surely, *never lighted on this orb, which she hardly seemed to touch, a more delightful vision.*"

The first part of this sentence merely informs us of the time and place at which he had seen the queen, and that she was then the dauphiness. It is, therefore, narrative. But the conclusion is the language of ideality, and strikes us as a happy application of the poetic art. The mind, in progressing through it, is so happily prepared by the image, which having "*lighted on this orb,*" must, of course, have come from another sphere, and, *hardly touching it*, flits before his imagination; that the conclusion, which, in ordinary language, would merely have embodied the preceding description in some delightful object of sensuous vision, now exerts a magic influence, and calls up the subject of some entrancing revery or ecstatic dream; perchance an angel form, which, in some bright moment of enchantment, has lent its celestial influence to the illusions of fancy. His imagination recalls the image fresh from heaven, too pure to touch our earth, or breathe an atmosphere so gross, but enveloped in a fleecy cloud of heavenly element, buoyant with purity, and deriving a pearly splendor from its unearthly transparency. The smile with which it vanished again beams upon him; he recollects the thrill of pleasure, the exaltation of feeling, — so pure, so ennobling, so pervading, that he felt as if he were all mind, and mind were all refinement and ecstacy.

The next sentence — "I saw her just above the horizon, decorating and cheering the elevated sphere she just began to move in, full of life, and splendor, and joy," naturally suggests the orb of day, decorating with its beams the loveliness of nature in the freshness of early morn, or its inferior only in splendor, shedding her more mild and benign influence over some tranquil and enchanting scene. And with these scenes may be recalled those moments, when their purifying and exhilarating influence imparted vivacity and life; and the animation around us had its analogy in the gayety and joy within. Such are the phantasms which these few words may summon from the shades of oblivion, and with magic power impart distinctness to the misty shrouding of departed feelings and forgotten scenes; which, in again vanishing, are concentrated in one ideal, and picture the young queen before us as an angel-form — of spotless purity, glowing with life, radiant with joy, surrounded with splendor — imparting ecstacy to all, and elevating and ennobling all within the sphere of her influence.

One of the characteristic qualities of this mode of expression is the rapidity to which it excites thought; an obvious consequence of a multiplicity of ideals being immediately made the objects of our perception, without the usual circumlocution of examining their relations through the medium of terms. This rapidity is frequently still further accelerated by one set of expressions giving rise to two trains of ideals and their wide-spread associations; each of which, by the delicate mechanism of analogy, exhibits the subject in some new position; sheds the light of illustration upon it; or reproduces and adds another ideal to the less expansive train which bears it forward in its already illuminated path.

When we consider this effect of accelerated mental excitement, and unite to it that which arises from the power of calling up ideals or perceptions, with all the vividness of reality yet divested of the modifying circumstances of real life, we perceive that we have advanced far in the discovery of the secret springs of poetic inspiration,— the hidden sources of that mystic influence, which rolls upon us a tide of feelings the most exquisite and exalting, or acute and overwhelming.

In the language of narration, our course is prescribed by the order of events.

In the language of abstraction, each step is controlled by the terms of those which precede it. They guide our reasoning. But as objects may be seen and emotions felt in any conceivable order of succession, or without any order at all, so ideals, their immediate representatives, may in like manner be presented; and the poet may freely follow the dictates of his fancy, till, lost in the mazes which he has rapidly threaded from one bright object to another, overpowered by their dazzling influence, confused and distracted by their multitudinous and disordered assemblage, his excited feelings are wrought to a state of incoherent energy, and he enjoys or suffers a poetic frenzy.

The division or classification of language which we have suggested, has its basis in the elements of mind. Memory is first supplied by observation with facts, from which both reason and imagination draw their materials. Among these facts, as expressed in the simple language of narration, the reasoning faculty perceives many which are similar in all respects, except that each relates to a distinct object. It divests them of this distinction, by substituting the generic term which embraces them all in one general proposition expressing an abstract truth. It then proceeds to form more propositions in the same manner, and, by a proper combination of these, to deduce others of a like character, or still more condensed.*

Imagination, on the other hand, avoiding those propositions which appear common, from their similarity to many others, seizes the more striking ideals, which, isolated and far removed from the limits of common observation, unite the charms of novelty with the illusions of distance. It is her province to form new and beautiful combinations of these; to present them with the advantages which varied light and shade can impart, and with the pleasing illustrations which refined analogies and associations may bring to their aid. She thus introduces us to an intimacy with those distant shadows of sentiment and feeling, which have often flitted just within the verge of our perceptions, but were never distinctly pictured to our understanding.

* Thus :

<table>
<tr><td>Oxygen resists less than stone,
Hydrogen resists less than stone,
Nitrogen resists less than stone, etc.</td><td>Gases resist less than stone.</td><td rowspan="2">Fluids resist less than stone.</td></tr>
<tr><td>Water resists less than stone,
Oil resists less than stone,
Spirit resists less than stone, etc.</td><td>Liquids resist less than stone.</td></tr>
<tr><td colspan="2">Fluids resist less than stone,
" " " " wood,
" " " " earth,
" " " " iron, etc.</td><td>Fluids resist less than solids.</td></tr>
</table>

Of these three divisions it may be said to be the province of the first to suggest; of the second to demonstrate and condense; and of the last to perceive, to amplify, to illustrate, and adorn. To make obvious these various effects, we have the language of narration, which is the instrument of memory; the language of abstraction, which is the engine of the reasoning faculty; and the language of ideality, which is the machinery of the imagination.

We have thus far made no distinction between material objects and feeling; or, in other words, between the external and internal objects of our consciousness. It is obvious that the former interest us only by their influence upon the latter; that, in real life, certain combinations of the one produce certain states of the other, some of which the language of narration has no power to describe. To depict these in their native simplicity, or as refined and improved by new combinations, is the province of the poet. As a means of effecting this, he makes use of the circumstances or the objects which produce them, or of the associations which experience and observation have suggested. It is in thus availing himself of the principle of association that he so often and so happily alludes to the effect — not unfrequently the physiological effect — of those feelings when excited. Of this we have a fine illustration in the expression, "All was still; still as the breathless interval betwixt the flash and thunder."

To elicit these emotions in a happy manner requires a knowledge, not only of the niceties of language, but of the intricate and delicate relations of the feelings, united to a discriminating taste, which neither perplexes by obscurity, nor wearies attention by prolixity, nor offends the vanity by being too minute. The poet must frequently give only the prominent ideals, and leave the imagination to supply the rest. The reader will thus have his faculties more excited, and fill up the blanks in a manner most agreeable to himself; and, revelling in what thus seem the creations of his own fancy, he will cheerfully award the meed of praise to that which has provoked him to thought, and imparted to him the elevation of conscious power. We may here remark that a little obscurity in expression, or ambiguity in terms, when so employed as to concentrate rather than distract attention, may greatly assist this effect, and, at the same time, repel the attention from the terms to the ideals, to which they allow a greater latitude, but may still, in some measure, control.

Extending the application of terms, and, at the same time, preventing ambiguity by skilful arrangement and other aids, constitutes an important portion of the poet's art. It is this which enables him happily to express what others have only perceived or felt. We may sometimes be led to fancy a connection between the undefined feelings and thoughts which we have experienced, and vague expressions which we meet with. Writers may have associated them in the same way, and this reflection may illustrate the remark of a popular poet, that, "when he wrote very fine, he did not always expect to understand himself." In such cases, the ideals, though perceived in a state of high mental excitement, are probably indistinct, and their associations with the terms used to indicate them, rather accidental than conventional, or the connection with them is so vague, so delicate, or so remote, as not easily to be traced by the writer himself. In some instances this would be the utmost limit of his art, thought penetrating so far that he could find no adequate means of portraying it. In other cases it might be but a false glare,— an abuse of that latitude which tne poet must always be allowed in the use of language.

Though the activity to which the mind is excited by poetic description obviates the necessity of being minute, and often makes precision tedious, yet, when the subject is either sufficiently absorbing or important, the poet may present in quick succession each separate feature of a particular ideal, until the whole is completely developed and fixed in the mind, with all the circumstances of reality; or, he may dwell only on those delicate and shadowy characteristics, which, recalling the more obvious, suggest the whole picture, and make it equally perfect and distinct. That description of Byron's, where the image is that of lifeless beauty and its apposite analogy — fallen Greece, is an instance of the first kind.

"He who hath bent him o'er the dead,
E're the first day of death has fled,
The first dark day of nothingness,
The last of danger and distress,
(Before decay's effacing fingers
Have swept the lines where beauty lingers,)
And marked the mild angelic air,
The rapture of repose that 's there,
The fixed yet tender traits that streak
The languor of the placid cheek,
And — but for that sad shrouded eye,
  That fires not, wins not, weeps not, now,
  And but for that chill, changeless brow,
Where cold obstruction's apathy
Appals the gazing mourner's heart,
As if to him it could impart
The doom he dreads, yet dwells upon;
Yes, but for these, and these alone,
Some moments, ay, one treacherous hour,
He still might doubt the tyrant's power;
So fair, so calm, so softly sealed,
The first last look by death revealed!

Such is the aspect of this shore ;
'T is Greece, but living Greece no more !
So coldly sweet, so deadly fair,
We start, for soul is wanting there.
Hers is the loveliness in death,
That parts not quite with parting breath ;
But beauty with that fearful bloom,
That hue that haunts it to the tomb,
Expression's last receding ray,
A gilded halo hovering round decay, —
The farewell beam of feeling past away !
Spark of that flame, perchance of heavenly birth,
Which gleams, but warms no more its cherished earth ! "

It is not our intention to attempt an analysis of the various artifices by which the pleasure arising from poetry is increased. But the allusion we have just made to one of the master-spirits of the art, and the recollection of his poetic history, has opportunely reminded us of the connection between poetry and love: a connection so universally believed, and believed to be so universal, that it has been doubted whether any one ever truly felt the latter, without some disposition also to the former. All — no, not all — the heart which has been petrified by avarice or corrupted by vice, whose sentiment and vitality are destroyed, may resist, or, rather, not feel its power — but the most abstract reasoner is not proof against it; the coldest mathematician, or the yet colder metaphysician, yields to its genial influence. Suddenly affected in a manner which he deems unaccountable, it is to him as though some law of nature had varied from its uniformity. Unaccustomed to such freaks of the imagination, he is unskilled in controlling them. Instead of being governed by his judgment, he seems impelled by some invisible agency, and the power of mystery is thus united to the spell of enchantment. His previous discipline of mind and accustomed scrutiny of its action, serve only to heighten his surprise, and to increase the difficulty of a rational solution. The more he contemplates it, the stranger and more peculiar his case appears. Not doubting that he had before known all the qualities of the human mind, he is ready to ascribe this new influence to a supernatural cause, and if such a vision as we have before endeavored to sketch should meet his wondering gaze, he may imagine — yes, imagine himself under the care of a guardian angel, who has suddenly imparted to him an elevation of soul, purity of sentiment, and delicacy of feeling, never before vouchsafed to mortal. All the terms by which other men might in some degree express their emotions are to him cold abstractions; he has already appropriated them; he has before located and limited their significations with a rigorous accuracy and precision which render them inapplicable to a new and expanded feeling. How, then, is he to express himself? The language of ideality is his only resource, and is naturally adopted; for his warm imaginings are primitive perceptions for which he knows no conventional signs. The solitude of his feelings finds relief in the objects around him; for all nature speaks the silent eloquence of love. Purified and exalted, those feelings are as inspirations from Heaven, and he takes pleasure in tracing their resemblances to other manifestations of the Source of all. His emotions are too strong to be repressed; too ethereal to find utterance in the common forms of discourse; too highly prized to be lessened by such diffusion. Throughout the worlds of matter and of mind he sees the beautiful, the delicate, the grand, the vague, and the infinite, with quickened powers of vision. He delights to dwell on the analogies they present, and to trace out the metaphors they suggest. He is treading on enchanted ground. He feels the force of those invisible links which unite the spiritual with the material world. Those mysterious associations, by which the most ethereal modes of ideality are connected with external forms and appearances, are shadowed out before him. He compares the emotions of his heart to all that is glowing and ardent, and the object of his affections to all that is pure and lovely in nature. He is thus introduced into the region of poetry, and his unskilful efforts in the use of its appropriate language often make him appear ridiculous. Added to this, he is acting under an excitement not imparted to those around him, and under circumstances, for which deductions from the past furnish him with no rule of conduct. He has already questioned the omnipotence of reason, and doubts the integrity of the magnet which has been his guide on the ocean of life. Unaccustomed to steer by chance, he acts either with that embarrassed indecision or restless energy, which has given rise to the assertion that the most sensible men are the greatest fools in love,— an assertion which would perhaps be more just if limited to men of the greatest reasoning powers. His mind, however, crowded by a rapid flow of ideals, seeks relief in a corresponding flow of words, and when these in their turn become too impetuous, or make harsh discord with thoughts attuned to love, he instinctively opposes to their vehemence the artificial obstacles of metre and rhyme, seeking, by this harmony of arrangement, to make them consonant with feelings which fill his whole soul with music. It is then the proper language of ideality — or poetry. Would it be wonderful if a man, thus suddenly metamorphosed, should question his identity? or, the habit of reasoning being still left him, that he should argue, that he, who was once proof against the charms of poetry and the fascinations of music, who would turn from the loveliest of nature's scenery to examine a triangle or a sophism, could not be the same person as he who is now warbling rhymes, and feasting his imagination with objects before unnoticed or unknown?

"Accustomed every thought to prove,
And by fixed rules each feeling try—
He might ascribe it all to love,
But cannot find a reason why."

We have seen that poetry, which term we now use as synonymous with the language of ideality, has only a remote and vaguely defined relation with words as generally used. This renders it difficult, if not impossible, for the poet to teach to others the knowledge of his art. Perhaps he himself does not analyze the process to which he is indebted for his inspirations; but, even when he is fully acquainted with it, the want of a direct and immediate mode of communication will present a serious obstacle to his imparting the secret of his power.

In the language of narration, the teacher may inform his pupil of the arbitrary but conventional connection between the terms and the things signified; or he may explain to him the necessary relations between the terms expressing the premises, the intermediate steps, and the conclusion of an abstract argument; and so instruct him that he may apply terms in a similar manner. But he who would seek an explanation of poetic imagery, or any other form of the language of ideality, must consult his own feelings; and his facility in understanding it will depend on the care which he has bestowed on these germs and vines of thought, which, in cultivated fertility and vigor, put forth numberless tendrils, uniting them all by delicate, elastic, invisible twinings, in one inseparable, tangled, yet free and flowing exuberance. Who, for instance, that had never known the mingled emotions of suspense and awe, or some analogous sensation, could understand what was meant by the "breathless interval betwixt the flash and thunder"? The expression "breathless interval" would be to him perfectly unmeaning. And suppose we should attempt to enlighten him. We might tell him that the phenomenon alluded to sometimes caused a momentary suspension of respiration. Our pupil would, no doubt, be astonished at the fact, would hold his breath, and thus get the new idea that lightning sometimes produced an unpleasant feeling of oppression about the region of the lungs, which he would probably ascribe to the effect of electricity. We would then strive to rectify his mistake, and to explain to him the corresponding emotions of the mind; but here, after exhausting all the appropriate terms which common language can supply, we should find that there were some of those emotions for which it had no appellatives, and which no appellatives could convey to one in whose mind they had not been impressed by experience or analogy; or which, at least, they could not shadow forth with all their delicate characteristics and finer influences. Here, then, our illustrations would fail; but, to the initiated, the expression "breathless interval" calls up all that may have been felt from the occurrence of the reality. It accommodates itself to the actual feelings, and is equally applicable to the strong and vivid emotions of the one, or the weak and glimmering sensations of another. Such expressions revive in every one the thoughts, the feelings, the unexpressed and unexpressible ideals he has respectively realized, or would realize, if the occasions, which the fancy of the poet has depicted, were presented in their reality.

If these considerations give us some idea of the language of ideality, they also suggest that it has its source in the deepest recesses of mind, and springs from those feelings which stir and quicken the soul, and the aspirations which lead it forward into the infinite; that the cultivation of these always elicits it, and that being thus the expression of the inherent and imperishable properties of the soul, or the consequence of their improvement, it must expand with it in its every state of èxistence.

It may be objected that this consideration is leading us beyond the proper limits of philosophical research. But some glimmering rays still light our path; and we will illustrate our meaning. Does temptation assail us? The gratification which is to be the result of yielding to error is presented to our thoughts, and so absorbs our attention that we do not see the more remote and less dazzling consequences. But, if reason is permitted to trace them all in the language of abstraction, or if ideality delineates the *whole* picture, the illusion is dispelled. On the other hand, does virtue prompt us to a good and generous act? She calls to her aid the very feelings which are to reward it.

The application of these facts to our argument must be obvious to all who believe in communications from the spirits of another world, and especially to those who also believe that some of these spirits have the will and the power to thwart the designs of Deity, and that, from the creation of the world, they have maintained a not altogether unsuccessful strife with Omnipotence for the mastery of man. To at least a portion of these, the facts we have mentioned may appear to lead us to the conclusion that the language of ideality, in its purest form, is the language of the higher orders of intelligence. To others it may still appear a visionary speculation, a baseless hypothesis, or vague conjecture. But, far as it evidently is beyond the reach of rigid demonstration, permit us for a moment to examine its probability. *

The hypothesis that death annuls all consciousness of our present state of existence, and all the mental qualities here possessed, involves that of annihilation. Or to suppose that it destroys the consciousness of the present state, while the qualities of mind are still retained, is supposing what is exactly equivalent to the extinction of one soul and the creation of a new one of the same material or essence. A moment's consideration will convince us of the correctness of these positions, from which we may fairly infer that the soul, in its separate state, retains the qualities and properties it here possesses, and the consciousness of having here enjoyed them. Analogy, too, clearly indicates that the faculties which we have been perfecting here should not be lost. Nature is always careful of even what is much less precious than intellect and moral feeling. Retaining, then, these qualities, and having this remembrance of the past, is it not exceedingly probable that some of the same sources of enjoyment, which have contributed to their happiness here, must continue to constitute a portion of the felicity of the future? Now, one of the most pure and

* The reader will observe that this essay was published in 1836, long before the outburst of what are called "spiritual manifestations" at present, and that our author is not discussing those curious phenomena. ED.

unalloyed gratifications arises from the improvement of our intellectual and moral qualities by advancing in knowledge. We all know how much this is accelerated by communion with each other; and yet how much it is retarded by the ambiguity and inefficiency of words. So much is this the case that many sciences are now only advanced by so advancing language as to improve the means of thought, and enable a number of kindred minds to communicate their views, and concentrate their power on the same point. But, even when success has crowned these efforts by the discovery of some new truth, how slowly is it diffused, how long before it enlightens the public mind! The language of mathematics is undoubtedly the most explicit, and best adapted to its subject, of any which we possess; and yet the controversy among the cotemporaries of Newton shows us that there was one of his discoveries * in that science, the reasoning of which was pronounced fallacious by mathematicians of acknowledged learning and acuteness, and which very few of its no less learned supporters then clearly understood; yet, from the improvement in the modes of illustration, it is now made familiar to schoolboys. But generations passed away before it admitted of being thus easily imparted and understood; and, in sciences of less perfect adaptation of language, the diffusion of truth in the higher departments is still slower.

If, from what we have said before, it appears probable that there will be some mode of communion hereafter, does it not now seem equally probable that, in that more perfect state, we shall possess a means of social intercourse free from ambiguity; that the pleasure of advancement will be increased by its consequent acceleration; that, when de-

* Fluxions; now called Differential Calculus.

prived of the material organs, words and signs will no longer be employed; in a word, that the language of ideality, which a partial improvement of our faculties has here elicited, will then be so perfected that terms will be *entirely* dispensed with, and thought be communicated without the intervention of any medium to distort its meaning, or sully its brightness; that ideas will flow directly from mind to mind, and the soul be continually exhilarated by breathing a pure, congenial atmosphere, inhaling feeling, poetry, and knowledge?

This conjecture derives a further plausibility from the consideration that our present language seems especially adapted to things material; that in the purely physical sciences we can communicate ideas with great accuracy and precision; that the difficulty of doing this increases in proportion as our feelings and the qualities of mind enter into the subject to which we endeavor to apply it, and that, when they become exclusively its objects, it almost entirely fails. Poetry has accomplished much more than other forms of language in portraying the passions, sentiments, and all the more striking and complicated mental phenomena; but even that has shed but a feeble light over a small portion of this interesting field of research, and in bright, but fitful gleams, shown the undefined vastness not yet explored. Our present language, then, is wholly inadequate to a subject which, of all others, must most interest a world of spirits, as if it were intended only to carry us to the point from which we are thence to start — to give us a glimpse of the infinite regions which imagination has not yet traversed — the exhaustless sources of thought which mind still possesses; the language of ideality having here accomplished just enough in the exhibition of the subjects of our internal consciousness to assure us that it possesses the elements of a power which, when matured, may become the fitting instrument to gather the treasures of that unexplored immensity. But may we not go further? May we not say that we have even here a foretaste, or, at least, a near approach to that angelic pleasure? Have we not witnessed the soul, in all its purity and vigor, throwing off the trammels which words impose on its highest action; and, as if anticipating its conscious destiny, in a transport of impassioned thought and feeling, almost entirely discarding the usual mode of expressing them; when the eloquence of the eye anticipates the tongue, when every feature kindles with emotion, and the whole countenance is as a transparency lighted with its glowing conceptions? It is then that terms are most nearly dispensed with, and it is in this sympathetic mingling of thought and sentiment that we enjoy the purest poetry which warms the soul in its earthly tabernacle. Those who have known the raptures of such converse, and have felt its exalting influence, will regard it as worthy a place in a higher sphere, and be willing to admit it to their most entrancing reveries of elysian bliss. Does not this view lend a delightful confirmation to our hypothesis? But the argument derives yet additional strength from the consideration that this faculty, — this power of silent yet vivid expression, — seems somewhat proportioned to moral excellence, or increases as the spiritual predominates over the material part of our natures; that in most men it is at best but dimly visible; that, in those of the finer grade of intellect, whose feelings have been cultivated, whose purity has never been sullied by corroding care and ignoble pursuits, nor their sensibility blunted by too rude collision with the world, it is more apparent; while in the sex of finer mould, who are elevated above these degrading influences, whose feelings are more pure, whose sentiments are more refined, and whose spirits are more ethereal, it manifests itself with a softened splendor, to which that of angels may well be supposed only another step in the scale of a magnificent progression.

It is to the superiority which woman has in this expressive language,—to her command of this direct avenue to the finer feelings,—that we must attribute her influence in refining and softening the asperities of our nature. And it is owing to the possession of this element of moral elevation that, while the finest and strongest reasoning of philosophy has, in this respect, accomplished so little, woman has accomplished so much. She possesses not the strength which has been exhibited by some masculine minds, nor perhaps even the brilliancy which has emanated from others; but the influence which the sexes respectively exert on society, appears in strange disproportion to the *apparent* causes. The one is as the sun which sheds his strong beams upon the waters, and the waves proudly reflect his dazzling brilliancy; the other, as the moon, whose milder light melts into the ocean, glows through all its depths, heaves its mighty bosom, and elevates it above its common level. The refined subtleties of an Aristotle, or the glowing sublimities of a Plato, though presented to us with all the fascinations of a high-toned morality, and clothed in the imposing grandeur of a lofty and commanding eloquence, are dim and powerless to that effusion of soul, that seraphic fervor, which with a glance, unlocks the avenues to our tenderness, which chides our errors with a tear, or, winning us to virtue with the omnipotence of a charm, irradiates its path with the beaming eye, and cheers it with the approving smile of loveliness. And hence, too, it is, that the degree in which this influence is felt, and its source appreciated, is justly considered as the test of civilization and refinement. Is there not in this mild, gentle, silent, persuasive, yet dissolving and resistless influence, a charm which bears witness to its celestial character? Do we not recognize in it a similarity to that of heaven? And, if we have ascribed it to its proper cause, does not this similarity at once stamp our speculation, if not with the seal of a moral certainty, at least with the impress of a cheering probability?

It is apparent that the language we have endeavored to portray as that of the future state, would embrace that of narration, and thus to the imagination unite memory, with its pre-requisites, observation and attention. But we are aware that a difficulty may here occur to the metaphysician, and that others may be ready to inquire how some of these views can be reconciled with what we before asserted, of the necessity of the language of abstraction in advancing knowledge. To the latter we would observe, that it is principally in the physical and intellectual sciences that this language is so indispensable, and we have already labored to show that it does not hold the first place as a means of moral culture. But to both we would urge that the necessity of the language of abstraction arises from the weakness and imperfection of our present faculties. If we could conceive of generals — of a whole species — as we do of an individual of that species, and retain distinctly a long series and combination of them, abstractions would be unnecessary as a means of thinking. It is our weakness, only, which obliges us to use symbols accurately defined, which, being condensed expressions, are easily embraced by our limited powers.

To obviate this necessity, it may at first be supposed that a new faculty must be given us. But we believe that even this hypothesis may be dispensed with, and, in lieu of it, would suggest that, if the faculty of attention were so disciplined and improved, that, when we considered the image of any species, we could at pleasure and with ease direct that faculty only to the characteristics which belong to all the species, and divest our idea of those which distinguish it from the same species, it would be precisely what is now gained by the substitution of terms for abstracted qualities. It would be free from those incidental associations, which produce error when they enter into the elements of a general result. And is it too much to suppose that, when no longer engaged in the dissipating cares of this life, nor surrounded by the distracting influences of the material world, our power of attention should become so perfected that we could then discover the relations among our perceptions without being obliged first to express them in abstract terms, and thus the language of abstraction and all the power which it imparts be merged in that of ideality?

All modes of language are then united in the anticipated language of heaven. Let us for a moment endeavor to form some idea of this combination, from the consideration of its distinct elements.

We have already remarked, that observation, through the medium of memory, furnishes the materials for both the reasoning and the imaginative faculties; and we may further observe, that, without a sufficiency of the solid realities which it supplies, the first would expend itself on chimerical and illusive theories, and the latter on weak and vapid conceits. There evidently is, in the union of ideality and abstraction (or, to speak of the faculties, instead of their means or mode of action, in imagination and reasoning combined), a peculiar adaptation to the advancement of knowledge. The one supplies the deficiency of the other. Imagination, by her superior quickness and greater reach, extends her flight far beyond the limits to which science has extended her empire. She penetrates and pervades the wilderness of the unknown, and frequently catches the first glimmering of truth, or shadows out the yet dubious relations between the most remote ideas, long before the approach of slower-paced reason, and thus guides the latter on the way, and facilitates her progress to more certain discoveries. It was thus that the poet first pointed to the position of a twinkling star, whose ray, sent forth at creation's birth, had not yet reached the eye of grovelling mortals, and the probable existence of which, astronomy has since put forth the powers of abstraction to demonstrate.

The language of ideality is perfect, in proportion to the facilities which it gives for portraying thoughts in their incipient state. By resorting to its various expedients, the poet exhibits casual and even indistinct associations, as they exist in his own mind, which, finding place in other minds, and brightening in their course, result in truths confirmed by common opinion and experience. These associations, when traced out, are often found to depend on some real — though perhaps before unnoticed — connection, the discovery of which is thus added to the common stock of knowledge.

In the following instance we are made to associate crime and misery, by having them presented to our mental vision, shrouded in the same intellectual brightness :

"His intellect so bright, that it could shed
A lustre o'er the darkest deeds of crime ;
So dazzling bright that it at once could dim
The sight of mortals, and from human gaze
Enshroud the misery itself produced."

We are aware that it is now too late to treat the connection of crime and misery as a truth in the poetic stage of knowledge. It has advanced nearer to the sphere of certainty, and we offer this instance only as an illustration of one of the modes in which such truths first find utterance, and finally become embodied in the generally admitted maxims or scientific theorems of succeeding generations. It is thus that the imagination is continually extending the vague boundaries of speculative science, while abstraction is as constantly following it up, by advancing the limits of probability and extending the less distant verge of demonstration. United, they enlarge the sphere of knowledge, fill it with the grandeur and magnificence of truth, and throw around it a garniture of all that is beautiful and sublime in the ideal. These faculties are seldom found united in a high degree of perfection in the same individual, but we hope we have already made it appear at least possible that the obstacles to their union here are obviated in the hereafter; that the unshackled spirit may there possess a quickened observation, furnishing an exhaustless supply of the new and wonderful, on which reason shall pour the sparkling brilliancy of demonstration, and which an active and versatile imagination shall adorn with the effulgence of poetic imagery, culled from creation's vast expanse; and, by their combined influence, that every idea will be presented with the vividness of fancy, the coherence of reality, and the certainty of demonstration, and imparted with all its primitive fulness and splendor; that there, the same individual may unite concentrated attention which, like perfect vision, observes all around it, with an imagination whose telescopic glance reveals the most distant mysteries of nature's amplitudes, and a power of reasoning that shall bring everything to the test of microscopical examination. What a combination! What a manifold fitness of purpose! What a power is thus presented! It increases while we contemplate it. It expands while we strive to grasp it with our feeble faculties, until it seems coëxtensive with that boundless region which is to be the theatre of its action, and its limits elude the eye in the shades of infinity.

The phenomena of sleep may elucidate the effect which we have ascribed to the abstraction of spirit from material influences. It may, in all that relates to our argument, be considered as a partial death, which abstracts us from the realities of sense, which shuts out the physical world; and the attention, being thus freed from the distracting influence of surrounding objects, acquires a concentrated energy, giving us that command of the processes of ideality which imparts such unearthly vividness to our dreams. The connection between reason and imagination is not yet sufficiently complete; we are not sufficiently habituated to dealing with ideals completely detached from signs and reality; some of the faculties necessary to a perfect action are dormant; and hence incoherence and error are most frequently the consequence.* But the great activity of the mind, the facility

* The apparent incoherence of dreams is probably very much exaggerated by our viewing them as abstract operations of the mind. Knowing that our senses are at the time inert, we very naturally class them with those mental exercises which we are accustomed to pursue with the least

with which it accomplishes many intellectual operations, and the unwonted vigor of its perceptions during this temporary suspension, may assist us to some faint idea of

reference to sensation, and suppose they should be connected by the same laws of association as govern this class of our waking thoughts. These failing to account for their singular combinations, they appear mysterious; but the difficulty will in very many instances be removed, if we look upon them as imitations of the effect of sensation, or ideals which the increased vigor of the imagination, arising from causes already explained, enables it to produce with great celerity. When we class them with abstraction, we state them in terms, and, in the relations of these terms, seek the associations by which one idea has been made to follow another. In this we are of course baffled, but objects, events, emotions, or their immediate representative, ideals, may accrue in any conceivable order of succession, and in our waking reveries are sometimes recalled with scarcely less incongruity than they assume in dreams. In dreaming, these are sometimes mingled with trains of abstraction, which, being expressed in terms, produce a heterogeneous mass of reasoning and imagery, the attention often oscillating between the two, so that, in the order in which they occur, they appear in strange confusion, when, if separated into two distinct trains, the one might assume the form of abstraction, and the other be within the usual limits of ideality. It is possible that when we dream of using terms (of reading, for instance) that we do not always do it, — the ideas, the manner, the sensations, incident to reading, all taking the form of ideals. However this may be, it cannot be doubted that this element of ideality preponderates in our dreams ; and hence the effect of applying the rigid laws of narration or abstraction to this poetic mode of mind. Many of our waking reveries, and some written poetry, would not bear the application of such a test. The following instance is selected as one of the most common and simple forms of what may be called incoherent dreams :

The narrator dreamed that he was settling a mercantile account. Having completed the additions, he said the balance is two hundred dollars, to which I must add the interest, — all the angles of a triangle are equal to two right angles, which makes the balance just two hundred and twelve dollars. He awoke, wondering what the theorem had to do with the balance of the account. But when awake, the presence of a geometrical work open at this theorem, might have forced it on his senses between the premises which he had stated and the conclusion which he had in view. Had an what a more perfect alienation from all that is material may effect.

There is a pleasant mode of investigation, which the mind often resorts to, in the form of ideal conversations with absent friends. We conceive them present, state our own views, and imagine what they would reply. From the knowledge which we have acquired of their intellectual habits, we adopt their modes, and endeavor to get into the same channels of thought which they would pursue. We follow them to their conclusions, and modify our own accordingly. The advantages which result from this practice are similar to those which arise from the actual interchange of sentiments and opinions with the persons supposed to be present. We are led to view the subject in various aspects; and we feel, to a sufficient extent, the excitement which usually arises from real conversations upon subjects and with individuals of our choice. In sleep,—that state which most nearly approaches to that of death, and in which the spirit acts most independently of external circumstances,—this power of adopting the thoughts of our friends is so greatly increased, that we hardly suspect it of being the same which we exert in our waking reveries. How often in our dreams are we surprised at the turn given to the current of our thoughts by a remark which we imagine comes from some one present! Sometimes, when dreaming that we are engaged in argument, and when we suppose we have demonstrated our position, we find our confidence shaken by some new view, or some argument presented so suddenly and so unexpectedly that it seems impossible that it should have had its origin in

ideal of any object usually connected with accounts thus presented itself, its intrusion might have passed unnoticed, or as no more than a common and natural occurrence.

our own minds. It seems strange that our own thought should come thus unexpectedly upon us. But we are sometimes no less surprised by a new view suddenly occurring to us when awake; and that which surprises us in dreaming is but a new view, to which we have been led by imagining how another would look at it. These views, and the terms in which they are expressed in our dreams, are strikingly true to the modes of thought and expression usually adopted by the persons to whom we impute them; and while, in many instances, if we had met with them when awake, we should without hesitation have ascribed them to the same individuals, we are struck with the fact that they are widely different from our own accustomed modes.

Such dreams present another phenomenon, still more remarkable and mysterious. In some instances we do not immediately understand the connection of the argument, which we think we have heard from the lips of another, with the subject under discussion. The question arises, how could we have ourselves framed the argument without having perceived the connection? Is it that the views, which we thus perceive through the optics of another, flit before us, as our own waking thoughts sometimes do, without our being able to arrest them; that we get a glimpse of an idea and of its application to the subject, then lose it, and are obliged to reëxamine before we can again perceive the connection? We confess that this is not a sufficient explanation of all the facts of this kind within our knowledge, and we apprehend that most persons will be able to call to mind some, for which it does not furnish a satisfactory solution. But that the mind has a power, by which it can, in some degree, avail itself of the aid of those which are absent; by which, though it cannot perceive their thoughts, it can determine what they probably would think, if the subject were presented to them; and that this power is manifested in a much higher degree in that state of mind which approaches most nearly to that of its separate condition, appears to us to indicate the existence of a latent faculty or sympathy, by which, in a more perfect state, each mind may avail itself of the thoughts of others without the medium of terms.

Will it still be said that this is but an empty speculation, having no practical application? To us it seems to bear upon a subject of great importance, and one in which all must feel an interest. We regard it as a ray of light gilding the closing scenes of life, and dimly revealing a connection with that future, where we delight to group all that ideality pictures as lovely or ennobling, and where we expect to realize those visions of pure felicity, which a partial cultivation of our spiritual nature has here shown to be congenial to its highest development. But how few, even of such natures, contemplate these delightful anticipations unalloyed with painful apprehensions! The isolated paradise they gaze upon is beautiful, but appears to be surrounded by a troubled and unfathomable abyss. It is the distance at which they locate it, and the dark mystery which superstition has thrown around it, which fill them with gloomy forebodings. Whatever, then, has a tendency to destroy this illusion and exhibit, however obscurely, the channels by which the present flows into the future, gives confidence to hope, and disarms death of doubt and despair. Such we believe to be the effect of contemplating the nature, and observing the influence, of the purer forms of ideality.

On this subject we apprehend that much error prevails. However highly wrought the popular notions of the future may be, they are generally of that vague and unsettled character which produce little or no practical influence. They interest only those feelings which are acted upon by the power of mystery; and even the virtuous shrink from it as from a dreaded unknown. It is indeed to them an empty speculation, having no higher influence on their thoughts than the baseless visions of hope or fear can produce. But such views as the one we have endeavored to exhibit, give this airy nothing a local habitation in our hearts, turn illusion into reality and body it forth in all its brightness; extend our thoughts and our affections to another life; attach to it all the interest of a future home, and identify it with all the glowing anticipations and noble aspirations of the soul, — enabling us to see the connection between our present and future existence, as clearly as we perceive that between youth and age, and to estimate the influence of the one upon the other, with as much certainty as the boy can anticipate the effect of youthful virtue and exertion on his future manhood. And it is the extension of such views that can alone dissipate the gloom which hangs over the entrance to futurity, and so strip death of its mysterious terrors, that we shall view it only as an event in the life of the soul, which increases its vigor and introduces it to a higher field of action. It will then appear as little more than a line in the path of our advancement, marking our entrance into another and a better territory, where the efflorescence of a milder clime bursts upon us; where the alluring paths of ideality never lead to error; where the frost of care and the blight of disappointment are unknown; but where, in the bland influence of a perennial spring, the flowers of fancy are continually opening from the buds of feeling, and at the same time maturing to the fruit of knowledge, refreshing and invigorating the soul with new and varied manifestations of beauty and excellence.

It may be apprehended that the tendency of such views of future happiness, and such unalloyed confidence in its being the immediate effect of the separation of what in us is pure and spiritual from what is material, would be to render us dissatisfied with our present condition. But, even in regard to things temporal, bright anticipations do not make us less happy; and if they sometimes induce a restless, feverish anxiety for their attainment, it probably arises from an impression that the season of their enjoyment is limited and will be shortened by delay; whereas, in our contemplations of eternity, although we may not be able to grasp its infinity, we are impressed with a consciousness that it is long enough for the fulfilment of our anticipations, at whatever period they may commence. It may also be remarked, that the increase of happiness, arising from that mental and moral cultivation which enables us to form these brighter and nobler views of our destiny, is more than sufficient to make us satisfied; it gives zest to life. To a mind thus accustomed to observe its own progress in virtue and excellence, there can be nothing terrible in that event which merely accelerates it. It is only those who are entirely absorbed in transitory pursuits, having no participation in the delights of a cultivated mind; no idea of bliss purely spiritual; no conception of a heaven not material, that the change wrought by death is associated with all that is gloomy and appalling. Remove from them the material world, and nothing but a fearful blank, an abhorred vacuum remains. Engaged only with objects of sense, ideality has not revealed to them the more exalted sources of interest, and the idea of separation from all that has engrossed their thoughts, from all that has made mind manifest, must appear to them scarcely less dreadful than annihilation. If such be the condition of those who have neglected to improve, the case is yet worse with those who have perverted their highest powers, who have called them into action only to degrade them; who have known and felt the powerful workings of the spirit, but only through its influence on lacerated feelings, its convulsive throes to extricate itself from the degrading shackles of vice, and its ineffectual efforts to rise and expand in its proper sphere. It is here that ideality, still vivifying and giving intensity to the feelings, portrays its darkest picture.

We have, before, incidentally remarked, and at the same time attempted to explain the fact, that poetry is the source of feelings the most exquisite and exalting, or acute and overwhelming. We ascribed this to its power of calling up ideals with all the vividness of reality, yet divested of the modifying circumstances of real life. We have since pointed out other causes of its increase of power, particularly those which we have supposed to arise from the separation of the soul and body by death. Tracing it in its progress, we see it, while yet within reach of our finite faculties, becoming a source of pure, unspeakable enjoyment to the elevated and virtuous; but it is an equally efficient means of punishment to the degenerate spirit. It reaches our innermost feelings, and puts in action all the dormant elements of pleasure or pain. We know not that any description of spiritual punishment has yet gone further than to picture, in that figurative language in which ideality is so frequently embodied, what we here observe. We here see those who are degraded by avarice incessantly turning the iron wheel; the man of low ambition forever rolling up the recoiling stone: he who seeks gratification in the perversion of his moral feelings, is continually drawing, from the wells of pleasure, vessels which will hold no water; and the heart and spirits of the voluptuary are perpetually renewed, only again to be preyed upon by the vultures, satiety and remorse. These are indeed but pictures, faint pictures of the mental inquietude, chagrin, and desolation, of the bitterness of disappointment, and the reproach of conscience, which in this life attend transgression; producing in the vicious a mental degradation, a hideous blight, a loathsome leprosy of mind rotting in endless decay, which, however pride may conceal from the world, or however he may strive to blunt his sensibilities, and to stupefy and engross himself with the distractions of sense, still rankle in his bosom, or in the anguish-riven countenance give convincing proof of the immutable and immediate connection between vice and misery. He may observe the aggravation of suffering which solitude and seclusion produce in himself; or the effect on others, when the certain proximity of death has destroyed all interest in former pursuits, when shades of horror are darkening sublunary scenes around him, and the mind, no longer buoyed up by the levities and engrossments of the world, reverts to itself, and there meets the long-smothered, the avenging secrets of the past, just bursting their chains, with resistless energy overpowering the soul, and exhibiting themselves in the diabolical contortions and horrid writhings of their victims. These effects of a partial withdrawing from material things furnish him with data, from which he may calculate with something like arithmetical precision, the climax to which this suffering must arrive, when the mind is entirely deprived of its present resources; when it can no longer drown an upbraiding conscience in the tumult, nor divert attention in the bustling pursuits of life; when the host of vile recollections, the remorse and bitterness of the past, are mirrored back with multiform and magnified reflection in the maddening anticipations of the future, or depicted with all the vividness of a dream, yet with all the coherence and all the consequences of reality; when the fire, which has long raged within, has burst its earthly bonds, and displays its volcanic energy in the uncontrollable ravings of torturing, frenzied feelings; while, from the abyss of the past, lava torrents of reproach and shame whelm the soul in a guilty delirium, and visionary and dreadful phantasms mock its nightmare efforts to escape these emanations and shadows of itself; all acting upon the fermenting energies of a mind nervously awake to the exigencies of its condition, and wrought to its utmost intensity, — not with the buoyant excitement of hope, but with the dreadful agony of despair. Will not the consideration of this rapid progression hurry him to the result, and force upon him the conviction that he has within himself, in a corrupted heart, a degraded intellect, and brutal passions, the crude elements of a hell, more terrific than any which has been realized from all the physical torture which superstition has conceived or fanaticism attempted to portray? The fact that he has already witnessed its commencement, and the conviction that its consummation depends only on the stability of the laws of nature (or, as we would rather say, on the continuance of the uniform modes of Deity, of which we already have the evidence, and can, in some degree, estimate), gives it an appalling certainty. We know that its fulfilment will be but the natural effect of causes which are attested by human consciousness, and hence we perceive that it needs not a special interference of

Deity to accomplish it, but that it would require a miracle, perhaps more than a miracle, to prevent it.

The imagination being the most excursive faculty, and describing that which it rapidly glances over, by analogies to what was before known, and by refinements of the language which already exists, has a greater celerity than reason, which follows with assured and cautious steps, and has to adapt a language of terms to every new discovery. The former sweeps the distant verge of the dim horizon, and communicates the results of her desultory search, in shadowy forms which the latter condenses into terms, and brings to the test of a more critical examination. She then embodies, organizes, and extends her dominion over the newly-acquired territory; forming on its remotest confines more distant stations, from which fancy may again take its survey, and extend its horizon, till yet more remote regions are embraced.

In the natural order of events, then, ideality precedes reasoning; and if poetry has not always presented the first indications of remote truth, it is because of the superior discipline and perseverance of men of abstraction; or, perhaps oftener, because her own votaries have abandoned their high office of telescopic observers, and ingloriously contented themselves with a more humble and limited occupation of their talents. Happy mortals! who, with the most exalting and soul-kindling endowments; with powers which might exert a happy and immortal influence on the destinies of man, are still content to tread the level and beaten track of unambitious life; who find ample amusement in gathering the flowers, and picking up the pebbles they chance to meet with; and sufficient excitement in the dubious and ephemeral fame which may attend their success! They suffer themselves to be quietly enslaved by these sweet enticements, and enervated in gentle dalliance with such pretty toys; their souls lose the power of lofty effort; they shrink from the contest, and are no longer candidates for eternity.

Some of these, more skilled than others in the mechanism of verse, form insignificant trifles into poetic kaleidoscopes, where they appear with all the charms which varied arrangement and multiplied and harmonious reflection can bestow on such common-place materials. We turn them round, and are amused for the moment; but change itself soon ceases to be novelty, and even variety becomes monotonous. He who aspires to immortality, must add to these every-day beauties of nature more rare and costly materials, derived from less accessible sources. He must labor in the mines of thought, and give the extracted gems the soul-lit, sparkling polish which genius can bestow; and, from ocean-depths of feeling, bring pearls of purity and loveliness. He must cultivate an intimacy with nature in all her forms. He must gambol with her in her frolics; he must meditate with her in her tranquil scenes; or rush with her into the tempest, and witness the strife of elements. With her he must seize the roaring ocean by its mane, and mingle with the lightning, and hold communion with the thunder of the storm; or, with nobler effort and higher aim, soar aloft on the aspiring wing of fancy, and, with the unshrinking eye and daring hand of genius, cull the radiance of the welkin arch, and bring its star-lit splendors, fresh and sparkling, to adorn his page. With such splendid materials, he must illuminate and adorn the path to those distant truths, which his far-searching vision has first distinctly revealed to himself alone. These he must amplify with the powers of that language which is exclusively his own; a language which, free from vulgar associations, elevates the reader into a higher, purer, nobler region of thought. His discoveries are primitive perceptions, and a skilful use of the language of ideality, can alone enable him fully to impart them to others. By this he exhibits them with the impress of his own intellect and sensibility. He portrays them as they exist in his own mind, with the same vivid coloring and sparkling radiance, illustrated by striking analogies, and connected with associations so varied and diffusive, that, to the utmost stretch of vision, they present new and delightful combinations, and in the farthest outline seem still expanding, like the inappreciable and intangible emotions of music.

"The inappreciable and intangible emotions of music," — these words have produced an effect which we have already ascribed to the language of ideality. They have led us on to a point from which we have a glimpse of another bright realm in this unexplored wilderness, in advance of that in which we have already expatiated. It is the connection of poetry with music. If we have observed the fitness of the former to the subjects of feeling and of spirit, do we not perceive something in the latter, still more evidently having relation to some higher purpose than that of our physical existence? Is there not in these indescribable emotions, something which we here in vain attempt to grasp, more comprehensive, more ethereal even than poetry — a benign influence, which gleams on the soul, and, as a ray of light in its rapid course, just rouses its energies, and sweeps endlessly on through infinity? With any power of attention which we here enjoy, and with the limited means which we here possess of imparting these emotions, the sounds by which they are usually communicated require to be dwelt upon and varied. The mind at each successive variation pauses to examine the sensation, makes an effort to identify the indistinct associations which seem hovering around it, and needs to dwell on them for a moment, before it can be satisfied that they are too ethereal to be fully appreciated by its blunt sensibilities, and too vast to be embraced by its limited comprehension. It is a series of excitements, an induced activity to which the soul is wrought without any conscious effort of its own. But suppose music divested of its sounds, which absorb a portion of the attention, and these unmingled emotions to be immediately imparted to spirit, when the concentration of attention will admit of their passing in rapid and intensely exhilarating succession, while the increase of its powers enables it to follow and pervade the circle in which each expands itself in feeling's boundlessness?

The associations of music with sounds is so general, that, to some, even the hypothetical separation of them may appear preposterous. We, however, think it perfectly conceivable. We apprehend that the composers of music* must have the emotions independent of the sounds, as the poet has the ideals independent of the terms; and we believe that Shakspeare's denunciation of him who has not music in his soul would have been more justly applied to those who are destitute of these innate emotions, than to those who, from organic defect, or perhaps from being conversant with a

* Beethoven composed his greatest works after he had ceased to hear. —ED.

superior harmony within themselves, are less influenced by mere sounds, however mellifluous and delightful to better ears, or less cultivated sensibilities.

In defence of the high station which we have assigned to musical emotion, we may remark, that it is in the highest exaltation of mental action that these emotions are most perceptible. The effect of refined music is very much enhanced, when the mind is under the influence of some absorbing sentiment which concentrates its energies while it withdraws it from narrow, selfish considerations, and inspires it with generous feeling. It is then that the fine tones within, responsively swell the harmony which blends with them from without. We find this to be the case, when it is kindled into enthusiasm by the high and hallowing emotions of virtuous love, when our conceptions of loveliness, purity, and bliss, so far outstrip our powers of expression, as to belong rather to the empyreal evanescence of music, than to the most ethereal forms of poetry. When this sentiment reaches a still higher elevation, when Infinite Goodness becomes the object of devotion, we find music, in some of its forms, almost universally associated with it. It exhibits itself in the rude worship of the savage, and attunes the heart of the most cultivated and refined sensibility. We find it in the devout homage of the heathen; and it lends its mellowing influence to the forms of a more enlightened religion. It softens the stern rigidity of the anchorite, and instils itself into the pious meditations of the disciples of a milder creed. It is an elastic element of mind, which adapts itself to the various conditions of humanity. Among savages, it manifests itself in rude, barbarous sounds, which appear to have more connection with physical than with mental exercises. From this low state it rises, through the successive stages of cultivation, to that divine harmony of the spirit, which imparts such a delightful charm, such kindling rapture to the silent meditations of the enlightened mind; and which, while in the outward creation it finds for itself innumerable types and resemblances, admits of no generic sign, and no external substitute.

We may here observe an effect of language, in all its material forms. Like the mechanical powers, it gives us efficiency; but, like them, only at the expense of time. In the language of narration, the memory is assisted by having two separate objects of attention, either of which will recall the event or subject spoken of. In respect to the language of abstraction, years have sometimes been employed in settling the terms of a proposition. This induces a more critical examination, and a more thorough acquaintance with the subject. In examining the relations among terms, many others are discovered, besides those for which we are particularly seeking. We have already mentioned the effect of metre and rhyme in restraining the impetuosity of the poet, and giving fulness and variety to his views. In music, there appears to be a yet further application of this principle, and an extension of it to the recipient, by dwelling on the sounds of this artificial arrangement. In all these forms it retards us. It is always an incumbrance, but, like the lever, an incumbrance which our weakness renders essential.

We have now seen language, in its simplest form of narration, elevating us above the brute creation, to social and intelligent beings. We have observed, that, in the form of abstraction, it becomes an engine for the acquisition of general knowledge, and thus carries us through another stage of improvement, but one in which narrow views still predominate. We have remarked that it still keeps pace with our intellectual and moral advancement, and when our enlarging views pass the boundary of common, direct expressions, it becomes elevated to poetry, which we have supposed to be perfected where spirit is purified from all selfishness, and in a future state to receive an accession of power, by embracing the preceding forms. And we have suggested that this combination may, in a yet further stage of advancement, be etherealized and sublimated to the more exquisite perfection of music, which, though here but a vague and misty shadow, may yet be the first indication of what is there to be embodied in the most comprehensive, perhaps infinite emanations of truth and beauty. This progression is facilitated by the generous feelings which carry us beyond the little circle of common affairs, and particularly by those excitements which elevate us far above them; for it is only in the further and higher departments of thought, that we are compelled to think only in the poetic form of ideals. Hence it is that this faculty is so often first developed, when love,

> "That feeling from the Godhead caught,
> Has won from earth each sordid thought,"

making us conscious of a happiness too generous and exalted, too pure and ethereal, too vast for words to express.

The effect of this expansive sentiment upon the modes of thought and expression is one of the most striking illustrations of the theory we have advanced, and as such deserves a further notice. In its most romantic, and also its most ennobling form, it is the result of all the estimable qualities which the excited imagination of the lover can combine, embodied and harmonizing in some pleasing object, which has, in some generally unknown manner, excited the first emotion. When these perfections are different from any which we are conscious of possessing within ourselves, we have no means of measuring their extent, and the imagination may expand, without limit, to meet the soul's conceptions or wants. The superiority of mind to matter, and the greater expansibility of its qualities, indicate it as the only terrestrial object capable of exciting this hallowed emotion; and the diversity, which is a necessary element of perfecting it, is found admirably designed in the modifications of the masculine and feminine characters. If these views of the romantic passion are correct, it is evident that the imagination will almost immediately have filled the measure of this ideal excellence; that it will have reached, and even gone beyond, the tangible object of its adoration; and hence, although it may still retain all that it has gained, that object must lose its power of impelling it forward in the flowery paths and bright creations to which it has introduced it. We trust that we shall not be suspected of intending any disparagement of the sex, from whose purer spirit first emanated the spark which kindled in the breast of man this ethereal flame. It is much that woman has made us acquainted with one of the infinite tendencies of the soul, to fill the never-ending expansion of which she must be more than angel.

Must this influence, then, be arrested, and the consequent improvement cease? Has this spirituality been awakened in the soul, only to shed a momentary gleam of romance over the realities of life? Analogy rejects the idea; it must serve some higher purpose. And, observing the law of progression, is it not obvious that this finite feeling may be merged in the love of that which is infinite, and, in the attributes of God, find an illimitable field for its expansion, where every new elevation but reveals more to admire, adore, and love, thus forever presenting a standard of superior excellence, and forever winning us towards perfection? There is, on this account, a manifest advantage in the Deity not being present to our senses in any definite, tangible form. His power, wisdom, goodness, and every perfection, are manifested to us only in the beauty, grandeur, and designs of his creation; but these evidences are so obvious, so numerous, and so varied, that every one may discern the qualities and combine them, so as to form the precise character which will correspond to his own idea of perfection, and which he can most admire, love, and adore; a beau ideal, in which increased clearness of perception will only discover new beauty, and on which he may forever expatiate, and yet not sum up all its excellences; in which his admiration will be perpetually excited by new and delightful discovery; which will continually adapt itself to the change and enlargement of his views of perfection, and appear more beautiful and lovely the more he contemplates it. His most exalted conceptions of excellence may here always be realized; and this mode of mind is love etherealized, love sublimated to devotion, resting not on the fleeting shadows of a feverish imagination, but on the infinite and immutable attributes of a Being, that can never be the subject of those changes and misfortunes, the thought of which will sometimes break upon the transports of the most impassioned lover. The thought of one beloved, and with whom fancy has associated every human excellence and angelic loveliness, has often elevated the mind above criminal or ignoble conduct; and, if religion had done no more than furnish us with an ideal in which we group every perfection, she would still have done much to purify the heart, ennoble the mind, and bless and protect our race. Whether the object, with which we associate this ideal excellence, be human or divine, the effect of contemplating it will be the same in kind, though varying in degree; the tendency in either case being to produce that elevation of soul, purity of sentiment, and refinement of feeling, which are the natural guardians of virtue. It is in this view that we may realize the fulness of an apothegm of Madame De Stael, and perceive how much more than the mere truism is conveyed in her expression, "to love God is still to love." We again repeat, that to a mind accustomed to observe and to contemplate its own advancement in this delightful progress, there can be nothing terrible in that which merely accelerates it.

The observed connection between refined intelligence, enthusiasm, love, poetry, music, and devotion, bears a striking analogy to that so often noticed by natural philosophers between heat, light, magnetism, galvanism, electricity, vitality, and the nervous fluid. An ingenious attempt* has not long since been made to elucidate the latter, by a division of matter into two classes; the one, called common matter, having the property of concreting by an attractive power; the other, or ethereal matter, having the property of expanding by an inherent repelling tendency. All the phenomena alluded to, and indeed all other in the material world, are referred to combinations of these two, varying as the one or the other predominates in a greater or less

* Ultimate Principles, etc., by Lardner. Vanuxum.

degree. Pursuing the analogy, we may divide our moral nature into two elements; the one having an influence to contract, and keep us within the narrow limits of gross and grovelling occupations, and to which we may ascribe all the selfish feelings, which have no higher object than physical existence, or sensual pleasure, and which, if unaided, even in the best estate, reach no higher elevation than mechanical reasoning; and refer the greater refinements of reason, and the generous and exalted emotions of enthusiasm, love, poetry, music, and devotion, to the predominance of a finer and purer essence, already exhibiting its infinite tendency, and destined, when freed from its connection with the gross and sensual, to expand in the purer regions of an undefined immensity.

The calculations of avarice, and the sordid maxims of selfishness, are easily embraced in finite terms; and the language of abstraction, even when directed to more ennobling pursuits, has a constant tendency to narrow the path of our advancement, and lead us to subtle, rather than improving results. The processes of ideality, on the other hand, are constantly widening and giving us more expanded views. We would therefore suggest that the latent connection, which exists between the purer feelings and sentiments, arises from their all flowing from this source, as well as the property which they consequently have of gratifying our desire for the infinite. Thus, for instance, arises the association of music with devotion. The former consists of sounds so contrived that no one appears ever to reach an end, but to elude us rather than to cease, and these in forms so varied as to create the impression that they flow from some exhaustless source; while the latter is an analogous system of ideas, expanding without limit and modified without end, and so habitual is the association of sounds with ideas, that the recipient of the former often erroneously supposes he is possessing himself of the latter. Music may thus satisfy the infinite tendencies of our nature, without affording it any substantial nourishment, and thus, instead of imparting energy to those exalted feelings, create a morbid sensibility, producing disease, debility, and decay.

If, however, the state of feeling which is produced by symphony, is similar to that which best appreciates moral excellence, music may he useful in religious exercises. It may assist in unfolding the moral harmonies; and, if the state of mind, which observes the delicate relations of sounds, is analogous to that which perceives the delicate relations of ideas, it may be useful in education. But in all cases care must be taken that it be made a means, and not an end. There are other sensible phenomena which are, perhaps, even more generally associated with devotional feelings than music. The vast expanse and endless roar of ocean, the never-dying murmur of the forest, mountains piled on mountains with no visible limit, the scenery of a nocturnal sky with its countless host of stars filling immensity, all awaken emotions which we feel to be closely allied to those which arise from the contemplation of the goodness and attributes of Deity. They all exalt to solemn thought and heavenly musings. There is infinity in all.

We have seen that language is one principal means by which the ethereal principle is first elicited, and that, by embodying the results of the processes of ideality, it sustains it through successive stages of improvement, until it expands itself in devotion, where it may forever continue its progress without arriving at any limit.

Observation is the first faculty brought into action, and is for a time a sufficient source of mental excitement. The child is pleased with every novelty; we may see him sound his rattle, pause, and shake it again, to assure himself that it is the effect of his own volitions, and he is thus continually exhilarated by the acquisition of knowledge, and the discovery and exertion of his own powers. His store of facts accumulates, the circle around him is culled, and a necessity for classification and invention (the two earliest stages of reasoning and imagining) is at once produced. These enable him to reduce his particulars, and to form new combinations of them. His mind expands until these appear too limited, and reason begins to form universal propositions, which are among the earliest indications of its infinite tendency. These, however, relating only to things in themselves finite, fail to meet the wants of his opening soul. The infinite begins to claim his attention. He fixes upon the most expansive of terrestrial objects, upon mind, but in a form so differing from his own, that he may conceive of it as imbued with qualities far surpassing any which he is conscious of possessing, and yet not feel himself comparatively degraded in his division of the species. This, as we have before explained, forms the poetic stage of his advancement. The finer feelings of his nature are now developed, and expand themselves with a rapidity proportioned to the vast range here opened to their exercise, until even this fails to meet their wants. The universal mind alone remains; and here all the infinite tendencies of the soul now expand themselves; here refined intelligence, enthusiasm, love, poetry, and devotion, are united in a delightful harmony — blended in one heaven of feeling. The religious sentiment is thus fully developed by the union of all the pure and infinite tendencies of the soul, which, traversing the finite, find no other sphere sufficiently comprehensive for their full development, and nothing which harmonizes wholly with their nature, but the manifestations and the attributes of the Godhead. In this combination the ethereal principle largely predominates, and the expansive tendency becomes so strong, that neither human force, nor human ingenuity, has yet been able to control it. It has been loaded with the chains of tyranny; it has been retarded and shackled by creeds; it has been diverted from its proper objects by cunningly-devised forms, and gorgeous and imposing ceremonies. It has been wickedly directed to inexplicable mysteries, and wasted in the vain endeavor to elicit truth from terms which contained no meaning. But, in despite of all these obstacles, it has advanced. It has set at defiance the power of princes, and broken the fetters they imposed. It has put at naught the subtlety of priests, and, with the energy of enthusiasm, penetrated beyond the forms and mysteries by which they have sought to conceal truth; and it has proclaimed its discoveries from the flames which surrounded it with glory, and shed lustre on its revelations. The only mode of preventing the development of this expansive principle is, by destroying some of its elements, or by taking away some of the steps which are essential to its progress. The experiment of shackling the mind with prohibitions, preventing the acquisition of knowledge, and restraining the reasoning faculties, has in part succeeded. But the step, thus removed, is too short to leave an impassable barrier. The mind gets over the abhorred vacuum, and its weakened energies expand beyond it. It is by removing the next and greater element of our advancement, by destroying the influence of woman on society, and with it the generous emotions, the exalting influence of love, that the progress of mankind has been most effectually checked. It is only where the female character is so degraded that its ethereal influence is no longer felt; only where from infancy man has been taught to look upon woman as a soulless toy, and woman to act as if unconscious of a higher destiny, that this sign of divinity has failed to exhibit itself. The same effect has been elsewhere produced by her exclusion from society, and by resorting to physical deformity, of a kind producing sloth of body, dependence, and consequent want of mental energy. Restore the soul of woman, and the Mahometans would soon have a better and a brighter revelation. Suffer the feet of Chinese women to grow, and the men could not long retain their grovelling, slavish dispositions, nor the government its narrow and exclusive policy.

It is worthy of remark, that a religion adapted to the wants of the ethereal nature, must, like that nature, possess a susceptibility to never-ending expansion. It must continually exhibit a higher and better state of existence than that to which we have arrived; and consequently, the professors of such a religion will always be manifestly short of its teachings, while the professors of a rigid finite system of ethics may fulfil every tittle of their law. The Christian dispensation certainly appears to possess this wonderful adaptation. Its broad principles include the whole duty of man, and apply in every situation and in every stage of his progression. Like the Source from whence they emanate, they always fulfil our views of perfection. It were to be wished that the views just stated would account for all the acknowledged defalcation of those who profess to be followers of its great founder. How delightful would it be to draw at once an illustration and a confirmation from such a fact! How encouraging to believe, that, because we had improved and were still improving, the horizon of perfection recedes! We fear, however, that we must look to other causes, for at least a portion of the disparity between the profession and practice of Christians.

But the application of this subject, and of some of the principles which this investigation of it has elicited, is so universal, that its full development would embrace all knowledge, and leave no department of mind unexplored. Leaving, then, this vast field of speculation, we will return to the consideration of some points, more immediately connected with the two principal forms of language.

The language of ideality admits of an almost universal adaptation to every grade of intellect. It calls up emotions such as the realities produce. It fits itself to the comprehension, and fills the capacious as well as the contracted mind. If the difficulties, which our imperfect modes of communicating thought here present, were removed, so that every mind might at once be easily made the recipient and dispenser of ideals, the disadvantages of inferior intellect, considered in its relations to society, would be in a great measure obviated. The less would then impart to the greater a measure which itself did not possess, and thus all be fitted for agreeable communion with each other. Besides, as the gratification of imparting or receiving knowledge is in well regulated minds just equal, they may be reciprocally the means of happiness to each other. Happiness will then depend on purity, sensibility, and a consciousness of advancement. In fact, all depends on purity. It is the vital element of the other two, without which the one would be dormant, and the other blunted or pained. So far as mere intellect is concerned, the greater weakness or ignorance will be compensated by greater capacity for improvement. The wise and the weak may both feel all the delight they are capable of feeling. Both may advance with a rapidity proportioned to their views of the sphere of excellence. Though the former may have arrived at what may be termed a greater and higher degree of enjoyment, yet they will also require all the larger and more elevated resources which they may be able to command; and where the measure of happiness is full in all it will be difficult to say who enjoys most. Nor is it improbable that we often err in our estimate of the effect of intellectual power. So far as a vigorous exercise of it advances us in the scale of moral excellence, it undoubtedly adds to our happiness; while, on the other hand, its perversion may sink us still lower in wretchedness. Moral purity is, then, the grand element of happiness; moral degradation the great source of misery. The proper object of all is improvement; and a consciousness of success in this great end of existence is a source of happiness which is accessible to all, and in which all may render mutual aid to each other. The inferior mind must receive more than it imparts, but, in thus receiving, it still conduces to the happiness of the more gifted, who are excited to exertion, not only by the consciousness of their own improvement, but by the pleasure which it gives them to improve others.

To omniscience the pleasure of acquiring knowledge must be denied, and enjoyment must arise from a sense of imparting its own perfection to finite minds. For even spiritual perfection, if it were wholly locked up in itself, and could impart nothing to other minds, would be of a character little higher than mere physical perfection. It is then principally through the medium of benevolence that much knowledge produces happiness. Without this attribute, even omniscience, deprived of the pleasure of acquiring and improving, would be a curse. Hence the desolation of those spirits, in whom the consciousness of superior powers and attainments is united to misanthropic feelings. To this misfortune the votary of ideality is peculiarly obnoxious. The man of abstraction goes little further than he can find words to sustain his thoughts; but the idealist knows no such bounds to his ardor; no limits are imposed on his fancy. His imagination revels in the infinite, and, great as his powers of expression may be, he cannot always clothe his conceptions in that palpable form, which will make them apparent to the multitude. He may have dreamed of improving the world. His fancy may have been warmed, his heart may have glowed with the purest enthusiasm for the advancement of his race. His whole soul may have felt the delightful influence of an expansive benevolence; and yet he may not have possessed that self-forgetting benevolence which would lead him, without any compromise of his own individuality and greatness, to accommodate his powers to the wants of society, and employ a portion of his talents in making his discoveries more accessible to common minds. He may be exalted, and yet not be wholly free from that vanity which induces him to expect applause as the reward of his genius. He expected sympathy, and the world views his enthusiasm with cold distrust, and refuses to bestow the praise which fed his hopes. Confident in himself, he imputes his failure to the stupidity of others. Disappointment produces disgust, and the bosom which once swelled with the most generous and glowing emotions, now inflated with the proud feelings of misanthropy, or chilled with contempt, exhibits only occasional manifestations of its native excellence.

We feel the want of the support of other minds, in proportion as our views extend beyond the pale of certainty. In matters which admit of rigid demonstration, we care little who differs from us; but in matters of opinion, we are pleased with the confirmation of other minds; and in subjects of mere speculation, are delighted to find a kindred spirit who has traversed the same ground and arrived at similar results, or is at least able to enter into our views and understand our imperfect descriptions of it. Hence, of all others, the poet enjoys most from the sympathy of congenial minds, and suffers most from the want of it. Hence, too, an intemperate zeal to make converts to a particular faith, often arises from an innate doubt, or latent conviction that the particular doctrine in question cannot be demonstrated, and requires to be supported by extrinsic testimony.

Even as a means of advancing knowledge, we apprehend the comparative power of reasoning is often overrated, or too exclusively relied upon. We give it credit for original discovery, when it has only attested the truth of what ideality has suggested. In some sciences it undoubtedly is all availing; but in the perception of moral truth it often falls short of that intuitive principle, that sensibility, which is most frequently found conspicuous in those destitute of great reasoning powers. A lofty power of generalization may bear forward the intellectual philosopher even in the field of morals; but how often will his fine-spun theories be found inapplicable to the endless variety of actual occurrences! His greater strength may enable him to penetrate gloomy forests, traverse mountains, ford rivers, and make his way against every obstruction, even beyond the usual limits of research, and he may, on his return, exhibit some remotely acquired truth; yet it is often as ill-shapen, and and as little adapted to the occasions of life, as the fragments which the traveller brings from some alpine height, as mementos of his useless toil. Others, less hardy, and seemingly less adventurous, are endowed with a more refined spirituality, which enables them to perceive the delicate relations among ideals. Their feelings assume a softer hue, on which the finest shades of truth are more nicely delineated, and, possessing in these feelings the most delicate tests, they are susceptible to the slight and beautiful indications of truth everywhere to be met with, and from which are deduced the most important consequences. If reasoning, with powers which may fitly be compared to those of the telescope and lever, has measured the amazing distances, and weighed the immense masses of systems of worlds, and overpowered us with astonishment at the stupendous results, it must be remembered that humbler instruments have elicited equal cause of wonder. The microscope has exhibited to us a world in every atom, and introduced us to that intimacy with creation, which has ever led to the most expanded views of nature and of nature's God; and the torsion of a single fibre of a spider's web has revealed that one of the laws by which He hurls the thunder and shakes the universe is precisely the same as that by which He has chosen to sustain it. If the one is a type of the masculine powers of generalization and abstraction, the other, like the softer sex, reveals the poetry and music of our nature; for the refined sensibility, ideality of character, and spontaneity of thought and feeling of women, enable them at once to pronounce on what accords and what discords with moral truth and moral beauty. It cannot, in the absence of the other powers, enable them always to appreciate universal propositions, nor can it protect them from the commission of great errors, when they attempt to express themselves in general terms; but it seldom allows them to go far wrong in a particular case. If they are asked for a reason, they can generally answer only from their feelings or convictions, the sources of which are to them as inappreciable and as intangible as the inspirations of poetry or the emotions of music. *I know*, or *I feel*, is with them an argument, against which it is in vain for philosophy to direct its reasonings, or for satire to point its ridicule. They pretend not to judge of the one, and rectitude of intention elevates them above the other. This confidence in their own perceptions is to them a conservative principle, which shields them from many errors that they would inevitably commit, if they endeavored to apply the results, even of those wiser than themselves, without understanding either their speculative subtlety or practical application, *which they neither know nor feel.*

This power of perceiving truth in the form of ideals is the basis of the intuitive principle, and though, like all the finer endowments, possessed in a high degree of perfection only by the pure and sensitive, is capable of extension, in some degree, to every order of intelligence. In finite minds it is of course limited. In perverted minds it will lead to mistakes. Yet, considering the rapidity of its action, it is much less surprising that it should sometimes be wrong, than that it should so often be right. Even experience sometimes misleads us, and a general rule, tested by the observation of years, is afterwards found to have its exceptions. As the opportunities for observation are lessened, the chances of mistake are greatly increased, and hence, of all sources of error, a too rapid generalization is perhaps the most prolific. What then would be the result, if men who have not cultivated this faculty, who are immersed in business, and whose examination must necessarily be hasty, should rely on processes of reasoning, in which an error in the signification or limit of a term would vitiate a conclusion, on which their correctness in a thousand other instances might depend? The consequences would be incalculable, and hence the importance of this intuitive principle, which appears to us to be but a process of ideality, a mode of reasoning or of examining the relations of things and ideas, without the intervention of terms. In this act of the mind, it glances through its primitive perceptions, surveys at once motives, actions and consequences, and forms its conclusions, in inconceivably less time than it would require to substitute the terms, test the precision of their limits, examine their relations, and arrange them into syllogisms.

From the quickness of the operation, and the absence of terms, it can give no account of its processes. How admirably does this facility of examining particular cases compensate for the want of generalization! It is evidently a mode of mind nearly allied to that by which we have supposed spirits to perceive truth, but often desecrated by its application to inferior objects. This principle, however, sheds light on some portions of our speculation, and strengthens some points of our argument; and particularly as it is developed with a clearness and extent proportioned to spiritual and moral excellence.

When this power of perceiving is sufficiently clear and

accurate, it enables its possessor to lay aside general rules, and to judge, or act, in each particular case, from his immediate perceptions and impulses, giving to his mind a reach of thought, and spontaneity of action, which we generally denominate *genius*. With a *poetic sense* he perceives the relations of ideas, and those little delicacies of propriety and association, which words can but feebly portray. He is thus enabled to act with a discerning judgment and taste in matters in which language affords him no aid, either in the way of general rules, or as a means of investigation. Hence it is that genius acts independently of general rules. It occupies a sphere too far advanced for their application, and in which the processes of ideality are alone availing.

The man of abstraction often acquires a power, nearly resembling this, and no doubt frequently confounded with it. In some cases his terms are already prepared, and habit enables him to substitute them, and to perceive their relations, with such facility, that the processes make no impression on his memory, and the result appears to be intuitive.

In the processes of ideality, the mind deals with the actual existences of the material or intellectual world, which present themselves with all their natural and wide-spread associations. In verbal reasoning it deals with words, and the limited, arbitrary associations, which form their definitions. The use of terms in the one case has the same effect in calling up these artificial associations, as the sight or recollection of an actual existence has in calling up whatever we have associated with it. The mode of mind is in both cases very similar, and if the former may be said to be a mode of reasoning without terms, the latter may with equal propriety be defined a process of ideality with them. We apprehend that this similarity has had some influence in obscuring the relations of poetry and prose. It makes the apparent difference in the processes less than it really is, and it seems altogether disproportioned to the results. But it must be remembered that, although these modes of mind are in this one respect similar, its action is very much modified by the nature of the materials which it acts upon. Ideals expand; terms narrow the path in which it advances. Ideality is coëxtensive with thought and sentiment; abstraction cannot extend beyond the contracted limits to which a precise language is applied. Here we perceive a vast difference; and we have endeavored to preserve the distinction, by applying the term reasoning, when used without explanation, only to the forms of abstraction. But if, in accordance with common custom and learned authority, we define this term to imply that process of the mind by which it deduces consequences justly from premises, or by which it arrives at the unknown by combinations of the known, it embraces both of these modes. The one is the reasoning of the nominalists; the other is the nearest possible approach to that of the realists. The nominalists compress a subject until the mind can survey it at once. Their definitions are often mere hypotheses, having no *necessary* connection with reality, but so framed as to involve certain consequences; and their reasoning is but an arrangement of terms, more clearly showing that these consequences are thus involved. This is emphatically the case in mathematics, the most perfect specimen of nominal or verbal reasoning. In this science the same definition always attaches to the same word, but in connection with these words, and more especially in the application of the algebraic modes, we use letters of the alphabet, or any other marks which have no particular meaning, but in each individual case are supposed to represent such quantity or property as renders them most fit for the purposes for which they are immediately wanted. These are signs to which any hypothesis may be attached; terms, whose significations are made to vary according to circumstances. The associations with them, or their definitions for the time being, are dependent on our will. We make them expressly for the occasion, we limit and fit them as we choose, and hence are in little danger of misapplying them. By this artifice, this mode of reasoning from definitions is extended to minuter divisions of cases, which, if terms with unvarying definitions were used, would require more words than now exist in our whole language.

Before we can apply the results of this or any other nominal reasoning to practice, we must be certain that we have a case conformable to the hypothesis. In the application of mathematics, we are often enabled to do this. In the measurement of matter, we can divide it into shapes nearly approaching to those of which it treats; and the motions of the heavenly bodies are, with small variations, in curves, whose properties are accurately expressed in their definitions. In point of accuracy, mathematical reasoning has an advantage in dealing with nothing but quantity. However different the shapes which it compares, they may still be considered as in this respect homogeneous; they are all quantity, and to the mind of the mathematician nothing but quantity. Every form is measured by a portion of itself, but how can we measure in the case of subjects which are in their nature indivisible, as love, virtue, honor, happiness, etc.? Still mathematical, in common with all nominal reasoning, goes no further than to meet specific cases. The general rules elicited may assist the judgment, and enter into the composition of that common-sense opinion, which is within the province of ideality. The mathematician, for instance, may calculate the flow of water in channels supposed to be rectangular, circular, or of any other given form, and tell us the effect of the increase or decrease of quantity, or of inclination, etc.; but, in the application of the formula deduced from such hypothesis to actual existences, to rivers in their unequal winding channels, so great and various allowances must be made, that at best the scientific calculations make but a portion of the circumstances which go to form our opinion. Considering this difficulty of making the definitions, or the hypothesis on which verbal reasoning always depends, conformable to actual existences, and that the process of ideality is always really based on these actual existences, it is at least conceivable, that the difficulties and chances of error, in the adaptation of the former mode, may be greater than those which arise from the vague and indefinite expansion of the ideals used in the latter; and that this may be preferable in many of the practical concerns of life, where circumstances and their combinations are so various that no general rules can embrace them all. No mode of applying to this variety variable terms, like those which give algebra such a diffused and universal application to questions of quantity, has yet been devised. It is conceivable that something of this kind might be done in other departments of thought, but when we reflect, that, in applying it to the every-day concerns of life, the principal object would be to estimate the effect of flowing events on our happiness, and then consider the endless variety, the infinite combination and *unde-*

finable nature of these circumstances, and the various effects of the same causes on different individuals, the obstacles appear insurmountable. An arrangement of terms, which would meet all the cases which actually arise, must be as subtle and diffusive as spirit, and its distinctions be as nicely shaded as those of thought itself. We apprehend that mind alone possesses the pliancy which admits of this universal adaptation, and that it must lose its expansive energy, before its primitive perceptions will be thus overtaken by terms.

But, to show how far these latter now fall short of the wants of our being, we will take a case of far narrower limits.

The combinations on the chess-board, though vast in number, are finite. Yet, how vain would be the attempt to give rules for every case which could possibly arise! It is conceivable, it is even obviously possible, that it might be done; but, when accomplished, a life would be too short to learn it. If, therefore, we cannot, by means of general rules, learn to play this game, which has only finite combinations, what can we expect from them when applied to the more complicated game of life, in which the combinations are infinite, and the circumstances often as little within our control, and as unexpected, as the moves made by an antagonist on the chess-board? We apprehend that in both cases the only proper way, after deriving what assistance we readily can from general rules, is to look at the actual existences, to combine and examine the particular circumstances as they arise, to suppose a particular course adopted, and then *see* what consequences will probably follow, and by this process of ideality to determine how to move or act. This mode seems to have been preferred by a large portion of mankind, especially in the great questions connected with morals and religion. It is not always as certain as if more time were devoted, and every conceivable case examined, in all its bearings and tendencies, with the aid of terms; but it is the only one which admits of practical application. It enables us promptly to apply that great moral law, "to do unto others as we would that they in similar circumstances should do to us," for the means by which we ascertain what we would they should do to us, is evidently a process of ideality. It is the only way in which a large portion of mankind are able to examine and determine on many matters in which they are greatly interested. We may often observe the failure, in stating general rules, of good men, whose consciences would leave them at no loss as to how they should act in any of the particular cases arising under these same rules. All have not the time, the skill, nor can all spare from other proper pursuits the intellectual capital necessary, to perfect the verbal machinery which is required to examine high and important questions; and the attempt, if unsuccessful, or not persevered in, would only entangle and perplex them. It is more prudent and safe, for such, to do what they require for their own home use in the simple, natural way, and leave to philosophers the business of supplying the world, by the operation of complicated machinery which they better understand. We cheerfully commit to them the task of fitting and regulating the action of that enginery, which is to convert the pliable materials of ideality into fixed and rigid maxims, meet every case of morality, and answer all the purposes of religion, by doing which, its advocates hope to give stability to the changing forms and hues, by which religious observances and opinions are adapted to the various conditions of society, and to reconcile their endless variety in one beautiful, harmonious system.

But they have not yet been able to exclude numerous errors and discrepancies; and, however rapidly they may perfect their mode, we apprehend that the equally improving optics of ideality will continue to detect imperfections. Still, their persevering industry has accomplished much; and we regard the deficiencies alluded to not as a fault of theirs, or of the means which they employ, but as necessarily connected with all subjects which admit of no limitation. Morality and religion, — the relations of man with his fellow-beings and with his God, are of this infinite kind. They cannot, therefore, be fully embraced by terms, and ideality will always perceive more of them than abstraction has reduced to order. This is the natural progress of knowledge; the vague and conjectural becomes distinct and certain; demonstration follows on the rear of fancy. Yet we do not apprehend that the progress of truth has the power to circumscribe her flight. Philosophy may condense the mists in which ideality shapes her fairest forms, and with them may vanish the gorgeous rainbow and the prismatic splendor with which this poetic power had adorned them. These beautiful effects of uncombined, confused, and perverted light, may no longer glitter in the eye of the poet, but the mist, condensing into the dew of science, has refreshed his imagination, and opened on his vision more distant prospects. With fresh hopes and invigorated powers, he takes a loftier flight, and, in the indistinct perceptions which still form the boundary of his extended vision, he shapes new and more perfect beauty, and finds sublimer and more exciting mystery.

Poetry is relatively further advanced in an uncultivated state of society, or rather when science is just dawning on a benighted age, because then the artificial language of abstraction is very imperfect, and thought is, of necessity, pursued by means of processes of ideality, and expressed in the language adapted to that mode. The genius of a people thus circumstanced, is forced into this channel, and poetic forms of thought and expression become habitual. The resources of the poet are then more various, and more accessible, for all the great truths are beyond the limits to which philosophical language has advanced. They are in the vague poetic state, and furnish ample materials for ideality. These are first presented in their most striking aspect, and associated in a manner, which, however beautiful, would not be likely to occur to those who discerned their real connections, but which, being always conceivable, appear as distinct creations of the poet. Our admiration of the genius which conceived these associations increases as the advancement of truth shows them to have little or no foundation in reality, and he who supposed himself only narrating his discoveries, obtains praise for inventing or creating. The language in which the early poets have thus expressed themselves, becoming identified with indistinct perceptions, or erroneous and delusive associations, is rendered unfit for philosophical accuracy, and hence it is allowed to retain its poetic expansibility.

From this view of the subject it appears that the sphere of poetry must be continually changing; that, in an ignorant state of society, it admits of a larger infusion of narrative and physical knowledge, and advances on the verge of literature to the higher departments of moral and intellectual science, which are now its principal elements. If ever the mysteries of our nature, and the relations of society, should be fully developed, and accurately expressed in words, it would be driven from these to yet higher objects. The mysteries of the infinite mind, in its various manifestations, and the numberless relations by which, through eternity, it is united to the finite, would then become more exclusively its appropriate themes.

As philosophy is extended, poetry, always occupying the circle beyond it, recedes, and fewer will get through the mass of science which intervenes. This is particularly the case when a sudden impulse is given to abstract knowledge. The progress of the poet is then impeded, and his vision obstructed, by the unarranged and partially condensed materials with which philosophy is engaged. The atmosphere is not then sufficiently clear for distant observation, and to make what is already within the sphere of concrete science the subject of poetry, would be to retrograde. It would be using a telescope to look at objects near to us. To versify its facts is an exercise of ingenuity very similar to that of arranging the mathematical shapes of a Chinese puzzle into given prescribed figures.

The novels of the present age are narration, with a large infusion of ideality, and the favor with which they have been received by the public is a cheering evidence that this principle has not been eradicated by the encroachments of physical science, and that it is not confined to a few who have successfully cultivated it, but is still diffused through all classes of society. We give them credit for something more than being evidence of this fact. We regard them as having conduced to it; as having at least aided to keep alive the germs of this high but unanalyzed endowment. In these works of fiction it has assumed the guise of reality, and mingled with the utilitarian topics which now almost exclusively occupy the public mind. In the productions of Scott it portrays character, sentiment, and affection, as they exhibit themselves in society; and in those of Bulwer it is advancing to still more remote regions of metaphysics.

Repressed by the force of circumstances, ideality still infuses its spirit into the material science of the day, and its animating beams, though shorn of their brilliancy, still light and cheer the path of improvement.

How far cultivation and moral purity may increase the clearness of perception, and give at once extension and certainty to the processes of ideality, we pretend not to know. There are those who, habituating themselves to silent meditation, and carefully avoiding the usual modes of reasoning, sometimes arrive at results so suddenly, so vividly portrayed, and by means so difficult to trace, that they appear to flash upon them from some unseen source, and they ascribe them to inspiration. We are not disposed to differ from them about this term, as thus applied, though we may deem it more nearly allied to poetic inspiration, than they would be willing to admit. To us it seems to be an inference, or impression, derived immediately from the perceptions or ideals in the mind, — a process of ideality, quickened by a pure enthusiasm and dignified by its objects. Being good, we agree with them that it comes from the source of all good. We agree with them that it is the reward of patient seeking and holiness of thought; but whether as a natural consequence of this hallowed meditation, or as an immediate and special act of divine favor, is a question which is involved in the more general and very interesting inquiry, whether the creation is governed by natural, self-sustaining laws, or by the immediate volitions of Deity, or by both.

We agree with them that it is, in every sense of the word, the *quickening* principle, that it is superior to all other human endowments, but we would still pronounce it human; or, if with them we admit it to be divine, we would call it the divinity of human nature. It literally is, as they express it, a working of the spirit, but it seems to be a common opinion with them that this spirit is not an attribute of themselves, but a distinct, independent power, over which they can exert no control, but of whose manifestations they must be mere passive recipients. The obvious tendency of such a belief is to prevent exertion, and their faith in it is probably strengthened by the greater ease with which truth is PERCEIVED in this mode than it can be ATTAINED by reasoning. The difference is analogous to that of observing the equality of two figures when one is applied directly to the other, or determining the same fact by means of a geometrical demonstration. In the first case we ascertain it without any conscious effort—we perceive it, as we perceive intuitive truth when we compare our perceptions immediately with each other. In the latter, it requires labor and attention to trace the equality of figures, as it does the agreement of ideas through the medium of terms. The error to which we have alluded is, however, principally in terms. Experience teaches the disciples of this doctrine that some efforts on their part, and some mental exercises of their own, are necessary antecedents to this working of the spirit, and the practical evil is thus, in a great measure, avoided. In these meditations, they arrive at higher views of their destiny; they more clearly discern the means of attaining it; and however deficient the views of any one may still be, or however short of what more gifted spirits may have entertained, it is still to him a revelation. The exalted pleasure they derive from these sudden manifestations, and a vivid perception of their real or supposed importance, united to a philanthropic and generous enthusiasm to extend the knowledge of these sources of happiness, often imparts to them a fervor and eloquence apparently supernatural.

Such, we apprehend, is the *rationale* of Quakerism. The practical application and improvement of the elastic principle of ideality, with its expansive power unshackled by creeds, has enabled an unlearned people to make great advances in spiritual truth; while their ignorance of this grand element of their own system will account for some extravagances or errors into which it has led them. Not recognizing this sublime agent of discovery and advancement as an attribute of humanity, they have ascribed its effects to the immediate and special interposition of the Deity, and thus overlooked all secondary means of his manifestation. A predominance of this principle, and an habitual reliance upon it, has had its influence upon the society to which we have alluded, to give them a character for caution and prudence in the management of their secular concerns, which probably has, in part, arisen from its protecting them from those visionary schemes which are based on fine-spun reasonings. To these schemes, from the importance which the absence of other sources of aggrandizement has led them to attach to wealth, they would be peculiarly obnoxious, were it not for the countervailing tendency of their belief to distrust results deduced from a skilful arrangement of terms, which they expressively call "vain reasoning." It is not unworthy of remark, that these same people believe, that, by attention to these inward teachings, they arrive at a higher degree of purity and refinement than can otherwise be attained; and that, when thus far advanced, they can, in some favored moments, communicate, one with another, without any external means. We must confess that, although this is precisely what we have supposed to be an effect of spiritual advancement, yet we can no more conceive that such an effect, without a greater change in the condition of man than is apparent in this world, is embraced in that hypothesis, than we can conceive intuition, as we have just explained it, to extend to those long arithmetical calculations made by persons who are apparently deficient in every other faculty. The great interest felt on such occasions may direct the attention with corresponding intensity, and all the circumstances in which the one is placed may be realized by the other in the form of ideals, and produce in him similar emotions. It is, then, only like causes producing like effects. It is a state of highly excited sympathy in which they enter into the circumstances and participate in the feelings of each other. In the exact sciences, a problem being mentally investigated by a number of individuals understanding the subject, and then expressed in the proper terms, would in most instances be recognized by each of them as his own train of reasoning; and, on many questions which admit of greater diversity, there will be a few channels of thought, some one of which those who think of the subject will pursue, and thus produce many coincidences of argument and conclusion. So, in the instances we are considering, the circumstances, being known and pondered upon, produce similar states of mind. It is true that it is more difficult to say precisely what feelings will be produced by known circumstances, than what thoughts on a problem. There is a greater latitude, and the coincidences will, from this cause, be less frequent. As an offset to this, the terms in which these excited feelings are expressed have an almost equal latitude. Added to this, the feelings themselves may be of a very vague and indistinct character, and, being expressed in terms equally vague, each may suppose his own ideals properly represented by the same form of words, though in reality they vary in no small degree from each other.

We will here remark on an evil, not attaching to this sect in particular, but arising among sectarians generally, from the exclusion or neglect of verbal reasoning. The want of the habit of thinking abstractly leads them to associate what they deem wrong principles so closely with sects and individuals, that their abhorrence of the erroneous doctrines becomes rancor towards those who profess them.

We have followed the views of the Society of Friends further than we at first intended, in order to point out what we believe to be errors arising from the exclusion of verbal reasoning, and to exhibit the effect of a steady disciplined attention to one of the forms of ideality. They probably prefer to be considered the peculiarly favored of Heaven, and the recipients of its immediate dispensations; but we deem it no less honorable among men, nor less unequivocal evidence of acceptance with God, that they have so cultivated this exalted principle, that its manifestations, true to its divine character, appear to them of celestial origin, and to exert a celestial influence.

As a means of human advancement, we are far from considering this high endowment as exclusively attaching to any sect. It is a mode which must be more or less resorted to, by all patient inquirers after truth. It is the poetic temperament, the expansive properties of the soul, which will extend themselves into the hidden infinite, but which are partially subdued and made subservient to the high purpose of human advancement. It exhibits itself not in lightning gleam, but curbed in its erratic course, and softened and diffused over the space which lies between that which is tangible and that which is inscrutable, revealing, in its gloaming light, truths over which abstraction has not yet extended the pale of demonstration. It requires great care and application to keep the mind in that state which admits of intuitive certainty, for, as we are not fully aware of the elements which go to form our conclusions, we have no opportunity of correcting them by an analytic examination, and a single error may warp and vitiate all our views of a subject. Indeed, it is one of the greatest defects of those who rely on this principle, to the exclusion of reasoning, that they cannot distinguish its results from other impressions unconsciously received, and hence they are as tenacious of traditional error as of revealed truth. This makes it necessary frequently to apply the test of reasoning; by expressing the ideals or primitive perceptions of the mind in terms, and examining their relations. This would be productive of the more happy results, as the votaries of abstraction are obnoxious to errors of an opposite character, being more liable to be led astray by the bewitchments of prohibition, and the plausibility which their reasoning gives to new opinions insufficiently investigated. They, moreover, of necessity, acquire a habit of regarding only the signs, and, however clearly and certainly they may arrive at conclusions, are apt to forget that these conclusions are founded on hypotheses involved in the definitions of their terms. They do not see *things* vividly, but perceive only the *signs* which they have substituted for them; and hence their power of examining actual existences is lessened. By degrees, abstractions obtain in their minds the place of realities, to such a vicious degree, that in some instances they become the ultimate objects of thought, and the signs are invested with all the attributes which belong to that which they signify. The expression, *natural laws*, or *laws of nature*, is a remarkable instance in point; some philosophers have not only fallen into the absurdity of giving to these mere words a power over matter, but, in their zeal to get rid of a Universal Superintending Intelligence, have adopted an hypothesis, which, of necessity, presumes that matter is universally intelligent. For it is obvious that government, *immediately* by law, presupposes a knowledge of the law, and, of course, intelligence, on the part of the governed.

The opposite evils of which we have spoken, as arising from the exclusive use of ideality or abstraction, are neutralized by a combination of these poetic and prosaic modes of investigation. This combination would naturally occur, and the language of precision would be continually adapted and applied to the suggestions of intuition, were it not that, on some important subjects, a sort of odium, a vague suspicion, has attached to those who attempt to apply this severe but essential means of correction. They are pragmatical with our household deities. They interfere with established prejudices, and make us distrust early impressions and endeared associations. They banish forms of expression hallowed by recollections of youth and purity, and which, however illogical, were, perhaps, so modified in our minds, as to harmonize with correct principles and exalted virtue. Still they must abide their fate. They must die the death of error. We are slow to admit the propriety of such harsh treatment of sentiments which we have long revered. If we suspect we are wrong, we are almost ready to wish to remain so; and, even when we assent to the justice of the sentence, we suspect the executioner of a reckless and unfeeling hardihood. Hence it is that errors are suffered to accumulate, until their glaring absurdity gives confidence to the votaries of abstraction, and induces them boldly to apply the test of terms. Then they modify the existing system, or frame a new one, retaining of the old all that will abide their test, and rejecting much that is absurd and contradictory. They thus form a foundation on which to erect a superstructure of substantial truths. Their thoughts partake of its strength and firmness, their philosophy is sound, and their perceptions vigorous and clearly expressed; but a religion which is contained in precise finite terms is inadequate to the boundless cravings of the soul. The ardor of discovery; the fervor of improvement; the confidence of demonstration; the pleasure derived from clearer, self-reconciling, systematic views, may, for a time, be sufficient to sustain its votaries; but these very causes will at length bring them to a point at which terms will fail to bear them forward, or even to express what their enlarged views have enabled them to discover of the numerous and delicate relations which exist between the finite spirit and the infinite. Their advancement in thought has then outstripped their improvement of its signs. Their attempts to express its results are consequently not understood, and the tower which they hoped to raise to the skies, is, by this confusion of language, arrested in its progress, and its founders dispersed, to cultivate various portions of the world of thought, and to seek their way to heaven, each in his own path of duty and virtue.

They have, however, accomplished something; they have discarded error, and acquired and made known the means of its exclusion. They have reduced knowledge to a form, in which it may be imparted and made useful to the ignorant, and, in the prosecution of this work, they have improved the means of social intercourse, and given to words a power, and expression, and pervading subtlety, little short of the original thoughts which they represent. Still it is insufficient. The more ethereal (probably the more ethereal sex) will be the first to feel that its abstractions are too cold to express their heartfelt emotions, too limited to meet their expanding views of moral excellence. They will be the first to discover that there is a spiritual refinement which it has not power to portray; a holy charm, a sublime mystery, which it does not approach.

The intuitive principle here again resumes its sway. Ideality is again in the ascendant. It commences in a higher sphere, and, with an activity increased by the accumulation of truth and freedom from error, advances with a rapidity which soon induces the want of something in which to embody its accumulated discoveries. Some of the most cultivated and gifted spirits will naturally adopt the language of ideality or primitive perception, and their most ethereal thoughts will bear the impress of their poetic origin; but in the dearth of language, and of skill in its application, ambiguous, unmeaning, and even absurd phrases may be adopted by the many, as the nucleus around which each arranges his own peculiar and indistinct notions. In process of time, some of the crude maxims of the one class acquire undue importance as relics of ancient wisdom; and the refined poetic illustrations of the other are received as literal prosaic assertions, but still carry with them all the authority of inspiration.

These causes, in addition to the constant mutations of language, give rise to mysticisms, which are too often imposed on succeeding generations as indissolubly connected with the brightest and purest truths which hallow the thoughts of man. Among those who thus receive them will be some with sufficient sagacity to detect the error; but, not having sufficient philosophy to separate it from the truths with which they have always seen it united, they discard the whole, as an imposition on common sense, and as insulting to their understanding. Finding that to be false which they had from infancy looked upon as indisputable, they view everything else with suspicion, and abandon themselves to a universal scepticism. Others, of the same class, scarcely less unfortunate, give up the matter in despair of understanding it, and passively yield to the faith of childhood and the nursery. From these nothing is to be expected; they make no effort at improvement, but sluggishly pursue the beaten track, with, at best, no higher virtue than the absence of crime, no higher motive than present enjoyment and exemption from present care and perplexity. Fortunately, for the cause of human advancement, there is another class, who will be at the pains to analyze these absurdities, to extract the diluted truths which have given them currency, and, concentrating them in the terms of an improving language, transmit them to posterity as pure crystals, unalloyed with error, unclouded by mystery, undisturbed by contradictions.

In the department of physics we often observe phenomena, which we cannot account for upon any known principles, or which we cannot class with any already established genera. These mysteries of the material universe are continually yielding to the advances of science, and opening the way to others before unnoticed. They are occasionally rendered more obscure by unskilful expressions and blind prejudices, but in the main are well defined. In this class we may rank what for the time being are ultimate principles; the polarity of light, magnetism, its connection with electricity, and other facts which have been observed, but which, apparently, are not referable to any known laws. In the moral and intellectual world, phenomena analogous to these are presented; but here, the difficulties arising from ill-applied terms, and from long-established prejudices, become much greater, and cause gross absurdities. Hence has arisen a feeling against mysteries, which disposes many to discard them entirely; but this is to circumscribe themselves within present defined limits, and to bar all further progress. Others, with the blindness of bigotry, admit the mysteries, whatever form they may have already assumed; and, however preposterous they may appear, deny the expediency of any change, and even the propriety of any inquiry. It is thus that what at first were cheering anticipations of truth, distorted by ignorance and clouded by superstition, are perpetuated as errors, and throw their darkening shadows over the very spots they at first illumined. The rational mysteries of the moral and intellectual world arise from those ineffable visions, which are arrived at when the noble sallies of the soul carry it beyond its usual limits, and afford it transient and indistinct perceptions of something which it cannot define or represent by signs, but which serves to awaken curiosity and stimulate inquiry.

This field of imperfect discovery, the mind fills with beautiful ideals, and in contemplation of them realizes, with delightful certainty, that it is still free, still expanding, and has ample space for the exercise and improvement of its invigorated powers. Such mysteries, and their happy influences, are the result of processes of ideality, leading us forward, sometimes so far as to strain our feeble powers, and far, very far, beyond the application of terms or signs. Their changing forms are seen only in the mists of poetry, but, yielding gradually to increasing light and knowledge, they assume a settled form, and are embodied in the language of abstraction, which changes them from the poetic form of ideality, and, as it is well or ill applied, converts them into philosophical truths or prosaic errors.

We have spoken of the happy influence of mysteries; but we must be understood as meaning only those mysteries which are continually hovering near the outer verge of knowledge, and which, however far we may extend our view, will continue to unfold themselves in the expanding horizon. These, as we have before remarked, are rational mysteries. Language not having been extended to them, they are exclusively in the province of ideality; and are widely different from those verbal mystifications, contradictions and absurdities, which in some instances have been substituted for them. The latter have been held out to men as false lights, involving them in inextricable difficulties. They have been presented as objects upon which to direct the sublime power of improvement, while all hope of advancement is denied. In very mockery of their human wants and divine aspirations, something, having the appearance of the unplucked fruit of knowledge, has been presented to them, but they forbidden, under the most terrible penalties, to taste or touch it; and, with the infinite tendencies of the soul thus shackled, they have been told to rest their highest hopes on the verity of verbal involutions, which they are authoritatively told they cannot and ought not to unfold. The expansive power of the mind thus directed against an obstacle which is deemed insurmountable, loses its elasticity, and learns submission to a state of passive, unchanging ignorance. On the other hand, the free spirit, which has escaped these fetters, is always pressing forward. In its bold incursions into the infinite, it is continually making discoveries; but superstition too often follows, and with the iron grasp of tyranny seizes the new domain. To rescue these fair provinces from this gloomy despotism, becomes the object of succeeding philosophers. They bring all the force of well marshalled terms to aid them in the enterprise. Yet, what avails this array of strength in a crusade against a subtle enemy, continually shifting its position, and always eluding attack? But, though the toil of philanthropic philosophers has apparently been in vain; though the life-stream of the inspired enthusiast has scarcely sufficed to moisten the arid sands on which it has freely flowed; though the very soil on which truth first shone may be held by the ignorant and benighted, and superstition still sway its sceptre over these fair portions of this holy land, Truth itself is ever gradually and silently accomplishing its objects, and at length manifests itself with such universal power that prejudice yields, and even bigotry feels its influence.

The mysteries of ideality are like graceful, yielding, glowing clouds, seen through the atmosphere of knowledge. Like the distant nebulæ, they tell the philosopher that all beyond us is not a void; that there still exists a field of discovery; that what now appears unconnected, or at best an excrescence, may, to his expanding view, become harmoniously reconciled in the arrangements of a larger sphere; and what now seems only an obscure speck, may, with distinct and brilliant rays, light and guide him on his way to unthought of discoveries. They thus awaken in the soul a consciousness of the boundless nature of truth, and of the infinite progression of its own immortal powers. They inspire it with enthusiasm, and rouse it to that exertion which is necessary to the fulfilment of its highest destinies. These indistinct primitive perceptions, these glimpses of truth, which dawn on the free and aspiring mind, are directly opposed to those spurious mysteries, which consist of artificial arrangements of terms, and are sustained by repressing inquiry, and keeping the mind in that state of darkness which precludes examination. The latter are as dense mists around us, in which we may conjure up many strange phantoms, but which must be dispelled before we can see anything clearly or aright. They obstruct our vision, weaken our powers, retard our progress, and some of them, especially the dogmas of religion, dampen ardor, and hide from us the brightest paths and fairest fields of human investigation. There is, however, one circumstance which gives these artificial mysteries an advantage over the natural. Having already assumed the concrete form, they are fixed and inflexible. Continually presented to us with the same aspect, they take a stronger hold of our perceptions. Through all the changing scenes of life they remain the same. They are as plants of the joyous spring of existence, which, however worthless, have not decayed. They have not improved by cultivation, but like noxious weeds, producing no good fruit, have been suffered to grow for want of it. In them mind makes no progress. On them time makes no impression. The observances connected with them being the same, carry with them into age the associations of youth. They form a continuous chain, to whose uniform links are united all the recollections of the past, and all the anticipations of the future,—a thread of fiction stringing together the realities of life. They make a portion of the uniform web, on which is woven the varied colors which brighten and shade existence. Nor are these counterfeit mysteries wholly without the better influences which appertain to the real. Those who are deceived by them receive a baser coin than is issued from the mint of truth; but that they have thus received them is an evidence that the love of truth remains. That portion of prospective happiness, which arises from the consciousness that mind has not yet filled the measure of its capacities, may be associated with them. They are all that some men are permitted to conjecture of the bright paths which would lead them to a higher sphere. Human skill may have made the perspective so imposing, that, instead of mere proximate illusions of light and shade, they appear to the victim of the deception as realities, extending far beyond his earthly hopes. To him they are still truth in an inscrutable guise, and may still excite in him that devotion, which, when rightly appreciated, truth always inspires. He may listen to the voice, which is his authority for what is yet undiscovered. He may, again and again, repeat the mystic rites, which serve to amuse his hopes without awakening exertion; and he may visit the scenes where these mysteries have been made familiar to him, and ponder on the visible types of invisible truth, as we linger around the grave of friendship, while we expect only in another world to meet the spirit which consecrates the spot. And this veneration for what he is told is the robe of truth, this devotion to all which bears her impress, may prevent a reckless scepticism, and sustain some of the better feelings, of the existence of which they are undoubted evidence. The evil is, that they will not allow these better feelings to expand and improve. They cramp the soul, and if it ever discovers that its affections have been misplaced, and fastened on worthless absurdities, its confidence in the virtuous principles which it had been taught to associate with them is weakened, if not destroyed.

In the formation of character, ideality exerts an influence of the highest importance. It is the channel by which the conceivable objects of desire or aversion are brought nearest to the springs of voluntary action. From those supposable events which are continually flowing through the mind, we form rules of conduct, or receive impressions, which imperceptibly govern us in the concerns of real life. It is in meditation that we nurture those innate feelings which give impulse to action, and determine its mode. He who accustoms himself to this discipline, who withdraws from the bustle of the world, and in tranquillity contemplates imaginary cases, and determines how he ought to act under them, frames for himself a system of government with less liability to error, than he can do in the tumultuous scenes of active life. He is not swayed by those interests and passions, which so often distort the views of those who act from the impulse of immediate and pressing circumstances. The beautiful and the good rise in glowing forms before him, and light his path to excellence. The processes of ideality in which he indulges may not exactly fit all the occasions which naturally arise, but no contingency will occur, to which some of the vast number of them, that even the life most engrossed in ordinary pursuits admits of, will not in some degree be applicable. They will at least furnish analogies, and give him habits of disinterested thought, which lead to high and correct views of duty and propriety.

He who habitually cultivates thoughts of peace, who lives in an ideal harmony with all around him, and moistens the tenderness of his nature at the pure fountains of an indwelling benevolence, renders himself more susceptible to the pleasures of society, and less obnoxious to the cross incidents which sometimes mar its happiness. If these inopportunely happen to disturb him, he finds, in his primitive perceptions of the moral beauty of kindness and social order, a balsam for his wounded spirit, which soothes the painful asperity of his lacerated feelings, and restores him to tranquillity and cheerfulness. He who, in all the fancied or expected collisions of interest or opinion, maintains a calm and unruffled temper, represses irritable feelings, and calls into action those which are mild and conciliating, is fortifying himself against the rude attacks of the world, and elevating himself above its petty conflicts. Thus prepared, he meets the crosses and trials, which are the lot of existence, with fortitude and serenity. To him they are but occasions for the exercise of those amiable virtues which he has drawn from the pure sources of ideality. They enable him to act out what he has conceived. Like the majestic oak, he derives strength from the storms which assail him. Without this happy internal agency, which is ever exerting its unsuspected power, the character would be formed and developed only by the occurrences of life, and we should always be obliged to judge of propriety, at the very moment when we should be most liable to be biassed by the influence of peculiar circumstances, interest or passion. Feelings, thus brought into exercise only amid the stir and strife of the world, would probably become coarse, harsh and selfish. The processes of ideality may correct this tendency; may refine the affections, and give liberality to sentiment. They can soften the rigid feelings, and mould them into their own forms of beauty, but, at the same time, when perverted, they greatly increase the evil which they should be the means of averting.

Situations of difficulty and danger induce a corresponding cultivation of those sterner qualities which are then required. The savage, in continual danger of attack, sustains his warlike spirit by imaginary achievements, accomplished in ideal conflict with the enemies of his tribe. He fancies himself in mortal combat, and feels the glow of martial enthusiasm thrill through his veins, exciting him to deeds of valor or desperation; or he conceives himself the fettered victim of the strife, and nerves himself to endure the torture with uncomplaining fortitude. Courage and a power of endurance are with him the highest attainments; these occupy his thoughts. And that their growth is stimulated by processes of ideality, is evinced in his rude songs, the barbarous poetry in which these processes naturally find utterance; depicting warlike courage, soul-inspiring danger, and heroic fortitude. All this may be necessary in the rude state of society, when there are no laws to counteract brute force; but, even in its more advanced state, analogous causes undo the effects of civilization, and generate the savage character in the midst of refinement. He who has been compelled into keen collision with others, fosters the energies which are requisite for the strife, and sometimes acquires a morbid taste for such excitements, after the occasions for them have passed away. When this is the case, his ideal processes flow in the same channel. Discord and its attendant train of disturbing influences continually occupy his mind. His spirit becomes fiery and ferocious; his will impetuous and impatient of control. The malignant passions habitually acquire a dreadful ascendency. Embittered feeling, demoniac rage, and furious revenge, become the elements in which he lives; inhaling thence a stimulus, which gives frantic vigor to the worst passions of the heart, while its poison intoxicates, convulses, and maddens the soul.

But, low as he has thus fallen, he has not yet reached the worst condition. While he acts from impulse, even though it be the impulse of fierce and disturbing passion, he will still exhibit something of the greatness of his nature. Unsubdued energy of purpose, strong determination, unconquerable will, and even recklessness, impress us as the over-excited action of a noble though perverted spirit — of a spirit, which, like the tempest-cloud, adds to the sublimity of the scene which it darkens. It glows not with the warm beams of heaven, nor reflects its softened rays, but from its dark bosom it emits its own fierce and terrific gleams. And with these workings of power, a sympathy is felt by milder and better natures. It is not until the processes of ideality, perverted to evil, and cramped within the little sphere of self, have gradually exterminated all spontaneous impulse, and substituted, in its place, cold calculation, low cunning, and mean artifice, that the moral nature becomes wholly repulsive and disgusting. This is premeditated depravity. It is poisoning the fountain from which every action flows. To destroy the natural or early-formed impulses is a work requiring no little pains. It is probably effected by magnifying the advantages of selfishness, by recalling events in which a yielding to general impulse has interfered with it, and by searching out the modes by which, under similar circumstances, a repetition of this interference may be avoided. These are processes of ideality, in which the individual wilfully excludes the pleasures which arise from the generous emotions, and by this means destroys their natural connection with the springs of action, establishing in their room a system of narrow prudential considerations, which cramps and degrades his moral nature, induces a meanness incompatible with the dignity of virtue, and shuts out all the finer feelings and nobler aspirations of his soul.

It appears strange that a labor, thus painful in its performance, and leading to such baneful results, should ever be accomplished. It is no doubt generally done with a view to some immediate object, without reference to its ultimate effect, and without a sufficient examination of the laws of our being. But even with the vision circumscribed by this culpable neglect, no one ever committed this cold-blooded mutilation of soul, without a sense of immediate violence and degradation, as none ever fostered the generous sentiments, without a feeling of exaltation, and a conscious susceptibility to purer pleasures. The power which we exert over our moral nature, though less nobly exhibited, is more strongly attested by its perversion, than by its improvement; in the formation of the avaricious character, for instance, more than in that of the most generous virtue. In the latter case, it seems to advance with perfect freedom in the path of its own choice, and to be led forward by the delights which attend its progress. In the former, it is forced back against the current of its affections, fettered and guarded with tyrannic vigilance, and made subservient to the most degrading purposes. The miser looks upon the man of liberality, as one too weak to resist the dictates of generosity. He knows the labor which his own prudence has cost him, and congratulates himself on his exemption from such benevolent frailties. The higher pleasures are to him unreal, and the pursuit of them visionary. In curbing the expansive tendency of his moral nature, he has shown us how great a power we may exert in controlling it, as the martyr, who held his hand in the flames which consumed it, gave more striking proof of the power of the mental over the physical system, than the most skilful and useful application of that hand would have done.

That we can modify our dispositions, is perhaps sufficiently obvious, though too often overlooked in its practical application. The great means by which these modifications are effected, we believe to be processes of ideality, and the principal causes of the wrong formation of character are the perversion of these processes to foster ignoble passions, and the want of their influence in counteracting the effects of external causes. Fortunately, the occasions of life which have a tendency to warp the disposition, though frequent, have their intervals, are transient, and in some degree neutralize each other. The forms of ideality may always be brought to mind, and, if we encourage the presence of those only which are pure and elevated, we shall, as a consequence, become more and more refined and ennobled. Without this countervailing principle, our moral nature would be the sport of chance, liable to be irretrievably driven from its course by every current of feeling and every storm of passion. Character would then depend on accidental and physical causes. But in the contemplation of the conceivable events which continually occupy the mind, and the careful retention of the primitive perceptions which inspire us with virtuous emotion, we find a more steady influence, which, with proper attention, may counteract the effects of accidents, elevate us above the power of circumstance, and effectually protect us from a fatality otherwise inevitable.

In the over active life of those who task their whole abilities in business pursuits, the succession of impelling circumstances is often so close as not to admit of a sufficient infusion of ideality to temper their irritating and engrossing influence, and the character is consequently in danger of losing its amiable and expansive qualities. The frequent occurrence of this has probably given rise to a not uncommon impression that moral character is necessarily the result of external circumstances; and this impression we believe to be one reason of the too little value usually attached to it. We too often regard its possession rather as an evidence of good fortune, than of a useful and wise discipline on the part of the possessor, and the exercise of it as a mere act of volition, involving no difficulty, and, though deserving praise, yet calling for no distinction. Hence, too, it is, that we are prone to make the more palpably active intellectual powers the standard of excellence, and the objects of our admiration.

But, when we consider morality as the result of the most delicate cultivation, it assumes a higher elevation. We then look upon the actions of the virtuous as but the indications of a harmony within; the expression of an instrument whose fine tones have been improved amid the discord of confused and troubled scenes. We are led to admire the moral energy which has infused itself into each delicate spring, and preserved its perfection, amid the agitations to which it has been continually exposed.

We have already spoken of the power of ideality, in enabling us to fall into the same channels of thought which our acquaintances would pursue. If we mistake not, this is particularly obvious in the application of it which we are now considering. How often, when we have determined on a course of conduct, particularly when that determination is formed under the influence of exciting circumstances, are we led to suspect the propriety of it, by thinking how some friend would view it. We put ourselves in his position, look at it calmly as he would do, endeavor to get the same aspect as would be presented to him, and then perhaps discover that our own vision had been distorted, and led us into error. In this way, through the medium of this faculty, we make the virtue and discretion of our friends available to us. We use their modes of thought to mould our own.*

There is peculiar consolation in the consideration, that mind possesses, in these varied forms of ideality, an inherent power of resisting or modifying the influence of material causes; that it has a mode which is as near to our moral, as sensation is to our physical, nature; which elevates it to a more commanding eminence, gives it a tone of conscious superiority, and makes us feel at once the meanness of yielding to the petty trials and temptations which assail us, and our ability to triumph over them.

The examination of past conduct, and of supposed cases, is no doubt frequently performed in the abstract mode; but, from the greater length of time which it requires, it is impossible that this method should always be resorted to, and when it is, although it may establish general principles, it is less moving, and has a less direct influence on the conduct, than those scenic representations which are so faithfully acted

* Charles Lamb, in alluding to his friend Coleridge, then recently deceased, says: "His great and dear spirit haunts me. I cannot think a thought, I cannot make a criticism on men or books, without an ineffectual turning and reference to him. *He was the proof and touchstone of all my cogitations.*"

in the theatre within us. Ideality is in this respect the nearest approach to reality.

This expansive element, which thus exhibits itself in the formation of the most common charactër, becomes more conspicuous in those extraordinary manifestations of mind which have occasionally illumined the world with a brightness almost superhuman.

In the most humble guise of ideality, that in which i mingles with the business of life, and in which its expansive power is almost neutralized by the predominance of the grosser nature, it is the basis of that common sense, which is universally regarded not only as differing, but as somewhat opposed to the verbal refinement of those who, arriving at their conclusions through the medium of terms, can state them, however chimerical, in the plausible and imposing forms of syllogistic reasoning. It is sometimes this which induces a man to withhold his assent from the results of an argument that he cannot refute. The processes of ideality do not reveal to him the relation which the terms of the reasoner have pointed out. From this, the most alloyed form in which the ethereal principle is observable, its inherent property is developed as it increases in purity, until it exhibits its discursive tendency in the random gleams of poetic phrenzy, giving, in the distance, transient and indistinct perceptions of whatever its uncertain flashes chance to beam upon; or, still controlled and directed by a firm philosophy and an ardent pursuit of truth, it expands under their influence, until, embracing in the form of primitive perceptions all the great attributes of man, and the laws which regulate his progression, it displays to its votaries the connection between the present and the future, with the clearness of revelation, and enables them to predict with inspired confidence. If, in the earliest and weakest manifestation, when directed only to the little circle of events around us, incited only by a selfish interest, obscured by the mists of an imperfect morality, and liable to perversion from the wishes, the hopes, the fears, and the darker passions which agitate and perturb the undisciplined and unpurified mind; if, under such circumstances, it can enable us to anticipate some small portion of the future,—can it be doubted that, in its highest state of cultivation, when capable of embracing "all this maze of man," when its perceptions are quickened by a pure morality, inspired by a universal philanthropy, and all the feelings and passions of the man are merged in an enthusiastic devotion to truth,—can it be doubted that then these anticipations may assume the importance, the reach, the dignity, and the certainty of prophetic revelation? Are not the superiority of the elements, which are thus brought into action, proportioned to such a result?

But we mean not to imply that this highly improved state of ideality is common. On the contrary, he who has arrived at this state of refinement, this freedom from selfishness and the distractions of sense, this purity of passion and angelic devotion, has already attained an elevation far beyond the ordinary lot of mortals; and we have before considered one essential element of this power, that of coping with general propositions in the form of ideals, as properly belonging rather to a higher state of existence. The spirit, then, which has attained such reach of thought and clearness of perception, has anticipated its destiny; and the attributes of humanity, by care and cultivation, have been early matured to the celestial. In such a spirit the ethereal principle manifests itself in unwonted purity: and the impassioned soul, though wrought upon by its most expansive influence, still preserves its integrity and unity of purpose. In the highest exhibitions of its power, it seems borne forward on a whirlwind of thought; but in this moral tempest it retains its self-possession, and, with a tranquil, godlike power, directs and controls its lightning energies.

We would not be understood to say that this spiritual refinement of the processes of ideality is the only source of prophecy. We are aware that knowledge of the future may flow immediately from that infinitely purer fountain of all knowledge, to which the most advanced terrestrial spirit is but in the earliest stage of a never-ending approximation. But we do wish to inculcate the idea, that, in that intelligence which is allotted to man, there is infused a principle which, in its lowest state, enables him to form probable conjectures of future events most nearly connected with the objects of his thoughts, and that this principle admits of indefinite improvement and extension; that, when redeemed from a narrow selfishness, and unencumbered by the gross and sensual,—in short, when exerting its influence under circumstances similar to those which we have supposed to favor our progress hereafter, it will advance us to that purer region of knowledge, from which a more distant futurity is distinctly visible; and we wish to direct attention to the similarity between the two sources of prophecy. They are both manifestations of spirit. One is infallible, and the other is the nearest approach of a finite intelligence to infallibility. With the exception of a few recorded instances, in which the great I AM revealed himself in articulate language, they are equally spiritual discernings of truth; and when God reveals the future, by imparting more power and penetration to the purified spirit, and thus making its discernings more clear and certain, it still differs not from the processes of ideality in kind, but only in degree. It is then only an increase of the power which he originally gave. We are not prepared to call the increase miraculous; for, as the Supreme Being governs inferior intelligences through the medium of fixed, natural laws, prophecy may be a natural effect of increased purity and cultivation; or, if he governs them by his immediate volitions, this result may still be conformable to the uniform modes which he has adopted.

We apprehend that, on this subject, the views of many have been perverted, in consequence of conceiving the Supreme intelligence as existing only at a great distance from the little sphere of humanity, and that there is a great void between, which omnipresence does not fill, and which omnipotence cannot traverse without an effort. But how much more just and ennobling is the conception, that we are in the midst of this omnipresence, that our finite spirits are blended with the infinite, associated with it by innumerable relations, and with affinities continually increasing, as they assimilate to it in purity and holiness; that we hold communion with omniscience; that, through the medium of the material world, we continually imbibe a knowledge of the ways of nature's God, while his spiritual revealings enlarge our views of moral excellence and light, and guide us in our progress toward perfection!

We do not wish to lessen the estimation in which prophecy is deservedly held, and, if we understand the application of our own views, they have no such tendency. He who has increased his powers, by cultivating and purifying the talents allotted to him, we deem as worthy as if a new talent had been suddenly conferred upon him. He whose spiritual light has been permanently increased, we believe to be as much favored by Heaven, as if he were only occasionally made the vehicle of its revelations to mankind.

Prophecy, immediately revealed from God, has always been, as indeed it must needs be, accompanied by such extraordinary manifestations, as not only to leave no doubt in its immediate recipient, but all who believe his account of them, must also believe the prediction to come from an infallible source; a simple narration of them being sufficient to produce undoubting faith.

But those prophecies, which are the mere discernings of an inspired spirit, are unsupported by such supernatural occurrences, and their credibility must rest upon other evidence. We can judge of them only by what they themselves present. They must bear the stamp of their high character and origin. Their own brightness must convince us that they come from the fountain of light. Such has been the case with those which have been accredited. They have contained their own intrinsic evidence. They have borne the impress, which attested that they were the emanations of a gifted spirit. They have been stamped with the purest ideality, and clothed in the loftiest strains of poetry. It is the universal adaptation of this language to every degree of intelligence, which has made for them an avenue to every mind, and inspired with equal faith the weak and the wise, the ignorant and the learned.

The exceptions to the influence of prophecy have generally been minds that disciplined the reasoning faculty in the use of terms to the exclusion of ideality, or that cultivated this latter faculty, but applied it only to the purpose of producing illusion, and hence had no good reason to rely upon its manifestations in others. They felt the movements of its power within them, but so blended with the gross and sensual, that they had no adequate conceptions of the greatness of its purified nature.

It is often asserted that the age of prophecy has passed. With regard to that which is the immediate and miraculous manifestation of Deity, it becomes not us to speak; but, concerning that which we have described as the result of processes of ideality, we may venture some remarks.

The effect which the sudden advancement of the physical sciences has had, in changing our modes of thought and expression, has wrought an important change in this particular province of mind. Instead of stating the result of a process of ideality in its appropriate language, in which it would appear more oracular, these results are minutely traced, and the train of connection carefully preserved, through the medium of terms; and, by this infusion of the prosaic, that which in its original poetic form would have appeared as prophecy is reduced to the standard of common sense. The power of reaching the future through the medium of primitive perceptions is the highest effort of mind, and requires the most concentrated application of its undivided energies. Whatever then excites it to activity, and increases its power of attention, is favorable to this development. Intense interest enabled the Empress Josephine to foresee the results of a certain measure of Napoleon's; and had she stated those results in the less precise language of ideality, and without exhibiting the connecting train of reasoning, they might have passed for prophetic revelations. It is not, then, surprising that, before the general introduction of the philosophic method, and especially in the times of high religious excitement which preceded it, enthusiastic devotees should have often penetrated the future through the medium of ideals, to which their glowing imaginations imparted such vividness, that, if not in reality, they might easily be mistaken for, inspirations of prophecy, by men who honestly believed themselves endowed with more than human foresight. What then would have appeared in the form of false prophecy, is now first converted into false philosophy, or rejected in the attempt to embody it in concrete science.

We need not urge that this power of ideality, by which we revive the past, brighten the present, and anticipate the future, is the highest endowment of humanity. It is also that attribute of the finite spirit which most nearly corresponds to that of omnipresence in the infinite. By the exercise of this faculty, every place and every object of its knowledge is made present to the mind; and, if it be not equally proper to say that mind is present to them, this power furnishes an equivalent, which in effect makes mind not omnipresent, because, and only because, it is not omniscient and omnipotent. For, if we knew all things, we could make them all present to us in the form of ideals; and, if there were no limit to this power, we could embrace them all at once; and this would be equivalent to being everywhere present at the same time; or, if we may so express it, mind, as manifested in man, has a *finite presence*, which has the same relation to *omnipresence*, which its finite knowledge and power have to the other two great attributes of the universal intelligence.

The revealings of ideality require a constant improvement of the language in which they are expressed; and this, in turn, demands a corresponding progression in the forms of abstraction, and induces a mode of mind, which forms the first stage of its advancement from the finite to the infinite, and admits of such varied proportions of the gross and ethereal, that it can descend to the most selfish and narrow concerns, or, closely following where ideality leads, rise in lofty and refined investigation to the most ennobling conceptions. Abstraction has a peculiar adaptation to our present mixed nature, preserving the physical, and improving the moral. It is the tempered light suited to our feeble vision. It has not the brilliancy of poetic fancy, but it possesses the enduring charms of substantial truth. The language of abstraction is seldom found wholly unalloyed. It generally contains an infusion of ideality, and by this combination acquires a pliancy, which makes it more universally applicable to the subjects of thought. Cheered by this enlivening influence, and keeping on the firm ground of demonstration, the man of abstraction pursues the even tenor of his way, amid all the trials and temptations which beset his path; or, rising in lofty speculation above the little world of human care and perplexity, draws consolation or happiness from sources purely his own, and of which no vicissitudes of fortune can deprive him. He returns fortified by the results of mature investigation, and invested with a panoply of principle which prepares him for all the chances and changes of life. It imparts firmness to his virtue, and decision and energy to his action. It gives him a tone of conscious elevation, which raises him above the ordinary vexations of life, and enables him to look on its joys and its sorrows with steadiness and serenity. He has measured the evils to which he is exposed, and knows his ability to endure them.

Nor are the effects of this power less happy when exerted for the general welfare. To superficial observers the man of abstraction may, for a time, appear a soulless, uninteresting object. They will wonder how he can find amusement in abstruse and perplexing investigation. They cannot perceive that, in the calm solitude of his bosom, a glowing ardor sheds its mild but steady light on the engrossing objects of his unremitted toil. They cannot feel the fervor with which the simple charms of truth have inspired him. They suspect not that one, apparently so cold and unyielding, is secretly actuated by the warm and generous feelings of universal philanthropy, and is unostentatiously bestowing the wealth of his time and talents for the permanent benefit of mankind. His mind appears to them a gloomy laboratory, enveloped in smoke and mist. They will not be at the pains to examine his chymic processes, and are astonished when they result in such gleams of thought as shed effulgence around him, and exhibit the bright truths which he has transmuted from error, or the pure and original excellence which he has freed from the dross which rendered it obscure. He has no servile regard for unfounded opinions; but, inspired with a fearless love of truth, pursues it regardless of consequences; and never despairs of vanquishing error, whether it seeks to elude him in the subtle and imposing forms of mystery and superstition, or openly resists him with the arms of prejudice, and the armor of ignorance. Throughout, language has been the means of his advancement; it led him forward in the path of demonstration; it directed and gave certainty to the processes by which he discriminated truth; and it furnished the weapons with which he has successfully combated its opposers.

The philosopher has thus attained a high elevation. But

the poet seeks a yet higher sphere. He sets at naught the plodding calculations of a circumscribed utility, and, disgusted with the grovelling pursuits which engross the attention of most men, he wings his flight high in the airy fields of speculation, and lavishes the exuberance of his fancy on visionary splendors and the enticing charms of sentiment. His spirit-like perceptions no longer assume the garb of language, and seraph-winged thoughts lead him into that higher sphere,

"Where each conception is a heavenly guest,"

far beyond the little circle where every idea is clothed and made palpable in words, as a soul animating its embodying clay.

From this poetic elevation he looks down upon this little world, and throws over it and its concerns the bright hues of his own fervor, till, in the distance, it appears as a luminary fitted for the vault of heaven. Its coarse intrusions no longer disturb him. He looks above and around, and everywhere sees nature unfolding her graces. He brings everything to his standard of ideal excellence, and revels in the luxury of his own creations. The visions of paradise float before his fancy, and the inspirations of his musings are as visitings from yet higher spheres. But how often, in some momentary pause, when the imagination has become enfeebled by such vast, exciting, and long-continued effort, does the thought, that it is but a creation of fancy, burst with dread reality upon him, and dissipate the illusion. The veil which ideality cast over the realities of life is withdrawn, and the morbid sensibility of a heart, accustomed only to sensibility and refinement, turns with loathing from their comparative deformity. Such is the regretted effect of this exalted talent when it acts in excess, or unconnected with the reasoning faculty which sustains it with its strength, and receives in return grace, purity, and elevation. Yet, if these inspirations have been embodied in language, they are not without their utility. They may then be made to mingle with the thoughts of less ethereal minds, and neutralize the degrading tendency of grosser pursuits. The influence of poetry is, in this respect, of great importance, and admits of almost universal application. It commands the avenues to feeling, and there is hardly any state of mind to which it cannot impart pleasure or consolation. It resorts not to the tedious manipulations of abstraction, but with a godlike power commands things to come forth, and light to be. Are the spirits gay and buoyant? it touches some chord of rapture, and the heart yields its ready response. Is the mind oppressed with care, has the morning ray of hope ceased to illumine it? it extends its magic wand, and, like the electric influence on the summer evening's cloud, suffuses it with the light which more sunny hours had bestowed. But an expression in words is still necessary to make these influences tangible; without it they would be mere shadows, far too ethereal for our ordinary perception, and so be lost in the abyss of oblivion, from which even the magician who had once called them forth might not be able again to summon them.

THE observation of the actual events and occurrences of life impels us to action. We witness misery, and are moved to relieve it. We see the weak oppressed by the strong, and indignation rouses us to their rescue. We observe virtue victorious, and join in the triumph. The language of ideality, conveying to us what is the nearest approach to actual observation of the reality, produces in us more impulse, more emotion, than that of abstraction, in which we expect only a theoretical consequence, expressed in terms that present no particular object to excite our pity, abhorrence or admiration. Our finite emotions are lost in the infinity of a general proposition, without a case for its immediate application. Hence, too, arises the distinction between the effects of the maxims of morality and of devotional feeling,— a distinction which, though often denied by philosophers who reason, has always been insisted upon by the multitude who feel and perceive.

Although the poetic and prosaic modes of mind are seldom found united in their highest perfection in the same individual, yet every aspect of the subject indicates that it is by a combination of them that the greatest intellectual power is produced. It is then the union of activity and strength — the beauty of poetry mingling its vivacity and softness with the sterner and stronger attributes of reason. So necessary does this combination appear, in order to give efficiency to talent, that we think we should hazard little in asserting that every great enterprise in philosophy had been accomplished by a powerful imagination, controlled and directed by yet more powerful reasoning faculties; and that every grand achievement in poetry had been effected by strong reasoning powers, sustaining and impelling a yet more vigorous imagination. In great minds it is not the absence of either endowment, but only the *predominance* of the reasoning or ideal faculty, which forms the distinction, and determines the character to the one or the other class.

The processes by which they accomplish their designs, and the pleasures resulting from their pursuits, may be more nearly alike than is generally supposed. Let us bring them to the test of language. A celebrated divine thus speaks of one of the ancient and most sublime of poets: "The Psalmist takes a loftier flight. He leaves the world, and lifts his imagination to that mighty expanse which spreads above and around it. He wings his way through space, and wanders in thought over its immeasurable regions. Instead of a dark and unpeopled solitude, he sees it crowded with splendor and filled with the energy of the divine presence. Creation rises in its immensity before him, and the world, with all which it inherits, shrinks into littleness at a contemplation so vast and so overpowering. He wonders that he is not overlooked, amid the grandeur and the variety which are on every side of him; and, passing up from the majesty of nature to the majesty of nature's Architect, he exclaims, 'What is man that thou art mindful of him, or the son of man that thou shouldest deign to visit him?'" We have here a glowing description of the poet, his pursuits, and his feelings; but, with Newton in our view, might we not apply the same to the philosopher in whom the powers of abstraction were most prominent? To preserve this distinction between poet and philosopher, we might change the one word, *imaginations*, for *investigations*, and say, "The man of abstractions takes a still loftier flight. He leaves the world and carries his *investigations* to that mighty expanse," etc., etc.

Let us examine a little more closely the mighty expanse which Newton opened to our view, and the means by which he accomplished it. Taking this earth for our pedestal, we first observe that it is but one of a number of planets which, with their satellites, revolve round the sun as their common centre, and, with the comets in their more eccentric orbits, compose the solar system. The nicety of their instruments has enabled astronomers to detect a difference which has taken place in the angular distance of the fixed stars, from which reason has inferred that our whole system is revolving round some other centre, which analogy suggests may be the common centre of many such systems, performing their cycles in times so inconceivably great, and at such immense distances, that a thousand years scarcely makes a perceptible difference in their relative positions. The telescope has revealed to us a number of nebulæ, which, it has been imagined, are clusters of stars with systems like our own. It has also shown us that the galaxy is formed by the greater number of stars in that portion of the heavens at great distances from us; and it has been inferred that all these with the other visible, and probably many invisible stars, form one nebula, in which we occupy a position near to one edge of the cluster, and that, by looking through the centre, we see more stars in that direction, whose light, blended and softened in the distance, causes the milky appearance there exhibited. And on this fact reason has raised an analogy in support of the conjecture. Imagination, as if despairing of any limit, next suggests that the number of these systems may be infinite, and reason has attempted to prove that, from the known laws of gravitation, it cannot be otherwise.

Thus supported, Imagination has ventured yet a farther flight, and not only conceived each of these stars as a sun, with systems of planets revolving round it, and thus gemmed with worlds the sublime immensity, but she has given to each the garniture of a resplendent canopy, animated them all with a teeming population, and clothed them with the verdure and variety, which give beauty and interest to our own little orb. And here she rests until these conjectures shall have been reduced to certainty, or rejected as errors or groundless hypotheses.

We learn that the diameter of the earth's orbit is nearly two hundred millions of miles, and we rack our invention for some means of forming an adequate conception of this immense distance. We next find — and it is reduced to demonstration — that this distance is but an infinitesimal part of that of the nearest fixed stars, that, whether we are at one end of it or the other, makes not the least perceptible difference in their relative situation, and that, in all probability, there is a continuity of these stars, extending through a number of like distances, before reaching the outer limits of our own cluster. Our feeble faculties are dismayed, and hardly attempt to grasp the reality of such grand and imposing calculations. Yet, what is all this immensity to the distance of the nearest nebula, from which, to the aided eye of the observer, the congregated splendor of all this host of suns would appear but a feeble glimmering; and in the circumference of whose welkin vault the opposite extremes, embracing these millions upon millions, would appear but a span? We stand aghast at a contemplation so magnificent and overpowering, and even the infinite tendencies of our spiritual nature seem to have found ample room for their dilation in the consideration of this merging of vast into yet vaster systems without end.

The perfection of optical instruments has enabled astronomers to possess themselves of the facts, on which rest the demonstrations of the truths and the probability of the conjectures which have raised their science to the highest elevation; and we know that some of those, who have been instrumental in this grand achievement of philosophy, had learned, by long habit and continued effort, to withdraw themselves from the ordinary distractions and engrossments of life, and consequently had acquired a power of concentrating their energies upon their favorite pursuit. They had then, observation, aided by the instruments of art, together with reason concentrated by abstraction from the usual cares of existence, and wrought to its utmost effort by the inspiring magnitude of its pursuits, bearing forward and sustaining a vigorous imagination, which is excited to enthusiasm by the grandeur and sublimity of its objects. In a word, the most stupendous conception of the material universe has been brought within the grasp of humanity, by a partial approach to that combination of the intellectual powers, which we have supposed to become more perfect hereafter, and by a partial improvement of some of the elements of that combination, through the action of the same causes which we have endeavored to show must there be more universal. And while we derive from this greatest, grandest achievement of mind, in the province of the material, some idea of the effect of improving and uniting the faculties of observation, reason and imagination, we may also observe, in the beautiful harmony with which these systems into systems run, as they diverge in the illimitable regions of space, a something which acts on our feelings like the ineffable power of melody, producing an emotion — may we not say an infinite yet tangible emotion of music? — elevating us to the confines of devotion. And the whole development bears witness, that this feeling had a great, though perhaps an unperceived influence, in directing those great strides of the imagination, which precede every great effort and advancement of reason.

It is in these sublime discoveries that mind has put forth all its power and exerted all its energies. It here appears in all its grandeur, and supported by all its dependencies. It is its last grand successful effort. We here see the utmost limit to which it has attained, and, in this farthest stage of its advancement, we find it progressing towards perfection, in the path which our speculation has already traced, and which we have endeavored to extend in shadowy outline into the dim futurity.

In this process ideality has performed its part; but the results have been reduced to the more definite form of abstraction. The great magnitude of those results, and the universal interest felt in them, has produced a corresponding effect on the age. Abstraction has acquired a supremacy, and is made the test of rationality on every subject. Ideality is not permitted to range far beyond its precincts. The noble sallies of the soul are repressed. Mind, limited to a particular mode of action, exerts itself on subjects to which that mode is best adapted. Physical science is the order of the day. It has advanced, and is still advancing, with astonishing rapidity. The great outlines, which Newton and his cotemporaries struck out, are nearly filled up. The impulse which they gave to intellectual exertion is almost spent. The world is nearly ready for some other grand enterprise; and who that has observed the mutual light which the sciences shed upon each other, and their tendency to preserve an equilibrium, does not see, in this accumulation of the knowledge of the laws of matter, an indication of a corresponding improvement in our knowledge of the laws of mind? Who that has observed the effect which increasing our physical comforts has to produce a desire for the more refined pleasures of intellect, does not, in the present condition of the civilized world, already see the workings of an impulse which is to advance us in this higher pursuit?

The laws of mind are confessedly not understood. Something has perhaps been done in training the reasoning faculty; but, in regard to that other mode of mind, to which we have applied the term ideality, we apprehend that very little has yet been accomplished. It appears to have been thought beyond the reach of any regulated discipline. Its processes have been regarded either as lawless workings of the spirit, or as subject only to the control of some higher intelligence. Thus unrestrained, its expansive nature has often dissipated itself in wild extravagances, or errors, requiring the aid of abstraction to correct. For want of proper restraints, it has sometimes been productive of evil, but we confidently look forward to a time, when its laws, and the means of directing its power, will be better understood; when we shall know how to limit its expansibility within our means of controlling it; and, as we become more and more acquainted with its nature, be able to use it in its most elastic form, and make it subservient to the most exalted purposes which are within the provinces of humanity. If we are not deceived, the time is not distant when some strong hand will break down the barriers which now obstruct our progress in intellectual science; or some aspiring and gifted spirit rend the veil which obscures it, and introduce us into new regions of light, illuminating mind, and displaying the true greatness of our nature.

THE ADAPTATION OF THE UNIVERSE TO THE CULTIVATION OF THE MIND.

To every individual who for the first time meditates on infinity, there is, probably, presented in some form, the portentous questions, what, and whence, and wherefore, this I, which thinks? and what, and whence, and wherefore, this universe, in which this I, which thinks, is placed? And with these questions, he may be said to commence his philosophic existence. In advancing to the consideration of them, he has stepped from the finite to the infinite. The worlds of matter and of mind open to his view. Around him, the fair fields of science and philosophy allure him to tread their pleasant paths; stimulating his curiosity by the exhibition of their partially revealed mysteries, and tempting him to exert his powers to cull the flowers of fancy, or reap the harvest of reason. Above him, the lofty sky of speculation seems rather to open infinity, than to set bounds to his vision. But with whatever avidity and accuracy he may observe; with whatever reach and acuteness of reasoning he may extend the results of his observations, and however far the loftiest flights of speculation may carry him into the unknown ethereal, still do the great questions with which he commenced bound his visible horizon. They are the ultimate object, the end as well as the beginning of all philosophy, and recur at every step of his progress. Partaking of the infinity into which he has entered, it were vain to attempt to compass them; and all that the most successful investigator of nature's mysteries can hope, is to advance from truth to truth, and from one combination of them to others more comprehensive.

But how often is he deterred by the difficulties which meet him at the very threshold of the investigation! He looks around, and is perplexed by the incongruity of what he observes. Apparently emanating from the same first cause, he sees good and evil; beauty and deformity; the creatures of benevolence, full of strife and cruelty; the very elements marring the universe by their violence. Or, turning within himself, he finds, that with pure and lofty conceptions, and ardent aspirations for the good, he is still liable to be tempted to evil. All is jarring discord.

I know of but one mode which gives any promise of reconciling these seeming contradictions; and that is, to suppose the whole universe as intended for the education of the mind; as a school in which to discipline the spirit.

Without now alluding to the many various cases in which the adaptations of nature to this object are manifest, I will only remark, that, on this hypothesis, the necessity of evil, or at least of different degrees of good, is obvious. For, otherwise, there would be no choice. Without choice, there would be no exercise of the will; and, wanting will, the powers of the mind would be dormant. Life, under such circumstances, would hardly assume any higher form than that of vegetable existence. Without evil, there would be no temptation; and the pleasures of self-restraint, with its ennobling influences on the soul, would be lost; there would be no exercise of moral power. From this it is manifest that we may reason to the conclusion that evil is not only a necessary condition of the greatest good, but that it is absolutely requisite to the existence of finite moral agents.

But I have introduced the subject here that I might draw from it an impressive argument in favor of mental cultivation. For, if our hypothesis reconciles the various phenomena of creation, we may safely adopt it as true; and if it be true that this universe has been brought into existence for the purpose of improving the spirit, how very important must be the object for which all this creative power and wisdom has been put forth! The question may here arise, why was man made so imperfect as to require such a vast apparatus for his improvement? As the ratio of the finite to the infinite is always the same, this question might be asked, with equal propriety, if a man occupied any position in the scale of being, short of perfection; and is, therefore, equivalent to asking, why man, or all intelligence, was not made perfect and incapable of improvement. To this it may be replied, that the universal perfection of intelligence is incompatible with its activity, if, indeed, it be not with its very existence. For, intelligence is active only from some motive. The only conceivable motives are, the desire of improving our own condition, or that of others; motives which could not exist if all were perfect. If we could no longer employ our powers to advance ourselves, or, through the medium of benevolence, derive pleasure from their agency in advancing others, there would be an end of all moral activity. Intelligence would have no object, mind no employment; and all the varied modes in which it now manifests itself would be annihilated. It would, to all practical purposes, cease to exist. That a portion of intelligent beings should possess a susceptibility to improvement, is then a necessary part of the system of creation; necessary that they may themselves have motives to action, and necessary that they may be the objects of that benevolence which must be the motive-influence, in a being incapable of self-improvement.

But this necessity a wise Providence has made the source of our highest happiness; and a just God, as if in further compensation for our imperfections, has made this universe, and adapted it, as one vast apparatus, to facilitate our improvement, and increase the happiness derived from the very deficiencies of our nature. This susceptibility to improvement is thus made the compensation for the imperfection which it presupposes; and so well does it atone for it, that, in view of the amount of happiness it affords us, we may even doubt whether the want of such a capacity for improvement would not be the greatest possible defect in an intelligent nature; and whether, if we consider the perfection of being as meaning the best possible condition of being, we are not imperfect only in proportion as we neglect to avail ourselves of this compensating principle. And from this aspect do we gather a new emphasis to our argument in favor of mental cultivation; an argument, which, as derived from the design of creation, addresses itself to all those nobler sentiments, which would induce us to carry out the beneficent intentions of Providence; while it also appeals to the more selfish and narrow feelings, which would lead us to avail ourselves of all the advantages of our position in the universe.

In conformity to this grand design of creation, progress has been made a necessary condition of happiness; and no one can be happy, or even long satisfied, who does not think he is advancing in something. He may direct his energies to some worthless pursuit, and amuse himself with accomplishing that which brings with it no real improvement, no substantial good. But he finds his error; and disappointment and disgust punish the attempted fraud on the law of his moral nature. Those changes of matter, which are within the compass of human agency, are evidently of little importance, except as they influence mind; which alone has a sufficient capacity for improvement, to gratify desires constantly extending, and aspirations which know no limit.

Progress of mind, then, being essential to happiness, and this universe having been constructed, by infinite wisdom, to facilitate that object, it behoves us, as rational beings, to apply ourselves to the investigation of its complicated machinery, and endeavor, as far as possible, to understand its application to the various conditions of humanity. The natural modes of its operation (of the supernatural I do not now intend to treat) are, obviously, three-fold. Firstly, by the influence of external *material* causes; secondly, by the influence which we exert upon each other; and, thirdly, by the influence of those powers which we are conscious of possessing within ourselves: in other words, the influence of the material world on mind, of mind upon mind, and of the mind upon itself. With regard to the first, the observation of material phenomena is so familiar to us that we almost fail to observe its most important influences. We look upon a gorgeous sunset, or on the rich and varied aspect of a beautiful landscape, and, perhaps, hardly suffer ourselves to be abstracted from the bustle and hurry of customary pursuits; or if, haply lending a moment to the luxury of the scene, we think only of the immediate and agreeable effect of color and form on the eye, nor reflect that the soul is taking from it an impress, which will forever help to modify its thoughts and mould them into forms of beauty. He who is engrossed with the ordinary physical cares of life, is not apt to observe such influences. But who does not sometimes recur to the period of childhood, when his feelings were in unison with nature,— when, on the wings of the morning, his spirit mingled with Aurora's glow; or, in the shades of evening, partook the universal repose; when every breeze came fraught with melody; when the gentle murmur of the sequestered brook ministered to the poetry of his soul; when the warm sunbeam seemed to pervade and dilate his whole being; when the returning verdure of spring brought freshness to his mind, and the sombre autumn taught its silent lesson of mutability, mellowed the bright coloring of his thoughts with softer shades of revery, and led him to feel, and to meditate on, the mysteries of nature; when the tempest-driven snow aroused his latent energies, and called them forth to the mastery of circumstance; or when contemplation of the boundless ocean suggested the first vague, but rapturous thoughts, of a restless infinity within him; or when, gazing on the stars, the ardor of his yet unconquered spirit, the aspirings of his heart, found there no limit. And who, when he recurs to these hallowing impressions of his youth, does not feel the glow of virtue reänimate his bosom, and the love of all that is beautiful and gentle and holy in moral character quickened and strengthened within him?

Nor are the benefits of these appeals of nature confined to the earliest stage of our existence; but throughout the whole of life, and even amidst its most bustling scenes, they continue to exert an influence, which, however unnoticed, is still not without its effects in softening its sorrows, mitigating its asperities, and strengthening the ties of virtue.

> "To him, who, in the love of nature, holds
> Communion with her visible forms, she speaks
> A various language. For his gayer hours
> She has a voice of gladness, and a smile,
> And eloquence of beauty ; and she glides
> Into his darker musings with a mild
> And gentle sympathy, that steals away
> Their sharpness ere he is aware."

In the stir and bustle of active life — the ardor of pursuit, the tumult of passion, the enthralments of avarice, the harsh conflicts of opinions and interests, even in the degradations of vice, nature still appeals to all that is left of the better affections. Still the beautiful landscape, the quiet or song-enlivened grove, the placid lake and stream, and the azure sky, never cease to woo us to tranquillity; the moonbeams, as ever, steal quietly upon the conscience, carrying with them a calm approval to virtue, and alarming the wicked, whose thoughts or acts contrast with their purity; the returning verdure of spring still brings its hope and buoyancy of spirits. Our forests, in their autumnal changes, continue with solemn influence to teach us a cheerful resignation to the lot of mortality, on the verge of decay wearing their brightest hues, as a gentle spirit puts on its loveliest smile in death. The boundless ocean, with its unceasing roar, still speaks to us of the infinite tendencies of our nature, and quickens us to the fulfilment of their demands for high and liberal thought. The solemn night still imparts its sublimity, while its twinkling stars beckon our thoughts from the petty concerns of this little sphere of action, to that contemplation of lofty truths, which seems to connect our lowly condition with a high and glorious destiny. Nor are the more terrible of nature's scenes without their proper influences. The storm-tossed ocean, the raging tempest, the rushing torrent, and the wild tornado, impart grandeur to character, and nurture the energies which are requisite to the fulfilment of the loftiest purposes of the soul. But why should I expatiate on these manifold influences, which, though appreciated wherever there is a mind to comprehend and a heart to feel, can be but feebly portrayed by any form of expression? The loftiest strains, the purest inspirations of poetic genius would be but imperfect copies of this original language, in which nature appeals to our sensibilities; the beautiful, the poetic language in which God, through the medium of his works, holds communion with the soul, and shadows out the mysterious relations which exist between the visible and the invisible, the finite and the infinite. It was by an application of this universal language, that the Author of our religion taught us from the beauty of the lily to infer the universal care of Providence; and it was under its inspiring influence, that the untutored Indian, gazing on one of our beautiful lakes, whose sunlit surface reflected its verdant banks and flowery islands, called it "the smile of the Great Spirit."*

Need we any other illustration to make us realize that this is a language which addresses itself to all, and which may be understood by all? But if there are any with sensibilities so blunted, feelings so dead, as not to regard these gentle appeals, these persuasive influences of external nature, she has sterner powers, the effects of which apathy will rather augment than diminish. Among these are the

* Winnipiseogee.

influences of soil and climate on national character; influences which go far to account for the generic differences which exist in different latitudes. It can hardly be doubted, that, in this country, the greater industry and economy of the Eastern States is owing to the comparative poverty of a large portion of the soil, to the short time which elapses between seed-time and harvest, and to the necessity of providing for long winters; and that, to the habits induced by this latter necessity, we may attribute the desire of accumulation, which unfortunately has become too prominent as one of our distinguishing characteristics.

Such influences compel us to conform, in some degree, to the circumstances of our position, but may, nevertheless, be modified and regulated by liberal thought, comprehensive views, and a just estimate of their tendency to promote or retard our improvement. To this end a correct knowledge of them is very important.

Another and a better influence of the same kind arises from the repeated exhibitions of the power which rules the universe, as manifested in the changes of the seasons, inducing more religious awe and reverence in those countries where the transitions are great and striking, than where they are so slight as to make little or no impression on the careless observer. Such results, verified as they are by observation, attest the existence of the most hidden and subtle of the influences which I have endeavored to portray.

I will close my remarks on this portion of the subject by merely adverting to those magnificent discoveries of the modern astronomy, which have given us a new conception of the magnitude and grandeur of the material universe; a conception which, by its vastness, its sublimity, and its harmony, excites our profoundest awe, and awakens in us that sense of the infinite, which is nearly allied to the highest development of our nature, the religious sentiment. Nor is it merely by vastness, grandeur and harmony, that this sentiment is affected, in this lofty contemplation. It is also, that here, arriving at the farthest verge of human science, we still seek something beyond, namely, the Cause which organized this stupendous system of worlds, and still sustains and directs their harmonious movements. We find this cause only in Spirit. It is before this mysterious power, that man, in the pride of science, and the confidence of demonstration, is arrested and instinctively adores, as the untutored Indian, in obedience to the same law of his nature, worships the Manitto of the ocean and the storm. In both, this law of the religious sentiment is the same. Both pursue their inquiries as far as their science permits, and find themselves in the presence of a God.

The Indian, viewing nature in its apparently disconnected elements, naturally attributes a spirit cause to each: the philosopher, whom lofty science has enabled to combine the whole universe in one harmonious system moved by one will, as naturally makes that cause one; and, finding no limits to the creation, makes the cause also infinite and universal. Thus does science, by its slower processes, reach the results in which it is anticipated by revelation.

Through all the stages of human progress the connecting link between the natural and the supernatural is Cause. Our inquiries after truth conduct us to it, and merge themselves in the infinite.

In entering upon the influences which we exert upon each other, I will first remark, that, for the advantage of communicating our thoughts, we are indebted to the material world. For no one can look directly into the mind of another, or know its thoughts and feelings, except as they are manifested in material action, or described by analogy to some external object, of which both have a common perception. Language, which expresses the passions, the emotions, and all the purely mental processes, must have had this beginning, and still retains much evidence of its origin. By degrees, terms thus acquire a common signification, as applied directly to the operations of mind; and the emanations of poetry, philosophy and eloquence, are then circulated in streams, whose pellucid flow no longer reminds us that their channels were worn out of turbid matter. Language is thus fitted for the direct action of mind on mind, and becomes one of the most important agents for the development and cultivation of its powers. The mutual aid which individuals render to each other, in correcting errors of opinion and practice, in the discovery and propagation of truth, and by the inculcation of correct principles, and sound maxims, by precept and example, are among the most obvious mental and moral benefits arising from the social compact — benefits in which all may participate, and to the common stock of which every one should contribute in proportion to his ability. If a man has not the talent to convince, nor the eloquence to persuade, he may yet, by a correct and conscientious discharge of all his duties, exhibit the power of virtue and the beauty of holiness, in his every act, and make his life a more impressive and useful lesson to all within his sphere of action, than the most refined argument or elegant diction could convey. To such a one it is encouraging to reflect, that such influence, however obscure in its exercise, is never lost. A good action never dies. It lives in the unfading glow of the moral beauty it illustrates. It flows from character to character, and reproduces itself in a thousand varieties. It may be forgotten, hidden in the accumulated aggregation of events; but its leaven is still there, mingling with and modifying the whole mass.

The importance of this practical individual influence is felt in every community, and, in most, is the principal barrier to the increase of vice, fraud, and violence. By those more gifted in talents, more industrious in their application, or more favored by circumstances, an influence more pervading and palpable has been exerted. The inspiring strains of Homer and Virgil, the fervid eloquence of Demosthenes and Cicero, the wisdom of Solon and Lycurgus, the integrity of Aristides and Cato, the devotion of Leonidas and his little band, will forever inspire the patriot, the statesman, and the hero. The dazzling exploits of Alexander and Cæsar will long kindle the flame of military ambition. The glowing pages, the sublime character of Plato, the calm fortitude, the uncompromising virtue, the unblemished life of Socrates, the hosts of martyrs who have suffered torture and death to advance truth, and preserve their own purity, will never cease to be regarded with the most profound admiration. Through all time they will continue to awaken enthusiasm, and enlist its resistless energies in the cause of truth. They will ever hold up to their humble followers the high susceptibilities of human nature, and incite them by lofty contemplation and arduous virtue to participate in that glory which has shed light on every succeeding age, and gained them the homage of the world.

Of the social influences, that which arises from the formation of governments is a very important one, and furnishes an ample theme for the speculations of the philosopher, the philanthropist, and the statesman.

In proportion as men are obliged or permitted to govern themselves, will their energies be directed to that object; and hence it is that under the elective form of government the people are grave, sedate and thoughtful. Take from them the care of civil government, and they become more light and frivolous. If, in addition to this, they are relieved from the cares of the soul by a religious despotism, they become still more volatile and trifling. Proceed one step further, and remove also the cares of providing for physical existence, and we reach the condition of the slave, who, when no immediate evil presses upon him, is the most merry, grinning, fiddling specimen of humanity. But he, who, from this volatility, would argue a high order of happiness, might argue a yet higher for the fragile leaf, which yields to the impulse of every breath, dances to every breeze, and glitters in every ray which chances to beam upon it. Such happiness is little more than negative; the mere ebullition of animal spirit freed from the immediate pressures of life. It is in that exercise of the mind, which the task of conducting our own lives imposes, that its faculties are developed, and kept in that state of healthful progress, which is essential to dignified and rational enjoyment. In providing for the order of society, then, as much should be left to the self-restraint and moral power of individuals, as is consistent with public safety.

We have sketched some of the results of a vigorous exercise of those powers by which we act upon, and, in some measure, control or modify the characters of each other. There are other consequences, of a more spontaneous kind, growing out of our social relations; consequences for which we might argue even more importance, from the fact that Divine Wisdom has not left their development dependent on our efforts, but has made them essentially a part of this "complex stupendous scheme of things."

In the interchange of the courtesies of life, in the glow of mutual interests, the generous warmth of friendship, the tenderness of affection, the devotion of love, all awakening kindred and reciprocal emotions, the kindly feelings of our nature are improved by a healthful and exhilarating exercise, while sympathy for others' woe, compassion for the errors, and pity for the frailties of humanity, paternal solicitude for helpless infancy, the bereavements of death, the pangs of sundered affections and blighted hopes, lend to those feelings a keener sensibility, and give them an acute tenderness, which is essential to the full enjoyment of all the brighter forms of happiness. Feelings so vital and sensitive may sometimes lend a deeper poignancy to sorrow, but when self-degradation and crime do not enter into the sources of our mourning, their vitality heals the wounded spirit. While they soften and subdue all the fierce and angry passions, they exalt all that is noble, and hallow all that is benign, and, by the conscious generosity of emotions in which self is forgotten, elevate the soul above the power of circumstances, and temper its distress with that consolation which Montgomery has so beautifully depicted as the "joy of grief."

The obligations of justice, the propriety of regarding the rights, the opinions, the feelings, and the happiness of others, offer abundant opportunities for the exercise of self-restraint, of benevolence and magnanimity; while the conflicts of interest, the ardor of ambition, the pride of emulation, the stimulus of opposition and excited resentments, nurture the sterner energies. Even the manifold devices, the overreachings, the petty frauds and contemptible banterings of trade, serve to stimulate and give acuteness to the faculties, and, perhaps, with no injury to those who encounter, without being degraded by them, and who learn them not to practise, but that they may more certainly escape their pollution.

The supply of many things being inadequate to our desires, induces competition for their acquisition, which, with the rivalry for distinction, for power and glory, makes a gymnasium for the understanding, in which we are compelled, by the joint influence of our physical and intellectual wants, to that vigorous exercise of all our powers, which forms habits of toil and perseverance, and imparts vitality and strength to the whole character.

The relations of thought, which are thus almost forcibly impressed upon us, serve as formulas for the investigation of higher truths, and furnish the elements for the solution of the sublimest mysteries.

It is with reluctance that I broach a theme requiring even for its partial development much analytic skill; but I feel that I should leave a wide blank in this portion of my subject if I were to omit to notice the influence of woman on society; of woman, with her deep-toned affections, her delicate sensibilities, her warmth and purity of feeling, her intuitive appreciation of moral truth and rectitude, her enthusiasm tempered with gentleness, and gentleness made potent by an ethereal efficacy, by spells and sympathies, which place it above all the coarser forms of human power. To her is given a moral influence pervading as spirit, and scarcely less mysterious. For her approval, high-thoughted genius takes its loftiest flight, and industry redoubles its exertions. Her smile rewards virtue, her frown banishes vice, her glance inspires courage, and her neglect withers ambition. In her soul-lit eye there is an eloquence more moving, and in its tear a deeper pathos than words can express. A potent charm is in her smile, the spells of persuasion are on her lips, and the inspirations of love obey her bidding.

With such power what may she not accomplish? — power, which, when properly directed, is only less irresistible than that of Heaven; and possessing, in common with its omnipotence, the attribute of being undiminished by its exercise, let her recollect, that, like the divine, her power should be ever silent and gentle, and persuasive in its application; and that, like it, it should also be united with an all-pervading benevolence, with a philanthropy too universal to regard the narrow distinction of sects, too expansive to be limited by any creed.

Let her hold the powers confided to her as sacred; as dedicated to the cause of human improvement; and, faithful to the important trust, let her exert her sway for the advancement of *all* mankind, nor suffer her influence to be misapplied to any unworthy object. It were better that churches should crumble to atoms, that missionary stations should be abandoned, and ministers forsake their calling, than that this, the greatest element of moral elevation, should be fettered by sectarianism, perverted by bigotry, or desecrated by its application to the degrading artifices by which cupidity and false zeal have impiously sought to make it available in obtaining money.

When that cheering approval of the most ethereal of earthly intelligences, which should be the reward of virtue, can be procured for gold,—no matter for how holy a purpose that gold is to be used,—it is depreciated in public estimation. It has submitted to a lower standard of value. It has lost the attribute which gave it the potency of magic. It could once call out all that was noble in human nature, for this was its only price; but, perverted to pecuniary objects — how fallen! Gold and virtue are then on an equality. When the acquisitions of fraud, meanness, oppression, or extortion, may obtain the prize which should be the spontaneous reward of what is noble, generous and good, that which is ignoble is placed on a level with revealing genius and heroic virtue. This is confounding the distinctions of good and evil, from the knowledge of which the aspiring nature of our common mother could not be diverted by the pleasures of Paradise, nor deterred by the fear of death. If her daughters cannot restore us the Eden she lost, let them not abandon what she obtained for us in return; but, by preserving the distinction, still lead us on in the path of improvement, and retain for humanity, unimpaired, that godlike attribute — intelligence — which distinguishes good from evil. I conjure them, as they value their influence, as they regard the advancement of our race, to keep aloof from the petty conflicts of party, and the machinations of avarice; to preserve their delicate sensibilities from the rude encounter in which even less ethereal natures suffer a loss of refinement and spirituality;

> "In which they roughen to the sense, and all
> The winning softness of their sex is lost."

Woman's gentle nature is scarcely less out of place in the public arena in which men dispute the prize of wealth and power, than her tender frame would be in gladiatorial and pugilistic contests. She, whose proper office is to elevate and ennoble, should rise superior to low ambition and sordid views; she should be the sanctuary, keeping all the finer feelings sacred from the contamination of low-thoughted cares and ignoble strife;

> "The intelligencer
> Between the grace, the sanctities of Heaven,
> And our dull workings."

It is principally in the endearing relations of mother, wife, daughter, sister, and friend, that woman exerts the most benign influence on society. In these it is hers

> "To touch the finer springs which
> Move the world."

Whether in maiden loveliness she breathes high ambition and noble sentiment into the soul of some aspiring and adoring youth, or in her varied relations diffuses cheerfulness, grace and elegance, in the social and domestic circle, her influence is felt as the poetry of life, blending with its rougher pursuits, and neutralizing their harshness, with a tender, gentle, and holy efficacy, an influence, which, like music, soothes the savage breast, softens its asperity, and banishes its care, ere it is conscious of its power.

In the relation of mother, a high responsibility devolves upon woman. To her the infant intelligence is first confided. The young spirit, passive and yielding, receives from her its first impressions. Her plastic power moulds its intelligence, and exerts on its destiny a greater influence than any other human agency. Let her ever bear in mind this high responsibility; nor forget that, to children, *acts* are vivid and impressive, while *words* are weak; that one unguarded impropriety of conduct, a single outbreak of passion, a weak petulance, or a moment of fretfulness, may make an impression too strong for all the precepts of wisdom, and all the maxims of morality to counteract. Let her also be cheered to the ever watchful fulfilment of her important trust, by the reflection that every grace and propriety in action, every exhibition of true tenderness and affection, every effort of self-restraint, every sacrifice of selfishness to principle, and of convenience to love and duty, will be delineated on the mind of the child, in the glowing colors of his young affection, and will furnish him with a conception of moral beauty, which no time can eradicate. Such a conception, thus incorporated in his very being, cannot fail to elevate his thoughts, and increase his ability to resist temptation. And if, unhappily, he should still deviate from the path of rectitude, it will, as a second conscience, follow him in all his aberrations, keeping in his view the beauty of virtue, rendered more striking by contrast; and will unceasingly appeal to him to return to that course of duty which is hallowed by the recollections of maternal solicitude and tenderness. Words would fail to express the dream-like vividness and spirit-stirring power of such recollections; but they will be attested by every heart whose affections have been properly fostered by a mother's care, by all who have truly known and felt a mother's love. "When," said Raphael, "I take my pencil for lofty and holy purpose, the spirit of my mother hovers over me." And how often does the spirit of the mother inspire the lofty thought, quicken the noble act, and hallow the generous motive! All cannot possess the talent, or attain the excellence, of a Raphael; but moral action frequently gives a scarcely less beautiful expression to conceptions, not less divine than those which gave a spirit-like immortality to the creations of his transcendent genius.

In treating of subjects so vast, and so fruitful in details, I cannot hope to do more than to present an imperfect sketch, and it is probable that I may have entirely omitted some considerations which should have been made prominent. But if I have succeeded in suggesting an adequate idea of our solemn relations with the material world and with each other, and of their influences, some may be ready to inquire, "What is left for us to do individually?" If causes without us have an agency so potent, — if they are really the master-springs of our actions, — what have we to do for ourselves?

This inquiry leads us to the remaining division of the subject, — the influence of the mind upon itself, or of those powers of which we are conscious. Among these powers there is none of which we have a fuller conviction than of that which modifies the influence of external causes, and determines, in a greater or less degree, their influence upon us. In proportion as we exert this internal energy, do we mould the external world, and compel it to minister to our improvement and happiness. Suffer it to lie dormant, and nothing but the intervention of Heaven can prevent our being the mere sport of circumstances. Apply it to the investigations of our relations with the universe, and we learn how to make these circumstances beneficial.

It is by thought, truth-searching thought, that we free ourselves from the controlling power of causes without us. In reference to fate,

> "He is a freeman only, whom the *truth* makes free."

The mind has a power of recalling and of reëxamining

the past. By this means it can apply a cool, deliberate judgment, and decide in what respect it has erred, when under the influence of the immediate exciting causes of action, and can determine how it may better act, under similar circumstances, in future. This is the benefit of experience. But, to meet the various exigences of life, the mind has a more comprehensive power — that of imagining events, and of settling how it should act in the various combinations which it forms of them. These mental processes are the foundation of our habits and principles of action, and may be so extended as to apply, with more or less precision, to every condition to which we are liable. The greater the number of cases correctly settled, the better are we prepared for all the occasions of life, and enabled to derive advantage from its incidents. In proportion, then, as we keep this power active, are we fitted to perform our part with propriety. He who neglects it, will be the easy prey of temptation, the ready dupe of error, while he who has improved it, establishes in his mind a test of truth, and derives happiness from all the trials and vicissitudes of life, by the exercise of that virtue for which they furnish the opportunities.

The heedless mariner, when he finds himself in difficulty, either passively yields to his fate, or vents his energy in worse than useless imprecations on his evil fortune. On the other hand, he who, by constantly reflecting on the various dangers of his occupation, has prepared himself for their occurrence, finds, perhaps, even a pleasurable excitement in the exercise of that skill which is necessary to his safety, and which his previous thought has rendered easy and natural to him.

He who employs this faculty of the mind for the contemplation of probable events, lays up stores of wisdom for the common uses of life. He will become sagacious and practical in all that relates to our immediate every-day concerns. He who seeks for its exercise higher conceptions, and more thrilling combinations, fosters the spirit of genius, kindles enthusiasm, unfolds the noblest faculties of his soul, and awakens in his bosom desires which continually require the sublime, the beautiful and the holy, and which incessantly demand high progression. Such mental exercise is in harmony with the religious sentiment—that craving of the soul for something better than it has yet distinctly known; that insatiable thirst for perfection and truth. For these wants the external world is insufficient, and the mind turns within itself for the contemplation of that beauty and excellence which its own revelations afford it.

But this internal sense of beauty is quickened by the external. The perception of natural beauty, or of that found in more chaste and elegant productions of art, prepares the mind for its reception in any other form; and he who cultivates a flower, improves a landscape, or erects a beautiful edifice, improves his own ideas of moral symmetry, opens to his soul new avenues for the admission of moral beauty, and adds to the means of moral culture.

If I am correct in the necessity of progress, mental repose, or perhaps I should rather say, mental *quiescence*, is not desirable; and those who seek, will probably find it only in an uninquiring submission to the dogmas of arrogant authority; in the crushing embrace of despotism.

It is in Meditation that the self-forming power of the mind is most beneficially exerted. When we are not hurried by the necessity of immediate action, nor excited by passion, nor swayed by interest, the judgment is cool and disinterested, and we may then establish principles, and form habits of thought, which will greatly assist us whenever unexpectedly assailed by temptation, or a sudden emergency requires our hasty decision. It is thus that the influence of the external is moulded by the internal, and made subservient to it.

But, independent of the important influence of this faculty on the formation of character, it would be worthy of cultivation, were it only for the immediate gratification it affords. It can make the mind a theatre for scenic representation, in which we may act any part which suits the humor of the moment. Whatever our situation, its delights are always at hand. It can impart an intenser glow to the ardor of youth, and brighten the reveries of age. It can beautify the desert with verdure of its own creation, people the solitude of the pathless woods with the beings of its fancy, or on the watery waste hold communion with the spirits of its choice. By it the mind assimilates every excellence and grace, and by their habitual combination with its feelings makes the beautiful and the good as portions of itself.

I have spoken of the mind as susceptible of vast, of unlimited improvement. This improvement, I think, is to be effected by the cultivation of all its elements, preserving their due proportions to each other, which, when thus properly balanced, will all be found conducive to grace and strength; none requiring to be wholly eradicated. Pride, vanity, ambition, anger, fear and the love of acquisition, all exert a quickening influence. Fear is necessary to our safety, and is, apparently, among our lowest impulses. But who has ever known thought more electric, will more decisive and energetic, that the higher excitements of fear can produce? In its more moderated forms, it habitually and unnoticed enters into that combination of feelings which excites interest in what is passing around us; inducing us to observe the flow of events, and to investigate the laws of their succession, that we may avoid injury, or enjoy the sense of security. The love of acquisition, though often perverted to inferior objects, stimulates us in the pursuit of knowledge; and, the benefits of most of the other impulses being even more obvious, I will only reiterate my conviction, that they will all be found essential to the formation of the most perfect character, as all the colors of the prism, in proper proportions, are requisite to the production of the purest white; and that the mind which is invigorated by the passions, agitated by emotions, and stimulated by the thrilling impulses of sense, if it be also ennobled by lofty sentiments, and purified by the contemplation of that ideal beauty and excellence which it has the power of creating or of abstracting for itself, will be found more vital and efficient than that in which the judgment is cold, the feelings inert, and passions extinct.

From these general considerations, most of which are universally applicable, let us return for a moment to our own locality, and note what advantages we possess, and what difficulties we have to overcome, in intellectual progress. Our geographical position has, heretofore, excluded us from the full benefits of that extended social intercourse which, by rendering us familiar with the habits, systems and views, of other sections, weakens local prejudices, liberalizes the mind, and enlarges its thoughts. Another and greater obstacle to our progress has been the want of education, which, though not wholly disregarded, has been quite too much neglected. It is true there are few among us who have not been taught the rudiments of knowledge (using the term in its limited popular sense), and I fear it is equally true that very few of us have received much more than this. It is encouraging to see that all these obstacles are gradually yielding to improvements already made, or in progress.

Greater facilities of travel have also brought us into nearer communication with other portions of the country. The changes in our local habits I have already adverted to; and, on the subject of education, there is a growing interest and a corresponding progress. Intemperance, once so rife among us, has greatly lessened; and with it the waste of time, of property, and of character, has also diminished. On the other hand, industry has increased, labor is more economically administrated, and we have acquired more thorough habits of business than those which, having obtained amidst the institutions of slavery, were perpetuated long after its abolition, and continued to exert an influence on our community, in some respects the more baleful in its consequences, as the system, with which those habits in some measure harmonized, passed away. The effects of the change in opinion which has made voluntary labor honorable, and of practice which has made it active and efficient, are palpable. Look around us where we will, the increase of the products of industry, and of the comforts of life, arrest the attention. Commodious mansions or comfortable cottages are fast taking the places of those squalid hovels, where the brawl of the drunkard so often told the sad tale of the hopeless, spirit-broken, and suffering inmates. It is pleasant to witness a change which has gladdened so many hearts, brought comfort and cheerfulness to so many firesides, and diffused a general feeling of independence and confidence, of self-respect and security. But a new feeling of delight comes over us when we contemplate this improvement as but the promise of yet higher advancement; when we regard this generally diffused feeling of independence as the surest guarantee of moral character, and the certain indication, the prerequisite and precursor, of moral elevation.

The proper condition of society, as well as of the individual, is continued progress; and so strongly do the infinite tendencies of our nature demand this progress, that a proper provision for our physical wants seldom fails of being succeeded by a desire for higher and more intellectual pursuits.

Still much remains to be done,— much more ought to be done. I would gladly have thrown a veil over our defects, but the very object of these lectures requires that they should be brought to view, that the proper remedy may be applied. This duty performed, I turn with pleasure to some spots of brighter promise. There are some points in our local character which I think will not suffer by comparison with those of any portion of our country. With some opportunities for observing, I am persuaded that in no section of it have I seen more native strength of mind, more energy of purpose, more of that independence in thought, and freedom from arbitrary restraints, which are so important in the pursuit of truth; and that no place has come under my observation where the distinctions between liberty and libertinism are better marked or better appreciated, where the rational desire of freedom is more harmoniously united with a love of order, or where the transactions between individuals are marked with greater confidence, than in this my native land.

Will it be said that this is but the common preference of every mind for the customs, habits and institutions, by which itself has been more or less moulded, or that it is but a natural partiality for the land of my birth? To such suggestions I can only oppose the fact, that the portion of my life in which those preferences and partialities are most strongly impressed, the period reaching from infancy to the verge of manhood, was spent in another part of our country.

But admitting that my observations have been correct, and my judgment impartial, it may still very naturally be asked how it has happened that a people, who confessedly have labored under some peculiar disadvantages, whose progress has been retarded by a revolution in the once established habits and customs of society, whose local position has been unfavorable, and who have comparatively derived little benefit from education, should possess this superiority.

In the solution of this question, I find even more encouragement than in the fact; for I find it in causes which promise a lasting and beneficial influence on the future. To natural causes we owe something. A soil which, while it does not tax the powers of the cultivator to a state of repression or exhaustion, does not permit luxurious indolence; a climate in which there is little to enervate, and a natural scenery in which there is much to inspire thought; all have their effect. These are, in their nature, permanent; and while our "rock-ribbed" hills resist the action of the elements, while the succession of seasons varies the aspect of our fields and woods, and the rains of heaven fill our murmuring brooks, and our iron-bound coast repels old ocean's surge, we may rely on *their* influence.

But there is a moral cause, to which I attach more importance, and that is the ennobling influence of soul liberty. Here thought has never been trammelled; here discussion has known no proscription; intelligence has here been free; spirit has been supreme, and nothing but the decrees of Heaven have been exempt from its jurisdiction.

Here mind has put forth its native strength, neither fettered by creeds, perverted by bigotry, nor distracted by the intestine broils of sectarianism. Every one has here wrought his portion of the realms of thought in his own way, and, choosing without restraint, the whole domain has been more or less cultivated. It may be true that we have not so often visited that portion which is consecrated to religion, as our neighbors profess to have done; but we have entered it, not as contending parties, seeking only the best positions it affords to defend our own peculiar tenets, or to attack the opinions of others, but as calm inquirers, to learn its truths, to enjoy its grandeur and sublimity, and refresh our fainting strength at its fountains of inspiration.

The effect of prescribing arbitrary limits to thought can hardly be over-estimated. It is true that many wear such fetters so passively as not to find them galling, but those who have once escaped can never again be subjected to the same bondage. The mind which submits to artificial restraints loses its elasticity and strength; accustomed to yield, the habit of submission fastens upon it; no conscious power incites it to vigorous action, no lofty sentiment inspires it with heroism, no emotion of victory cheers it in the contest with error, no enthusiasm warms it in the pursuit of truth; it becomes cold, sullen and dissatisfied with itself, or, throwing off all care and thought of its destiny, abandons itself to frivolous or unworthy pursuits.

This evil becomes incalculable, when the mind is authoritatively restrained from the free examination of all the great mysteries of its own being, when it is not permitted to know itself, to commune with itself, and to improve itself in the contemplation of those sublime truths, the investigation of which furnishes the highest and amplest exercise of its powers, and elevates it to the loftiest eminence of intellectual aggrandizement. From such restraint we have been comparatively exempt. Religious freedom is almost of necessity associated with a corresponding system of civil government; and in this state there has been not only much less legislation than among our neighbors, but vastly less practical application of the laws which regulate society. More has been left to the self-restraint of individuals, and the moral power of the community; elements in the formation of individual and national character, which, within certain limits, increase as the absence of legal restraints makes them necessary, and decrease as the adaptation of the laws to the circumstances and contingencies of social intercourse usurp their place.

Rigid laws often create their own necessity. It is related that a citizen of Milan voluntarily resided sixty years within its walls, and felt no disposition to pass their limits, until his prince commanded him not to do so.

The mind spurns that authority, which, depriving it of the exercise of its powers in the choice of action, degrades it to a machine, and, taking from it the merit of voluntary performance, robs it of the cheering influence of self-approval. This induces a disposition to break despotic laws. The most noble and generous spirits rise in opposition to them. It is not, therefore, strange that those who live under such laws are prone to think that there is no security where every right is not guaranteed by force, forgetting that the disposition to do wrong is often not so much a desire to do the thing forbidden, as to break the fetters, and assert the dignity and supremacy of the mind. Hence, too, it is, that scepticism in religion is most prevalent where its forms are most despotic.

I am aware that this very freedom, which I think so beneficial and creditable to us, has been made the theme of ridicule and obloquy by our neighbors. That we have no law and no religion, is their constant gibe. But, so long as by law they mean those legislative enactments which are rendered necessary by the fraud and violence of the governed, and by religion they signify those arbitrary forms and systems which are supported by the zeal of bigots and the craft of hypocrites, so long may they justly continue to reproach us with having neither. We might ask them, where is the utility of a religion which does not purify and ennoble; or of that extensive system and minute adaptation of laws, which, dispensing with moral power as a means of social order, banishing all natural restraints, and crushing the generous impulses in its serpent-like folds, still sanctions enormities which savages would not permit?

Much of this difference in character may probably be attributed to early legislation. Roger Williams, by proclaiming universal liberty of conscience, produced an influence on the character of this state widely differing from that exerted by those colonists whose first governmental act is said to have been an agreement to abide by the laws of God until they should have time to make better. He asserted freedom in its broadest rational form — the freedom of intelligence. They asserted the prerogative of authority, of force, and legal coercion. He made conscience supreme; they sought to supersede its *divine* action by human institutions. They persisted in their plan, and made a church and civil establishment of rigid forms and rules. He enthroned the spirit; they subjected it to arbitrary laws.

Need we inquire which of these systems has most claims to religion? Their respective influence is obvious in the formation of sectional characters so radically different that ages of proximity and habitual intercourse will hardly suffice to wear away the distinctions.

We have been thrown more upon our own thoughts; and I have now spoken more freely, from a conviction that, if mistaken in any of my views, the expression of them would do little harm to a community so accustomed to examine and determine for themselves.

They are superior to us in education; they have been more wrought and burnished in the schools; they are more skilful in the weapons of controversy, and, with that advantage which learning and skill will sometimes gain over truth and strength, they have almost succeeded in producing an impression that we ought to follow in their steps; that we, too, ought to have what they would call law and religion. Heaven forefend!

The native character of our state has been preserved in greater purity in this * than in any other portion of it. For this we are indebted to the hale and unyielding spirit of our ancestors, and to the isolated position we have occupied. But their heroism can no longer defend, nor our position protect, us from foreign encroachment. Already have the latest improvements in the enginery of fanaticism been directed against us.

With such causes of apprehension on the one hand, and on the other with the hopes arising from improvement in

* This lecture was delivered at a Lyceum in Kingston, R. I.

our habits, increased attention to the subjects of religion and education, a more free communication with the world, and the earnest and laudable efforts making by some individuals to spread truth and excite inquiry, we seem to have arrived at a crisis, on the event of which much of our future character may depend. Let us meet the emergency, resolved to hold fast to that which is good, and take truth from any hand which proffers it. To those who seek to change our opinions by argument, or even by rational persuasion, let us not object. To those who come prepared by their researches to instruct us, who bring with them knowledge from afar to enlighten, pure sentiments to elevate, and lofty thoughts to ennoble us, and, above all, good examples to illustrate their precepts, let us extend a cordial welcome, liberal aid, and generous confidence. But let us regard those who deny to us the freedom of thought, and thus aim to establish religion by the destruction of all her allies; who seek to frighten the timid, and impose on the weak and credulous, and who, instead of the mild influences which come from above, arrogate to themselves the power of demons, and expect to make us worthy the hopes of heaven by terrifying us with the fears of hell; who, adopting the principle that religious faith is not only essentially distinct from reason, but incompatible with it, carry it to such extreme as to seem to think insanity the only conclusive evidence of its existence; let us regard all such either as foolish fanatics, or knavish impostors, and traitors to the cause of human advancement. But let us carefully discriminate between these, and such as, seeking to advance the highest interests of man, are no less arduously, or beneficially, or honorably employed, than they who hold the venerated plough. From such as these let us invite truth; but suffer none to encroach on the freedom of thought.

It is the one cause of liberty; for, without this freedom of the mind, all other freedom is but a tinkling sound. Witness the numerous attempts which have been made in South America to engraft free political institutions upon a religious despotism. They have all been abortive; they must ever be abortive; the two are incompatible. And nearer to ourselves we may observe how far the ennobling influence of knowledge may be counteracted, even by the decaying remnant of a religion of authority. The highest faculties of the soul interdicted, the mind excluded from its most ennobling pursuits, from all that gives sublimity to thought, and elevation to moral feeling, vents its activity in the stir and bustle of the world; and intelligence, confined within too narrow limits, reduplicates itself in mere ingenious contrivance, and seeks its advantage in the shallow artifices of trade.

But, though under certain conditions it would almost seem that a people may be instructed without being enlightened, and educated without being elevated, let us not hence infer that knowledge is of little importance. I have said that our neighbors of another state have been better, perhaps I should say *more* educated, than ourselves. Of its benefits many of them have given illustrious proof. It has gradually weakened the bonds imposed on the intellect, enabled many to throw them off entirely, and others to exhibit much energy, even in fetters. But it is when removed from these mental restraints that the benefits of the knowledge they have acquired becomes most apparent.

The facility with which intelligence passes from one system to another, and discovers that portion of truth and harmony which exists in each, is not the least of its advantages; and they, accordingly, when brought in contact with other systems, soon find that legislative enactments are not the only basis of social security, or the highest rule of action.

Aware of my incapacity to do justice to so vast and important a subject as that of mental freedom, I rejoice that it is one to which your interest has ever been alive; that the mention of it will here touch a sympathetic chord in every bosom. Is there a son of Rhode Island whose enthusiasm is not spontaneously kindled by it; who does not proudly feel that the glory of his forefathers is reflected upon him; and that through them he shares the transcendant honor of having emancipated the mind?

While, then, with feelings elate we reflect that our ancestors made this inestimable gift to the world; that they first threw wide open the portals to those sublime truths, those realms of lofty thoughts, where the feelings are hallowed, the intellect is ennobled, and the whole spirit is in harmony with itself and the universe; that they first claimed for earth this freedom of the skies; let us determine that we will be the last, ay, that we will never relinquish the proud inheritance. And, while with patriotic pride we recur to that brightest page of our history which records the first act of universal toleration known to the world, let us with firmness resolve that here mind, as it ever has been, shall continue to be free. Let us adopt the motto, worthy to be engraved on the vaulted sky, inscribed with sunbeams on the portals of heaven, displayed in the lightning, and proclaimed in the thunder of the universe — HERE MIND IS FREE.

THE PHILOSOPHICAL CHARACTER OF CHANNING.

WHEN a great and good man dies, it is a generous impulse which prompts us to redeem from oblivion those incidents of his life, and those traits of his character, which may serve to gratify a laudable desire to know as much as possible of the benefactor of our race; to sustain a praiseworthy interest in all that makes us more familiar with the thoughts and actions which comprise his history, and to hold up to the present and succeeding generations an object for those feelings of admiration and gratitude, which nurture pure purpose and noble sentiment in the living, while they render merited homage to departed worth.

It is the part of wisdom to preserve, in the most enduring forms, the lineaments of his mind, that, by an immortal influence, they may perpetuate and enforce the precepts and examples, by which he has contributed to the happiness and progress of his fellow-men. A generous and philanthropic regard for the living, and a natural and commendable desire to serve posterity, no less than reverence and gratitude for the illustrious dead, demand the performance of this duty.

In the death of Channing we have lost the brightest

ornament of our literature, the able sustainer and promoter of a pure morality and rational piety, and the strong and fearless champion of human rights. We would that all which pertained to him should be held in enduring remembrance, that, by an ideal presence, his purity may forever encourage virtue, his calm energy continually sustain the weak and assure the timid, and his moral dignity and elevated piety perpetually exhort the degraded and sensual to a nobler and more spiritual existence.

Even the artist who portrays the external features of such men, with some faint approaches to the expression which soul has given them, performs no mean service to his race; and while pure and lofty thoughts, clothed in harmonious and beautiful expression, shall continue to delight, to elevate, and refine the mind, will the canvas on which the pencil of genius has delineated the benign countenance of Channing, awaken in the beholder the sentiments of admiration and reverence, and inspire him with high and disinterested principle, earnest and manly purpose, and firm and magnanimous devotion to truth and virtue. We gaze on those calm features, moulded by benevolence and philosophic meditation, and are again and again carried back to those cherished hours of converse, when their vital expression betrayed the varying emotions of his soul, as "calmly he uttered his beautiful thought," or as "bravely he spoke to oppression and wrong," till, kindling with the associations thus recalled, we breathe the thought, we give utterance to the wish, that some intellectual artist would portray the moral beauty and spiritual energy, which tabernacled in that feeble frame.

We aspire not to such a work. Abler hands have not unwisely shrunk from the task, and our purpose is only to give such profile sketch as we may draw from the unforgotten past, in aid of the hand which shall essay a more perfect portrait; to give form to our recollections of some aspects of his mind, which we had opportunities for observing, before time shall have dimmed their lines on the tablets of memory, or imagination shall have removed the landmarks of reality, and blended them with those ideal conceptions of moral beauty and excellence, to which they are nearly allied.

Willingly would we linger yet longer amid these cherished recollections, and enjoy in soothing revery the retrospection glowing with such benign light. But the spirit which sheds its radiance over it, and whose influence we would now invoke, summons us to a more earnest and arduous duty. In his presence we are reproved when we relax in that labor for the progress of our race, in which he never seemed to tire; and in this cause we now proceed to offer some remarks upon his philosophical character. Partial and imperfect, we are aware, our analysis of it must be; but if, in conformity to our design, as already expressed, we can reflect a ray of light on some phase of his mind, or render any portion of its outline more distinct, we shall not deem the labor bestowed in vain.

The mind of Channing, as viewed in the abstract, with reference only to its truth-discovering powers, separated from the impulses which gave it activity, and from the motives which directed its energies, presents, as one of its most striking characteristics, the important aid which the intellectual faculties derive from the moral qualities. This is so apparent in his writings that it can hardly escape the notice even of a superficial observer. It was yet more obvious in his conversation; for, in the familiar colloquial expression of his views, upon subjects which he had not made his particular study, he habitually gave utterance to the dictates of his moral sense, before he had constructed any argument to sustain them, or even distinctly ascertained their relations to any preëstablished principles.

In him this was not the effect of intellectual temerity, or even of a want of caution, but of a firm reliance on the dictates of the internal consciousness. This influence of the moral qualities is a very important element in the philosophic mind, and one which, perhaps, is not generally estimated so highly as it deserves. Moral sentiment gives a sensibility which enables the mind to recognize truth in its most ethereal forms, and to detect error in its most subtle disguises. Without it, the intellect may be acute, but cannot attain that wisdom which lays the foundations of its knowledge on the rock of truth. Even in those who are not remarkable for the possession of it, opinions are modified, and judgment improved by its influence. It would be but a truism to say that the sense of right runs through all our convictions of every kind, but we may also add, that the sense of justice, either directly, or by close analogies, pervades and binds together all truth. This is the case, not only with the abstractions of ethics and metaphysics, but even with the conclusions of mathematical reasoning, of all truths the furthest removed from the jurisdiction of the moral sense.

In the spontaneous suggestions of this sentiment, Channing had himself great confidence. The accuracy with which he had settled great leading principles, the purity of his morals, the sensitiveness of his mind, his inflexible justice, and the clearness and extent of his spiritual perceptions, all combined to give them a truthful aim, which seldom failed to direct their conclusions within the limits of moral certainty.

They were in him revelations which mere argument could not supersede; and, highly as he estimated the reasoning faculties, he never exalted them above intuition, nor deemed their authority paramount to the dictates of the moral sense; but, on the contrary, in any apparent collision between them, he was more prone to suspect error in the reasoning processes than in the moral judgment.

In his mind conscience was supreme, and established and preserved a beautiful harmony in the movements of all its powers. From his own convictions he thus speaks of it: —

"It is conscience within us which, by its approving and condemning voice, interprets to us God's love of virtue, and hatred of sin; and, without conscience, these glorious conceptions would never have opened upon the mind. It is the lawgiver in our breasts which gives us the idea of divine authority, and binds us to obey it. The soul, by its sense of right, or its perception of moral distinctions, is clothed with sovereignty over itself, and through this alone it understands and recognizes the Sovereign of the Universe. Men, as by a natural inspiration, have agreed to speak of conscience as the voice of God, as the Divinity within us. This principle, reverently obeyed, makes us more and more partakers of the moral perfections of the Supreme Being, of that very excellence which constitutes the rightfulness of his sceptre, and enthrones him over the universe. Without this inward law, we should be as incapable of receiving a law from heaven as the brute. Without this, the thunders of Sinai might startle the outward ear, but would have no meaning, no authority to the mind. I have expressed here a great truth. Nothing teaches so encouragingly our relation and resemblance to God, for the glory of the Supreme Being is eminently moral." — Vol. III., p. 234.

The tendency of this influence of the moral qualities, in their full development, is to give greater sensibility, reach and certainty, to the perceiving and intuitive faculties, and, at the same time, induce a firm reliance in their revelations. A large infusion of these qualities, thus exerted and in combination with the reasoning powers, forms the basis of the *poetic order of philosophic minds.* By this phrase we do not mean that order of mind which delights in fiction, nor even that which, of necessity, pursues the imaginary and beautiful in preference to the real. We do not so understand poetry. On the contrary, we believe it to be the result of that faculty of the mind, by which it is most nearly allied to the actual, and which most especially seeks truth through the medium of reality; — that its processes are carried on by means of the original impressions which the mind receives of the objects of thought, whether these impressions are the result of observation or reflection; — that it thus brings actual existence before the mental vision, enabling it to observe their relations without first substituting arbitrary signs for them, and it is thus contra-distinguished from the prosaic or logical mode, in which abstract terms or signs are substituted for realities, as a means of comparing their relations, and of which mathematical reasoning, based entirely on hypotheses, involved in the definitions, and carried on by arbitrary signs, having no *natural* connection or analogous relations to the things they represent, is the most perfect specimen.

These two modes of investigation,—the one carried on by means of a direct examination of the realities themselves;

the other by means of words or other signs substituted for those realities, — constitute the most important distinction in the means of philosophic research and discovery. Each has its peculiar advantages, and both are perhaps equally necessary to the advancement of knowledge. Like the external senses of sight and feeling, they mutually confirm or correct each other.

The prosaic mode has the advantage in condensing and generalizing, and perhaps we may add, that its results are more distinct and definite; but it is confined to a very contracted sphere of action, and can be extended little, if any, beyond the limits within which a philosophical or scientific language has been constructed; while the poetic is coëxtensive with thought, and freely traverses its boundless domain.

In its least ethereal form, it is the element of that common sense which, perceiving the reality of things and events, and their relations to time and to each other, is enabled to form just opinions of propriety, and probable conjectures of immediate consequences; and, as it is aided and elevated by the moral sentiments, combined with intellectual power, and invigorated by warm feelings, pure passion, and fervid enthusiasm, it rises to the dignity of inspiration, and the sublimity of prophecy.

It does not follow that a man possessing this order of mind, inspired poet though he be, will seek to express himself in poetic diction. He will almost of necessity acquire a love for beauty, harmony, and sublimity, and this sentiment will naturally manifest itself in his style, and mould it into a correspondence with its own character. His thoughts extending beyond the limits of definite or conventional terms, he must, if he imparts them at all, present them by means of some other representative of ideas, — by literal description, or by analogies and associations which will convey his views to the minds of others; and this power of bringing the mind in immediate contact with the actual, we hold to be the distinguishing characteristic of poetry, which, consequently, is the nearest possible approach which language can make to reality. It pictures to the mind all the objects, occasions, and results of thought, with almost as much certainty and precision as the eye presents to it the external appearances of nature, and scarcely less immediately; for, when poetry assumes its purest form, we are as unconscious of the medium of words which it uses, as we are of the motion of light, or of the image on the retina, by which we are made conscious of the existence of external objects.

The power of advancing beyond the limits of concrete science, which is conferred by the poetic mode of mind, makes it the all-important element of discovery and invention, and hence it is the essential attribute of genius. That most minds, with capacities for this higher sphere of action, should be absorbed by it, and attain excellence in it only by fervent devotion to the improvement and enlargement of those capacities, is not remarkable; and that they should neglect to cultivate the arts of logic, is as natural, as that the genius of Milton and Shakspeare should not have been directed to mechanical contrivance or arithmetical calculations. He who, by the exercise of the poetic faculties, can summon before him, from the whole universe, all the objects of his knowledge, is under no necessity to substitute visible signs to make those objects tangible to his thoughts. He who, by the same power, can observe all the properties and all the relations of those objects, has no occasion to marshal words in their stead.

He who can thus bring the result of his observations directly to the view of the mental perceptions, and make them bear immediately on the springs of moral action, has no need to approach reason or conscience through the cold medium of artificial signs and soulless abstractions. He wields a mightier sceptre. He possesses a more godlike attribute. He commands light to be, and there is light.

We have already suggested that the mind of Channing was of this *poetic order*, and to this we may attribute not only his lofty aspirations, elevated sentiments, and reach of thought, but also that directness, and sound, practical common sense, so conspicuous even in the most ornate productions of his pen.

It also imparts that persuasive power, which, with few exceptions, pervades all his writings. There are exceptions, however, where the logical processes usurp the place of the poetic; where, for the moment, he throws off the mantle of inspiration, and meets his opponents with the earth-made weapons of polemical discussion. For, though the prominent characteristic of his mind was poetic, the logical modes of investigation were far from being wholly neglected. He made use of them as auxiliary to his own progress, and as a vehicle of truth to others. By the exercise of his mind in these two modes, the perceiving and reasoning faculties were kept healthy and vigorous, and, as they grew, acquired strength and acuteness. It was indeed the harmonious combination of these powers which made the action of his mind at once so strong and so graceful.

These, taken in connection with great moral power and purity, combine all the mental elements essential to grandeur of character, and the successful investigation of truth, and leave us only to regret that the physical frame in which they were embodied was too frail to admit of the full and continuous action of such powers.

And yet we can conceive that the very weakness of his material nature may have made the spiritual more sensitive to truth, and more ethereal in its thoughts.

The clay-built prison-house yielded to the spirit it imprisoned, and the mortal coil could only partially restrain the aspiring nature it seemed so feebly to enthrall. It is not improbable, too, that this physical weakness gave him a more acute feeling of the supremacy of moral power, and the necessity of relying upon it to overcome all the ills of life, and to grapple with its numerous trials and temptations. In the spiritual energy which he put forth, under circumstances which so often enfeeble or crush effort, we have a sublime manifestation of that moral grandeur, that real greatness, to which human nature, through the medium of the true and the holy, may be elevated, and fulfil the noble destiny indicated by its pure and lofty aspirations. That he sometimes felt the subduing tendencies of bodily infirmity, and suffered from that keen sensibility it often imparts to the soul, rendering it painful to come in collision with a selfish and unfeeling world, is manifest in occasional passages of his writings; but they also contain abundant proof of the lofty determination which elevated him above these depressing influences, and enabled him to meet the conflicts of life, not merely without fear, but with a serene confidence in the ultimate triumph of truth and virtue, which sustained his hopes, and inspired his efforts with the emotion of victory. We think these feelings are indicated in a passage, which we extract from his Essay on Milton.

"We will not say that we envy our first parents, for we

feel that there may be a higher happiness than theirs, — a happiness won through struggle with inward and outward foes, the happiness of power and moral victory, the happiness of disinterested sacrifices and wide-spread love, the happiness of boundless hope, and of 'thoughts which wander through eternity.' Still there are times when the spirit, oppressed with pain, worn with toil, tired of tumult, sick at the sight of guilt, wounded in its love, baffled in its hope, and trembling in its faith, almost longs for the 'wings of a dove, that it may fly away,' and take refuge amidst the 'shady bowers,' the 'vernal airs,' the 'roses without thorns,' the quiet, the beauty, the loveliness of Eden." — Vol. I., p. 18.

This occasional shade of despondency only exhibits in stronger light the general tone of hope, strength, and elevation, which pervades his works, and which is sustained against bodily weakness by the happy constitution and assiduous improvement of his mind; a mind which, in view of the strength of his intellect, the reach and clearness of his perceiving faculties, and his moral power and purity, may in its action be compared to a strong and healthy eye aided by a telescope looking at remote objects, through a medium so pure that the slightest cloud might easily be detected in its remotest bounds.

The moral qualities were the foundation of his elevated character. The poetic power which we have ascribed to him, though, from its capacity of extension, beyond the limits of language and of the senses, susceptible of the most ethereal elevation, does not of necessity aspire to it. In this utilitarian age we make the lightning run upon our errands, and toil in our work-shops; and poetry, though electric in its nature, may be employed in every department of mind, and has a universality coëxtensive with its thoughts. It may have for its object the discovery of native, unadorned truth, or it may put forth its powers to render it more attractive, by clothing it in beauty. It may seek merely to entertain or amuse us, to minister to our immediate gratification, and, in doing this, it may still elevate the taste, purify the heart, and strengthen its hold upon virtue; or it may throw its bright and glittering hues over the deformities of vice, and, desecrated by grovelling passions, become the pander to the lowest appetites, and cater for their wants, by drawing from the regions of sensuality and impurity.

In all these manifestations, it is still power, and, degraded as it may be, still spiritual power. The thunder-cloud, lowering upon the earth, still bears in its dark bosom celestial light, and thrills us with its fitful gleams, while it sheds its blasting influence upon or around us. We gaze upon it with breathless attention, with awe, and with apprehension of its erratic brightness and power.

How different the feelings with which we contemplate the beautiful cloud, already elevated by its purity to the serene azure, illuminated by the softened splendor of heaven, and reflecting upon us its benign radiance; cheering the earth in its sunshine, or dissipating its bright existence in the renovating dews which it sheds on a benighted world! Thus is it with those in whom high moral and intellectual endowments are brightened and etherealized by the poetic element; and thus, looking upon the bright side of humanity, no one had more cheering words of encouragement than Channing, or, turning to its darker aspects, none offered to its weaknesses and its misfortunes more sincere and heartfelt sympathy, or more tender consolation; while none visited its errors with more inflexible judgment, or more just and effective reproof.

He reasoned strongly; but it was not when he reasoned that his power was most felt. By the poetic element of his mind, he presented reality so clearly, that error found no hiding-place. In the light of truth, it stood convicted and was abashed. By its obvious power to supply the deficiencies of experience, he was enabled to reflect upon the wicked their own deformity, and make them feel the upbraidings of a violated conscience, and the pangs of a debased and mutilated soul.

We have been thus particular in defining the poetic character of the mind of Channing, and solicitous to show that this, harmoniously coöperating with high moral qualities, was the principal element of his power, because we are aware that there are many who look upon his views as wanting in that fervor which is allied to poetry, and in that faith which it often instinctively opposes to syllogistic argument, and who regard his theology as the result of cold reasoning and heartless verbal theories. Such, if they have observed his life, and studied his writings at all, have done it to little purpose. For confirmation of our position in this particular, we would open his works almost at random. The high estimate which he himself had formed of this most ethereal attribute of the mind is of itself evidence that he possessed it in no small measure; for the possession of it is essential to the very conception of its true character. He probably had not examined it with the eye of a mere metaphysician, but he *saw* it as it existed in his own mind, and in such combinations as it there found most congenial to its own nature.

Glowing, indeed, must have been the original from which he drew the following description:

"We agree with Milton in his estimate of poetry. It seems to us the divinest of all arts; for it is the breathing or expression of that principle or sentiment which is deepest and sublimest in human nature. We mean, of that thirst or aspiration, to which no mind is wholly a stranger, for something purer and lovelier, something more powerful, lofty and thrilling, than ordinary and real life affords. No doctrine is more common among Christians than that of man's immortality. But it is not so generally understood that the germs or principles of his whole future being are *now* wrapped up in the soul, as the rudiments of the future plant in the seed. As a necessary result of this constitution, the soul, possessed and moved by these mighty, though infant energies, is perpetually stretching beyond what is present and visible, struggling against the bounds of its earthly prison-house, and seeking relief and joy in imaginings of unseen and ideal being. This view of our nature, which has never been fully developed, and which goes further towards explaining the contradictions of human life than all others, carries us to the very foundation and source of poetry.

"He who cannot interpret by his own consciousness what we have now said, wants the true key to genius. He has not penetrated those secret recesses of the soul, where poetry is born and nourished, and inhales immortal vigor, and wings herself for her heavenward flight. In an intellectual nature, framed for progress and for higher modes of being, there must be creative energies, powers of original and ever-growing thought; and poetry is the form in which these energies are chiefly manifested. It is the glorious prerogative of this art, that it 'makes all things new,' for the gratification of a divine instinct. It indeed finds its elements in what it actually sees and experiences,— in the worlds of matter and mind; but it combines and blends these into new forms, and according to new affinities; breaks down, if we may so say, the distinctions and bounds of nature; imparts to material objects life, and sentiment, and emotion, and invests the mind with the powers and splendors of the outward creation; describes the surrounding universe in the colors which the passions throw over it; and depicts the soul in those modes of repose or agitation, of tenderness or sublime emotion, which manifest its thirst for a more powerful and joyous existence. To a man of literal and prosaic character, the mind may seem lawless in these workings; but it observes higher laws than it transgresses — the laws of the immortal intellect. It is trying and developing its best faculties; and in the objects which it describes, or in the emotions which it awakens, anticipates those states of progressive power, splendor, beauty, and happiness, for which it was created.

"We accordingly believe that poetry, far from injuring society, is one of the great instruments of its refinement and exaltation. It lifts the mind above ordinary life, gives it a respite from depressing cares, and awakens the consciousness of its affinity with what is pure and noble.

"In its legitimate and highest efforts, it has the same tendency and aim with Christianity; that is, to spiritualize our nature. True, poetry has been made the instrument of vice, the pander of bad passions; but, when genius thus stoops, it dims its fires, and parts with much of its power. And, even when poetry is enslaved to licentiousness or misanthropy, she cannot wholly forget her true vocation. Strains of pure feeling, touches of tenderness, images of innocent happiness, sympathies with suffering virtue, bursts of scorn or indignation at the hollowness of the world, passages true to our moral nature, often escape in an immoral work, and show us how hard it is for a gifted spirit to divorce itself wholly from what is good.

"Poetry has a natural alliance with our best affections. It delights in the beauty and sublimity of the outward creation and of the soul. It indeed portrays, with terrible energy, the excesses of the passions; but they are passions which show a mighty nature, which are full of power, which command awe, which excite a deep, though shuddering sympathy. Its great tendency and purpose is to carry the mind beyond and above the beaten, dusty, weary walks of ordinary life; to lift it into a purer element, and to breathe into it more profound and generous emotion. It reveals to us the loveliness of nature, brings back the freshness of early feeling, revives the relish of simple pleasures, keeps unquenched the enthusiasm which warmed the spring-time of our being, refines youthful love, strengthens our interest in human nature by vivid delineations of its tenderest and loftiest feelings, spreads our sympathies over all classes of society, knits us by new ties with universal being, and, through the brightness of its prophetic visions, helps faith to lay hold on the future life.

"We are aware that it is objected to poetry, that it gives wrong views and excites false expectations of life, peoples the mind with shadows and illusions, and builds up imagination on the ruins of wisdom. That there is a wisdom against which poetry wars,— the wisdom of the senses,— which makes physical comfort and gratification the supreme good, and wealth the chief interest of life, we do not deny. Nor do we deem it the least service which poetry renders to mankind, that it redeems them from the thraldom of this earth-born prudence. But, passing over this topic, we would observe that the complaint against poetry, as abounding in illusion and deception, is in the main groundless.

"In many poems there is more of truth than in many histories and philosophic theories. The fictions of genius are often the vehicles of the sublimest verities, and its flashes often open new regions of thought, and throw new light on the mysteries of our being. In poetry, when the letter is falsehood, the spirit is often profoundest wisdom. And if truth thus dwells in the boldest fictions of the poet, much more may it be expected in his delineations of life; for the present life, which is the first stage of the immortal mind, abounds in the materials of poetry; and it is the high office of the bard to detect this divine element among the grosser labors and pleasures of our earthly being. The present life is not wholly prosaic, precise, tame and finite. To the gifted eye it abounds in the poetic. The affections which spread beyond ourselves, and stretch far into futurity; the workings of mighty passions, which seem to arm the soul with an almost superhuman energy; the innocent and irrepressible joy of infancy; the bloom, and buoyancy, and dazzling hopes of youth; the throbbings of the heart, when it first wakes to love, and dreams of a happiness too vast for earth; woman, with her beauty, and grace, and gentleness, and fulness of feeling, and depth of affection, and blushes of purity, and the tones and looks which only a mother's heart can inspire; — these are all poetical. It is not true, that the poet paints a life which does not exist. He only extracts, and concentrates, as it were, life's ethereal essence, arrests and condenses its volatile fragrance, brings together its scattered beauties, and prolongs its more refined but evanescent joys. And in this he does well; for it is good to feel that life is not wholly usurped by cares for subsistence and physical gratifications, but admits, in measures which may be indefinitely enlarged, sentiments and delights worthy of a higher being. This power of poetry, to refine our views of life and happiness, is more and more needed as society advances. It is needed to withstand the encroachments of heartless and artificial manners, which make civilization so tame and uninteresting. It is needed to counteract the tendency of physical science, which being now sought, not, as formerly, for intellectual gratification, but for multiplying bodily comforts, requires a new development of imagination, taste, and poetry, to preserve men from sinking into an earthly, material, epicurean life. Our remarks in vindication of poetry have extended beyond our original design. They have had a higher aim than to assert the dignity of Milton as a poet, and that is, to endear and recommend this divine art to all who reverence and would cultivate and refine their nature."— Vol. I., p. 7.

And again, in his essay on the Life and Writings of Fenelon, he says:

"Let not beauty be so wronged. It resides chiefly in profound thoughts and feelings. It overflows chiefly in the writings of *poets* gifted with a sublime and piercing vision." —Vol. I., p. 211.

In his address to the Mercantile Library Company,

delivered at Philadelphia only a few months before his death, we find a more full confirmation of the views we have advanced of the essential truthfulness of poetry:

"The great poet of our times, Wordsworth, one of the few who are to live, has gone to common life, to the feelings of our universal nature, to the obscure and neglected portions of society, for beautiful and touching themes. Nor ought it to be said that he has shed over these the charms of his genius; as if in themselves they had nothing grand or lovely. Genius is not a creator, in the sense of fancying or feigning what does not exist. *Its distinction is to discern more of truth than ordinary minds.* It sees, under disguises and humble forms, everlasting beauty. This it is the prerogative of Wordsworth to discern and reveal in the ordinary walks of life, in the common human heart. He has revealed the loveliness of the *primitive feelings*, of the universal affections of the heart."—Vol. VI., p. 155.

Those who accuse him of leaning to the side of a cold philosophy, and an exclusive and narrow rationalism, will hardly expect such sentiments from him as,

"Men may be too rational as well as too fervent." "Men will prefer even a fanaticism, which is in earnest, to a pretended rationality, which leaves untouched all the springs of the soul, which never lays a quickening hand on our love and veneration, our awe and fear, our hope and joy."—Vol. III., p. 147.

That he was philosophic and rational, we freely admit

and assert; but his philosophy was not the mere unpractical result of abstract investigation, nor his rationalism the aimless refinement of cold reasoning. In both there was infused the electric influence of the poetic element, which quickened them into life glowing with vital warmth, and gave them a pervasive expansibility, by which they reached the most pure and delicate sensibilities of the heart, wrought upon the sublimest and profoundest sentiments of our nature, lent a kindling spark to the deepest feelings and warmest affections of the soul, and inspired it with those fervent hopes, and lofty and holy aspirations, by which the religious sentiment is most fully developed.

In further illustration of the greater faith which he reposed in those truths which are perceived and felt, as compared with those which are the results of reasoning, we quote from his "Discourse on the Evidences of Revealed Religion:"

"There is another evidence of Christianity, still more internal than any on which I have yet dwelt; an evidence to be *felt*, rather than *described*, but not less real because founded on feeling. I refer to that conviction of the divine original of our religion which springs up and continually gains strength in those who habitually apply it to their tempers and lives, and who imbibe its spirit and hopes. In such men there is a consciousness of the adaptation of Christianity to their noblest faculties; a consciousness of its exalting and consoling influences, of its power to confer the true happiness of human nature, to give that peace which the world cannot give; which assures them that it is not of earthly origin, but a ray from the Everlasting Light, a stream from the fountain of Heavenly Wisdom and

Love. This is the evidence which sustains the faith of thousands who never read and cannot understand the learned books of Christian apologists, who want, perhaps, words to explain the ground of their belief, but whose faith is of adamantine firmness, *who hold the gospel with a conviction more intimate and unwavering than mere argument ever produced.*" — Vol. III., p. 132.

He recognized these internal convictions as the immediate result of purity of mind; and, though susceptible of advantageous combination with logical and scientific attainments, yet capable of distinct and independent manifestations. Speaking of religion, he says:

"It is a subject to which every faculty and every acquisition may pay tribute, which may receive aids and lights from the accuracy of the logician, from the penetrating spirit of philosophy, from the intuitions of genius, from the researches of history, from the science of the mind, from physical science, from every branch of criticism, and, though last not least, *from the spontaneous suggestions and the moral aspirations of pure but unlettered men.*" — Vol. I., p. 207.

In conformity to these views he had great confidence in all the elements of human nature, and sought to give a good direction to its impulses, to elevate its passions rather than to eradicate them, and to make its instincts intelligent rather than to crush, or wholly subjugate them to the despotism of the reasoning faculties.

For the reasons already stated we have dwelt upon this feature of the character of Channing, and endeavored to fortify our view of it with copious extracts from his own record of his mind; but we deem its importance a sufficient apology for remarking yet further upon it.

That he possessed great power of some kind, is universally admitted by those who differed, as well as by those who concurred with him in his opinions and beliefs. That it was spiritual power none will deny; and moral qualities of the highest order are accorded to him by all. But it is remarkable that, while his theological opponents accuse him of having converted religion into a philosophy, and of reaching his results through cold and barren abstractions, and arid and heartless theories, many of his friends appear to think him, at least comparatively, deficient in philosophical power, in metaphysical analysis, and in logical acuteness. By some his influence is attributed to the peculiar beauty in which, with rare endowment, he clothed his thoughts. But it is not by mere coloring that genius manifests itself and makes its impression on the world. It is the conception which it embodies, the thought, the truthfulness, that takes strong and lasting hold of us; and, however successful Channing may have been in rendering his thoughts attractive, we have no doubt that the great source of his power is to be found in the direct, strong, natural, and earnest expression of great doctrines which he clearly perceived and firmly believed to be important to the progress and happiness of mankind; in the clear enunciation of that order of truths which are yet elevated beyond the reach of philosophical analysis, or, if thus accessible to gifted minds, are susceptible of being presented to the great mass of men only by means of the poetic power, which he so happily and successfully applied to this object. But the diversity of opinion, to which we have alluded, indicates, of itself, that his mind was well balanced in this respect; and that, without any deficiency either of the poetic or logical powers, it accorded supremacy to that which in its own nature is supreme.

But, though his elevation and sensibility rendered the poetic mode most congenial to his thoughts, and made controversy, in all its forms, repugnant to his feelings, yet, when, in resisting the attacks of his opponents, he meets them upon their own ground, and returns to those proximate principles which are within the limits of demonstration, or of logical deductions, we find no want of skill in the use of the weapons they have thus forced upon him. Do we often meet with more acute and conclusive logic than that with which he thus meets one of the arguments of a sect strongly opposed to his views?

"It is no slight objection to the mode of reasoning adopted by the Calvinist, that it renders the proof of the divine attributes impossible. When we object, to his representations of the divine government, that they shock our clearest ideas of goodness and justice, he replies, that still they may be true, because we know very little of God, and what seems unjust to man, may be in the Creator the perfection of rectitude. Now, this weapon has a double edge. If the strongest marks and expressions of injustice do not prove God unjust, then the strongest marks of the opposite character do not prove him righteous. If the first do not deserve confidence, because of our narrow views of God, neither do the last. If, when more shall be known, the first may be found consistent with perfect rectitude, so, when more shall be known, the last may be found consistent with infinite malignity and oppression. This reasoning of our opponents casts us upon an ocean of awful uncertainty. Admit it, and we have no proofs of God's goodness and equity to rely upon. What we call proof may be but mere appearances, which a wider knowledge of God may reverse. The future may show us that the very laws and works of the Creator, from which we now infer his kindness, are consistent with the most determined purpose to spread infinite misery and guilt, and were intended, by raising hope, to add the agony of disappointment to our other woes. Why may not these anticipations, horrible as they are, be verified by the unfolding of God's system, if our reasonings about his attributes are rendered so very uncertain as Calvinism teaches, by the infinity of his nature." — Vol. I., p. 634.

And from another portion of the same argument:

"It is an important truth, which we apprehend has not been sufficiently developed, that the ultimate reliance of a human being is, and must be, on his own mind. To confide in God, we must first confide in the faculties, by which He is apprehended, and by which the proofs of his existence are weighed. A trust in our ability to distinguish between truth and falsehood is implied in every act of belief; for, to question this ability, would, of necessity, unsettle all belief. We cannot take a step in reasoning or action without a secret reliance on our own minds." — Vol. I., p. 226.

And again he thus contends for the necessity of exercising the reason in matters of religious belief:

"But, if once we admit that propositions which, in their literal sense, appear plainly repugnant to one another, or to any known truth, are still to be literally understood and received, what possible limit can we set to the belief of contradictions? What shelter have we from the wildest fanaticism, which can always quote passages that in their literal and obvious sense give support to its extravagances? How can the Protestant escape from transubstantiation, a doctrine most clearly taught us, if the submission of reason, now contended for, be a duty? How can we even hold fast the truth of revelation? For, if one apparent contradiction may be true, so may another, and the proposition that Christianity is false, though involving inconsistencies, may still be a verity." — Vol. III., p. 68.

"We answer again, that if God be infinitely wise, he cannot sport with the understandings of his creatures. A wise teacher discovers his wisdom in adapting himself to the capacities of his pupils; not in perplexing them with what is unintelligible, nor in distressing them with apparent contradictions, nor in filling them with a sceptical distrust of their own powers. An infinitely wise teacher, who knows the precise extent of our minds, and the best method of enlightening them, will surpass all other instructors in bringing down truth to our apprehensions, and showing its truth and harmony. We ought, indeed, to expect occasional obscurity from such a book as the Bible, which was written for past and future ages, as well as for the present. But God's wisdom is a pledge that whatever is necessary for *us*, and necessary for salvation, is revealed too plainly to be mistaken, and too consistently to be questioned by a sound and upright mind. It is not the work of wisdom to use an unintelligible phraseology to communicate what is above our capacities, to confuse and unsettle the intellect by appearances of contradiction. We honor our heavenly teacher too much to ascribe to him such a revelation. A revelation is a gift of light; it cannot thicken our darkness and multiply our perplexities." — Vol. III., p. 68.

And even in the didactic statement of his views he often exhibits much logical skill in such an arrangement of the terms as presents the thought in clear and strong light; as, for instance:

"God indeed is said to seek his own glory; but the glory of a creator must consist in the glory of his works; and we may be assured that he cannot wish any recognition of himself but that which will perfect his sublimest, highest work, the immortal mind." — Vol. III., p. 216.

"In our apprehension, a conspiracy against the rights of the human race is as foul a crime as rebellion against the rights of sovereigns; nor is there less of treason in warring against public freedom than in assailing royal power." — Vol. I., p. 128.

The fact, however, that some of his most intimate friends and warmest admirers have suggested a deficiency in the power of metaphysical analysis, and in logical acuteness, seems to require some explanation, as well as, perhaps, some apology from us, for entertaining and expressing opinions differing from those of persons who, to such opportunities for observing, united such abilities to judge correctly. In reference to this difference of opinion, we would observe that it was Dr. Channing's habit to endeavor to advance men, and to encourage their efforts in any good path which he found them pursuing, rather than to turn their thoughts into other channels. He took position beyond them, and led them on. "He had a thought beyond other men's thoughts;" and we apprehend that few have entered with him into the discussion even of the most abstract portions of ethics and metaphysics, without feeling the truth of this marked expression of one who knew him well, and well knew how to appreciate his excellence; and it was upon these subjects that he usually chose to converse with the writer. On the other hand, those who have described him as wanting in metaphysical and logical power, are professed theologians, — men who were engaged with him in inculcating the loftiest truths of a spiritual religion, — in discoursing with whom these truths were most probably the absorbing theme; and upon this sublime subject his aspiring and fervent spirit would naturally soar above the limits of philosophical discussion, and lead him, in the didactic language of inspiration, to speak of what he perceived and felt, rather than of what he had investigated with metaphysical accuracy, or reduced to logical demonstration. With such men he would portray his ideal of moral beauty and grandeur, his lofty conceptions of the real dignity of man, and of that progress in virtue and religion, which he deemed not merely a means of reaching heaven, but as heaven already attained.

With such men he would unfold his idea of the True, the Beautiful, the Godlike, and those sublime conceptions which he had reached, not by acute reasoning, but by calm contemplation of divine perfections. From these perceptions of grandeur and goodness came his clear views of that delightful progression in truth and virtue, which he held to be the appropriate condition of man. It was not with men who agreed with him in these views, and who, from his utterance of them, derived a kindred inspiration, that he would feel the necessity of descending from such high themes, to make a logical examination of the foundation on which he had reared the lofty and beautiful superstructure. With such men he would practically illustrate his own precept to one about to assume the high functions of a spiritual teacher. "You will remember that good practice is the end of preaching, and will labor to make your people holy livers, rather than skilful disputants."

Such were the subjects, and such the manner of treating them, most congenial to his feelings; and, in this view, the testimony of those friends and coadjutors to whom we have alluded merely confirms our position, that his was of the *poetic order of philosophic minds;* while, on the other hand, the manner in which he met the arguments and assertions of his opponents exhibits an ability for abstract reasoning of no ordinary character. Of this we deem the passages we have selected sufficient proof; but the best specimens of logical power appear weak, cold, and narrow, when compared with the strong and fervid utterance which, in other forms of discourse, he gave to his expansive views, and which carried conviction to the heart and to the intellect, through a higher and purer medium than that of verbal reasoning; and this is another reason why the logical power in him was not conspicuous. It paled under the influence of superior light. Besides, the most marked and striking manifestations of the logical power are when it appears to succeed in forcing conviction against our consciousness, and boldly defies its supremacy.

Thus the apparently conclusive reasoning of Edwards against the freedom of the will, and the subtle argument of Berkeley to prove the nonexistence of matter, being processes of logic, which, if erroneous, elude detection, while they contradict our consciousness, are deemed masterpieces of the art. But Channing's reverence for the dictates of the moral judgment was so great, his confidence in them so unwavering, that he never attempted such a display of his reasoning powers. He would have looked upon it as moral treason — as an effort to dethrone the legitimate sovereign of the mind.

But there are other reasons for the impression alluded to, as having obtained with some of his friends, which we will proceed to examine. And, in the first place, we would remark that the temperament of Channing was of the most ardent character. Of that calmness which in him was so marked, apathy was no element; nor was it natural to him, but rather the effect of strong and steady discipline, of great moral dignity, and an elevated, rational, and holy faith, which raised him above the petty disturbances and conflicts of life. Yet this ardor occasionally broke through the self-restraint he habitually imposed upon it, and especially when his benevolence called it into action; when indignation for the oppressors of his race, who fettered the mind with error and tradition, or destroyed personal rights with the strong arm of despotism, kindled its latent fire. Though this spontaneous energy was, from its very nature, more apparent in his conversations, yet it is occasionally manifested in his writings; as, for instance:

"This system of *espionage* (we are proud that we have no English word for the infernal machine) had indeed been used under all tyrannies; but it wanted the craft of Fouché, and the energy of Bonaparte, to disclose all its powers." — Vol. I., p. 85.

"Whoever gives clear and undoubted proof that he is prepared and sternly resolved to make the earth a slaughter-house, and to crush every will adverse to his own, ought to be caged like a wild beast; and to require mankind to proceed against him by written laws and precedents, as if he were a private citizen in a quiet court of justice, is just as rational as to require a man in imminent peril from an assassin to wait and prosecute his murderer according to the most protracted forms of law." — Vol. I., p. 123.

"To such I would say that this doctrine (Unitarianism), which is considered by some as the last and most perfect invention of Satan, the consummation of his blasphemies, the most cunning weapon ever forged in the fires of hell, amounts to this: that there is One God, even the Father; and that Jesus Christ is not this One God, but his son and messenger, who derived all his powers and glories from the Universal Parent, and who came into the world, not to claim supreme homage for himself, but to carry up the soul to his Father as the Only Divine Person, the Only Ultimate Object of religious worship." — Vol. III., p. 165.

"Did I believe what Trinitarianism teaches, that not the least transgression, not even the first sin of the dawning mind of the child, could be remitted without an infinite expiation, I should feel myself living under a legislation unspeakably dreadful, — under laws written, like Draco's, in blood; and, instead of thanking the sovereign for providing an infinite substitute, I should shudder at the attributes which render this expedient necessary." — Vol. III., p. 196.

With what significance could he at a later period of his life say:

"*I call not on God to smite with his lightnings, to overwhelm with his storms*, the accursed ship which goes to the ignorant and rude native freighted with poison and death — which goes to add new ferocity to savage life, new licentiousness to savage sensuality. I have *learned* not to call down fire from heaven." — Vol. VI., p. 166.

With such ardent feelings, and that intense interest in the welfare of his race, which was manifested in his every thought and act, how could he wait the slow inculcation of metaphysical abstractions, and their yet slower influence upon the practical opinions, the habits, the sentiments, the feelings, and the voluntary actions of the mass? His sympathies were with the whole human family. He sought to increase the happiness of all, and, through the medium of periodicals, popular lectures, and professional discourses, brought himself most immediately in connection with the multitude. He saw them degraded by sordid and narrow views, and strove to inspire then with high and liberal thought — to awaken in them a sense of the true dignity of their nature, and animate them to noble and virtuous effort. In accomplishing this, he knew human nature too well to rely mainly upon the arts of logic. He knew that the loveliness of virtue, and the brightness of proximate truths, have a stronger hold upon the affections, and a more direct influence on the moral feelings and actions of men, than the subtle abstractions from which the acute metaphysician may deduce their verity, or into which he may generalize and condense them; that the foliage and the flowers have more direct influence to gladden the heart than the roots which sustain them. Yet no one better appreciated the value of that deep research which determines the firm foundation of truth, and, surrounding it with logical defences, renders it impregnable to the assaults of scepticism, and secure from the wily approaches of sophistry. He knew that the tendency of all error and of all truth, however apparently removed from the springs of action, was eventually to work out some practical result; and he knew that, in the last analysis, the deep thinkers are they who move the world; that they give impulse and direction to the great current of events and ideas, in which shallow errors, superficial thought, and perverted action, only cause some temporary eddies and counter-currents, destined to be swept away in the tide of truth that rushes resistlessly onward.

In the following passages we find this great and cheering thought shadowed forth:

"The great sources of intellectual power and progress to a people are its strong and original thinkers, be they found where they may." * * * * "The energy which is to carry forward the intellect of a people belongs chiefly to private individuals who devote themselves to lonely thought, who worship truth, who originate the views demanded by their age, who help to throw off the yoke of established prejudices, who improve old modes of education or invent better." — Vol. I., p. 162.

"But, as society advances, mind, thought, becomes the *sovereign* of the world; and, accordingly, at the present moment, profound and glowing thought, though breathing only from the silent page, exerts a kind of omnipotent and omnipresent energy. It crosses oceans and spreads through nations; and, at one and the same moment, the conceptions of a single mind are electrifying and kindling multitudes through wider regions than the Roman eagle overshadowed. This agency of mind on mind, I repeat it, is the true sovereignty of the world, and kings and heroes are becoming impotent by the side of men of deep and fervent thought." — Vol. III., p. 141.

"Perhaps some silent thinker among us is at work in his closet, whose name is to fill the earth. Perhaps there sleeps in his cradle some reformer who is to move the church and the world, — who is to open a new era in history, — who is to fire the human soul with new hope and new daring." — Vol. VI., p. 181. "Great ideas are mightier than the passions." — Vol. V., p. 184.

And his mission was to unfold great ideas, to ennoble his fellow-men by lofty thought, and encourage them to virtuous effort. But, as we have already observed, he did not present these great ideas through the medium of metaphysical reasoning, nor make its abstractions the foundation of his notions of virtue. Though the result of deep and fervent thought, there is in them no appearance of laborious or ingenious manipulation of words or ideas. He seemed to perceive them merely because he had attained an elevation, from which his sphere of vision was enlarged. They were the revelations of an inspired mind, acting under the stimulus of intense interest in all that affected the welfare of his race. He ever preferred the useful to the curious. He saw his fellow-men enslaved by their own passions and prejudices, or by an external, arrogant authority, and was more solicitous to inspire them with the spirit of freedom, than to investigate the sources of ecclesiastical and political power. He saw them suffering from error, and preferred rather to inspire them with a love of truth, than to trace out the subtle distinctions between the relative and absolute; and was more anxious to turn them from evil, than to discover its origin.

He chose to encourage men to make those voluntary moral efforts, which he considered as the essence of virtue, rather than himself engage in the controversy with the advocates of necessity, or attempt a verbal demonstration of free agency. With his acute sense of the suffering and degradation which arose from erroneous and narrow views, his clear convictions of the happiness and elevation of which man is susceptible, and his intense anxiety to relieve and to advance his condition, he could not coldly apply such slow remedies, and wait the tedious result of the circulation of doctrines, so apparently remote from the practical concerns of life. Yet he did not undervalue the investigation of these truths, and many were the words of encouragement which he spoke, to those whose dispositions led them into these abstruse inquiries. To such, he had not only words of encouragement, but aid; for few men had a clearer perception of the actual position of such problems, and of their various relations, than himself; and few could more readily detect a too hasty generalization, or point out any portion of the subject, or collateral question, which had been passed without sufficient examination; and though, as we have observed, the action of his mind was generally in the poetic mode, yet the student of mental philosophy cannot fail to observe that some of his most beautiful and popular thoughts appear to have been evolved from abstruse metaphysical inquiries, and that a large portion of them bear the impress of its influence; — that beneath them lies the intricate and unseen apparatus of mental assimilation, which penetrates, with innumerable fibres, the richest soil of the intellect, and thence derives sustenance for the bloom and verdure which appear on the surface.

To elicit deep and hidden truth, by the logical processes,

is a high effort of philosophy; but it is yet a higher to give these truths a practical application, and make them immediately conducive to pure feelings, elevated piety, and energetic virtue. This, the highest of all philosophical attributes, was Channing's peculiar power, and will ever give him a high rank among

> "The dead but sceptred sovereigns, who rule
> Our spirits from their urns."

Among those legitimate sovereigns of the world, "who, by their characters, deeds, suffering, writings, leave imperishable and ennobling traces of themselves on the human mind; who penetrate the secrets of the universe and of the soul; who open new fields to the intellect; who give it a new consciousness of its own powers, rights and divine original; who spread enlarged and liberal habits of thought, and who help men to understand that an ever-growing knowledge is the patrimony destined for them by the Father of spirits;" * * a high place will be assigned to the "moral and religious reformer, who truly merited that name; who rose above his times; who, moved by a holy impulse, assailed vicious establishments sustained by fierce passions and inveterate prejudices; who rescued great truths from the corruptions of ages; who, joining calm and deep thought to profound feeling, secured to religion at once enlightened and earnest conviction; who unfolded to men higher forms of virtue than they had yet attained or conceived; who gave brighter and more thrilling views of the perfection for which they were framed, and inspired a victorious faith in the perpetual progress of our nature."

Such was Channing as a philanthropist and philosopher;

so nearly realizing his own ideal of the lofty and noble in humanity, that his eloquent description of it seems better to delineate his own character, than any other language in which we can portray it. His whole mind partook of this excellence. Gifted with clear and far-reaching poetic vision, which made him familiar with the loftiest sphere of human thoughts, and the sublimest of human aspirations; with reasoning faculties, and a power of philosophical analysis, which restrained and diffused the electric fervor of the poetic element, checked its exuberance, and enabled him to give its discoveries and inspirations that palpable form and practical application, to which he was strongly moved by a benevolence which warmed his whole soul; — and these faculties, thus harmonizing and lending mutual aid to each other, warming while they enlightened; deriving energy from the earnestness of his disposition, yet preserved by the purity of his life in all their native delicacy and sensibility; made vigilant by an abiding sense of the just responsibilities of man to God, to his fellow-beings, and to himself; by his high susceptibilities and great sense of the duties of self-restraint and self-cultivation; he was stimulated to an intense, a burning interest in the welfare of his race, and to the highest and most constant activity which his fragile health permitted.

The result was such as might be anticipated from so rare a combination of mental faculties, directed by such pure and lofty motives, animated by such glowing thoughts, and invigorated by such virtuous and thrilling impulses.

He consecrated himself to the elevation and advancement of his race, and few have so happily moved the world with great truths, or so successfully warmed into activity the intellectual and moral effort which had been rendered torpid by the chilling influence of religious despotism. We cannot name a writer who has done more to awaken in his readers a true consciousness of the sublime attributes of their spiritual natures, or who has contributed so much to enlighten and liberalize the public mind upon the high truths of religion, and to place these truths on a firm and rational ground, or who has breathed into it a more vital, purifying and ennobling influence.

The perusal of his works must ever awaken the soul to the contemplation of sublime and glorious truths, animate it with lofty and magnanimous purpose, quicken its hallowing aspirations for moral beauty, truth and holiness, and incite it with glowing ardor to press forward, in the path of duty and virtue, to the fulfilment of its noblest destiny.

The improvement of his fellow-beings was the great object of his life. This was the absorbing theme of his philosophy, and the incentive to his action. His prevailing ideas of the proper condition of man may be comprised in three words, freedom, progress, happiness. And, in his view, freedom was mainly important as it accelerated progress, which in its turn derived its value from its relation to happiness.

Hence, his whole theology was based on freedom, as essential to that elevation and improvement of the moral nature most favorable to the development of the religious sentiment, and to the highest and purest enjoyment of spiritual existence.

But with these ultimate and prevailing views of the chief value of liberty, he did not overlook its important influences on the physical and social condition of man.

He occupied a similar position in regard to physical advantages arising from any other cause. His benevolence led him spontaneously to rejoice at their increase, and to regret their absence or diminution, while his more matured thought found, in their influence to elevate the mind, their principal utility and final cause. In this respect he may be said to have united the old and new philosophy,—through the material, comfort-seeking utilitarianism of the Baconian, ariving at the soul-elevating, ethereal views of the Socratic school. With reference to the popular opinion of the two systems, we might say the means he employed or indicated were often Baconian, the end he proposed was always Socratic.

His effort to place theology on a rational ground; to test its formulas by the results of observation, and give it a more practical influence, were consistent with the new philosophy; while his desire to make the power, which, through this philosophy, mind had acquired over matter, conducive to a higher spirituality, was in harmony with the sublime doctrines of the leaders of the ancient school. The disciples of Socrates and Plato disdained the application of philosophy to material objects, for the purpose of contributing to our physical wants.

The followers of Bacon, receiving their impulse rather from their leader's prevailing bias, than from any necessary consequence of his theory, directed their efforts principally to this object. Under the varying circumstances which existed at the two periods of their action, both were probably right. In the times of Socrates and Plato there was little diffused intelligence among the people, and the quintessence of it, which constitutes the philosophy of every age, would not bear general diffusion as to the objects of its power. It was then a wise foresight, or a noble instinct, which directed it exclusively to the greatest object of all philosophical thought—the moral and intellectual condition of man. By thus separating it from the vulgar uses of organic life, they maintained its purity and brightness unsullied, gave it a dignified and lofty character, which commanded the reverence and admiration of the world, thus rendering it attractive to a portion of that talent which had previously found exercise only in warlike achievements, or dissipated itself in wrangles for political supremacy, and which, accustomed to such exciting and brilliant modes of aggrandizement, would have found no allurements in a utilitarianism which had for its end the mere addition to human comforts, or in a philosophy which proposed for its object anything less than the grandest achievement of thought — the elevation and improvement of the soul. Its application then to the common uses of life would have protracted the iron rule of military despotism, and probably also have led to low and grovelling views among those who might still apply themselves to philosophical pursuits.

But, aside from these speculations, the results of the efforts of the Sophists and the Epicureans indicate that at that period, and for a long time after, the union of philosophy and the arts was impracticable, or at least incompatible with the highest interests of humanity. That early stage of society, in which physical force is the principal element of government, was not yet past. It was first requisite that philosophy should bring to its aid precisely that order of talent which was quite as likely to seek distinction in the camp as in the portico. It needed this active power to influence the popular mind, to diffuse the desire of knowledge by making its possession honorable, and thus multiply readers to an extent which should stimulate invention to supply the increased demand for books. It was further necessary that the increased means of circulating information should have time to produce some practical effects. To have proposed the application of intelligence to the manual arts, when the artists had no intelligence to apply, and before there were any means of communicating to them the results of philosophical investigation, would have been at least premature, and would have produced no beneficial result. By the invention of printing, intelligence became more abundant and more diffused. Philosophy was carried to every man's door, and every artist, and eventually every laborer, could apply its discoveries to his daily pursuits. This movement had commenced before the time of Bacon, but the feeling against such application, to which we have alluded, had an influence in retarding it until his vigorous mind, confident in clear perception, and unswayed by those sentiments which, in reverence for time-honored doctrines and sympathy with lofty views and noble thoughts, might have restrained a less hardy intellect, broke down the barriers, and the accumulated power of the age acquired an impulse towards material science, which was soon after much accelerated by the magnificent discoveries of Newton and his contemporaries. The splendor and magnitude of these discoveries, in those portions of physical research which are furthest removed from a narrow and selfish use of the intellectual faculties, were associated with the utilitarian movement, and gave it a dignity which reconciled it even to those who would otherwise have contemned it as a desecration of mental power.

It has since been long sustained by the rapidly increasing demand for the tangible comforts of life, to the production of which it has been made subservient.

These in turn have reached a point where they are again conducive to spiritual progress. The great current of philosophic thought has ever been in that channel, and we here find that the Baconian system is but a collateral portion of it, which, during an overflow, has found or formed a new channel, but eventually returns with accumulated volume to the parent stream.

To hasten this return was a grand result of Channing's efforts, and though in the progress of knowledge this reünion was necessary, and the tendency of the age had already set in that direction, yet we deem the services he performed in its achievement sufficiently important, and sufficiently in advance of his contemporaries, to entitle his name to the most conspicuous place in the history of its accomplishment. His partiality for the spiritual side of philosophy was not exceeded by that of Socrates, Plato and Seneca, yet he did not contemn the material, but, on the contrary, endeavored to make it the vehicle of the most sublime and ethereal truths to the mass of mankind.

Practically to unite intelligence and elevating thought with the pursuits of the artisan, the laborer, and the distributor of their toil, is the prominent and ostensible object of many of his essays, among which we would instance his "Address before the Mercantile Library Association of Philadelphia," "Lectures on Self-Culture," and those "On the Elevation of the Laboring Portion of the Community."

In the aid which philosophy brought to physical effort, he saw a means of lessening the manual labor required to supply our bodily wants, and of thus relieving the mind of the laborer from the depressing influence of physical exhaustion, while, by making thought a necessary portion of his occupation, he was elevated above the mere machine of sinews, bones and muscles, to which he had been degraded by an ignorance which rendered him unable to resist oppression. In the increased physical comforts produced by this aid, he saw the basis of a higher spiritual condition for all classes, though more especially for those to whom education had already been one of its results.

In the less time required to feed and clothe the body, he saw the means of applying more to the cultivation of the mind. In short, he looked upon the whole movement as a means of accelerating that higher progress, which God ordained to be the chief end of man's existence, and to which all his designs, as manifested in his works, so obviously refer.

From causes, to some of which we have alluded, the time of Bacon was favorable to the impulse he gave. The incipient stage of abstract thought in physics had passed; the time to make it practical,—to reap the fruit,—had arrived. We have witnessed its prodigious results; the discoveries of the modern astronomy displaying the wonders of the heavens; geology divining those of earth; the time-and-space-destroying railroad and telegraph; the servitude of steam, light and lightning, and the universal subjugation of less ethereal forms of matter, attest the magnificent and stupendous achievements with which his name is so gloriously associated. The labors of Channing embraced a period when these results were consummating, when success and the plenitude of acquirement in physics led men to look for a higher application — an ultimate use for the accumulation. The victories of mind over matter had been so splendid and so rapid, that it began to feel the want of another world to conquer. It was the office of Channing to direct this victorious energy to spiritual progress, and in this object to find the ultimate use of its previous acquisitions. The utilitarian was thus again merged in the parent philosophy.

The results of this union are yet to be unfolded. Imagination can hardly picture them so vast and brilliant as those just developed; yet, when we compare the mundane character of the region which philosophy has just traversed, with the ethereal sphere which is to be the theatre of its future progress, we ought not to anticipate less either in magnitude or splendor. The union of the two philosophies indicates a further change. The Baconian had inclined far to the material side, and its junction with the main current must now have the effect to give the whole a more spiritual direction than its usual channel. The metaphysical age must succeed the mechanical age; — an age commencing, like that which had preceded it, with abstract speculation and disinterested thought, which, in the uniform mode of progressive knowledge, will also at last work their way to a practical result, and lend their influence to quicken the moral sensibilities, ennoble the sentiments, purify the affections, and strengthen and refine the whole spiritual nature.

This is obviously the goal, or one goal, of mental science; and it is because these practical results are not yet developed, that the philosophy of mind finds so little favor with the great majority of mankind. Before the sowing of the seed is completed, they complain that the harvest is not ready to be gathered. We think it requires no supernatural prophetic vision to see these results in the future. When they shall be realized, a just and impartial judgment may be formed of the incipient efforts to reëlevate the spiritual, and make it the great object of thought and progress.

In that day, the services which Channing has performed in uniting the new and the old philosophy, though now little thought of, and perhaps unconsciously performed, may appear the most prominent of his useful life; and, constituting an important epoch in the history of philosophy, place him in a rank as high among the great and wise who have contributed to its advancement, as his benevolence has already obtained for him among the benefactors of his race; and give him as valid a title to philosophical fame, as, by elevated virtue, enlightened philanthropy, and disinterested devotion to the cause of humanity, he has acquired to the admiration, love, and gratitude of mankind. In this view we have endeavored to exhibit the influence which he has had on that great current of philosophy, whose present force and direction is the composition and last result of the individual thought of past ages.

In this connection we would also mention another instance of his influence, more immediately relating to political and social improvement.

The progress of social organization is from physical force to intellectual power; from intellectual power to moral influence. In his articles on Napoleon, Channing gave the first decisive blow to the prestige for that manifestation of intellectual energy, which is most nearly allied to brute force, and thus, bringing into question the legitimacy of the alliance of the intellectual with the physical, as a means of government, prepared the way for the substitution of the intellectual united with the moral powers, which makes the next step in that progression, of which *love* is the last term.

There are some cheering indications of progress in this respect. Governments are learning to recognize the rights of subjects, and in their intercourse with each other the obligations of justice are more regarded. They are now ashamed to confound might with right, and the strong deem it necessary to preserve at least the appearance of fair dealing with the weak. In glancing over these marked results of his labors, we are again reminded of that harmony in his intellectual and moral character, to which we have before alluded, and which thus made his efforts equally effective in the loftiest region of speculation, and in the ordinary sphere of practical life. We have already suggested that it is yet too early to estimate the extent of his influence on human progress; but it is even now obvious that he has made benevolence more universal, religion more rational, philosophy more spiritual, and action more moral.

CHARACTER AND WRITINGS OF CHIEF JUSTICE DURFEE.*

GENTLEMEN OF THE HISTORICAL SOCIETY:

This return of our anniversary comes attended with circumstances which awaken in our bosoms the conflicting emotions of exultation and sorrow. With its recurrence, the elate feelings of patriotic pride, with which we here listened to the last annual discourse, again spring into being, with all their kindling and elevating influences. But, with these feelings, comes the painful reflection that he, who contributed so much to the glory of that occasion, is no more amongst us; that the voice, which then so delighted and instructed us, is hushed in the silent grave.

The events of that celebration may well form an era in the history of this society and of the state. By an effort, most felicitous and powerful, the orator of that day so successfully wrought all our past history — facts and principles — that little seems left to those who may follow him in the same field of labor.

The relations he held to this society, his zealous efforts in aid of its objects, the fact that he officiated as orator at the last annual celebration, and then delivered the first of the

* A Discourse delivered before the Historical Society of Rhode Island, Jan. 18, 1848.

contemplated series of yearly discourses; the important and honorable position he long held in the government of our state, his conspicuous literary position, the general expectation of the public, and the expressed wish of many of your number, indicate the character, services, and writings of our late honored and beloved Chief Justice, as the prominent topic of this discourse, and which, could I do them any justice, would certainly form an appropriate and congenial theme for the occasion.

I am not, however, insensible either to the difficulties of the task, or of my own inability properly to perform the duty, which the partiality of my friends has assigned me; and am oppressed by the conviction, that others more immediately connected, and more intimately acquainted with metaphysical and legal science, would have better conceived and better portrayed his services in these important departments, than any efforts of mine can accomplish. I feel my incapacity to do justice even to my own conceptions of his vigorous mind and philosophic spirit; but, most of all, do I feel incompetent to present to you any condensed and adequate idea of that towering fabric of philosophy he embodied in "Panidea," and which, almost without a figure of speech, may be characterized as an intrepid effort of genius to connect earth and sky.

The intelligence of his death came suddenly upon us; and the acute sense of unexpected and unestimated loss, which at first startled the public mind, reflection has now matured into a calm, but deep-felt conviction that it is irreparable. In recurring to the events of his life, the most important of which seem clustered round its close, our first feeling is that of keen regret that his intellectual labors were thus suddenly arrested, just as he had begun to make his long-hoarded thoughts known to the public, with such promise of celebrity to himself, of lustre to our state, and of utility to the world. Another moment, and we shrink, as from a danger which we suddenly perceive we have narrowly escaped, and rejoice that he lived to give us his Commencement Oration, Panidea, and his Discourse before the Historical Society. But for these, though he would still have been long remembered as the amiable and talented citizen, and the enlightened and upright judge; and though, by his "Whatcheer," his claim to poetical genius of no common order would have been established; his philosophical abilities would have been known only in a limited circle, and, even there, he might have been generally regarded as one possessed of mental powers which he was too indolent to use. And this view would, perhaps, have been rather confirmed, than otherwise, by the unfinished versification of his poem. Now, how different! The works alluded to attest that the intellectual labor and persevering efforts of his whole life must have been applied to the vigorous and ardent pursuit of philosophical truth. They entitle him to a high place among those who have devoted their best energies to the advancement of their race. They are his title-deeds to an enduring fame. Through them his voice will be heard over a realm so extensive, that the time between their publication and his death was not sufficient for the return of its echo from the nearest boundary of the subdivisions of the wide domain. Had he been taken from this sphere of action before these fruits of his philosophical labors had been matured, the voice of eulogy might have been required to grace his exit; while only that of friendship could have done justice to his talents, and disclosed the industry and zeal with which he devoted them to the advancement of truth and the welfare of his race.

But he has now spoken through his works a language which even eulogy need not wish to alter. I shall not, then, seek to praise; nor is it my purpose to attempt to stir the fountains of grief, already so deeply moved; nor yet to assuage the sorrow which this event has occasioned. But I would avail myself of the sensibility, which it has naturally produced in the public mind, to impress it with some of the lessons of duty, virtue, and wisdom, bequeathed us by our departed fellow-citizen.

When we can no longer profit by the presence, when we can derive no further instruction and encouragement from the flowing precepts and living examples of the wise and good, it is well to study such record of their thoughts, and meditate on such mementos of their actions, as may still be within our reach, and to give them that enduring place in the memory and affections which shall continue, as far as possible, their happy influences. Let their lives, perpetuated by the pen of the historian, and their virtues, embalmed in the verse of the poet, still lend attractions to pure principles, and incite to noble actions.

Nor let humble and more transitory efforts to kindle interest, such as those in which we are now engaged, be wanting. The sympathetic and social feelings, which make a part of our being, seem to indicate these as the first appropriate mode of commemoration; a means of at once manifesting our admiration of the conduct, and our gratitude for the services, of the deceased, and of securing, in frail material, the first impressions of those models of character, which, in some more enduring form, we would transmit to posterity. To *us*, memory, vivid memory, can still supply much which *they* can only receive through the labors of the painter and the sculptor, the historian and the poet. Low indeed, degraded beyond all precedent, must be the character and the destiny of the people, when they shall cease to profit by the lessons of their illustrious dead. Through all time these have exerted the most powerful agency in moral, political, and social regeneration.

And there is much, in the active life and recorded thought of the distinguished citizen, whose loss we now deplore, worthy to be treasured up for the benefit of our own and succeeding generations. It is true, his fame, though it had long since passed the boundary of his native country, and was extending, with a rapidity accelerated by his recent achievements in the highest department of thought, had not yet become so brilliant or so universal as to make the event of his death of marked importance in distant lands; yet the sphere of usefulness he here filled, the place he held in the confidence and the affections of the community, the efforts he made to preserve and improve our institutions, his influence on our local character, and the glory he reflected on our literature, make it an occurrence of absorbing interest to the people of this state. If the most notable event to the world is the arrival in it of a great thinker, surely the departure of one, whose labors seemed only just commenced, must be of corresponding importance.

The themes suggested by his position, and his writings, claiming our principal attention, we will present only a very brief chronological statement of the events of his life.

Job Durfee was a native of Tiverton, and son of the late Hon. Thomas Durfee, for many years Chief Justice of the Court of Common Pleas for the county of Newport. He was liberally educated; and took his bachelor's degree at Brown University, in the class of 1813. In May, 1816, some months previous to his admission to the bar, he was elected a representative to the General Assembly from his native town, and continued to be returned for the same place, by semi-annual elections, for five years successively.

At the March term of the Supreme Judicial Court for the county of Newport, he was admitted to practice, as an attorney and counsellor in all the courts of this state. In October, 1820, he was elected, conjointly with the Hon. Samuel Eddy, a representative to Congress, and served through the seventeenth and eighteenth Congresses. Having failed of his election to the nineteenth Congress, he was again returned by his fellow-citizens of Tiverton, to the State Legislature, and was speaker of the House from October, 1827, until May, 1829.

He then declined a reëlection, and remained in private life, occupied chiefly with literary and agricultural pursuits, until May, 1833, when he was once more returned to the General Assembly. At the meeting of the two houses that year, for the purpose of election, he was chosen an Assistant Justice of the Supreme Judicial Court, then consisting of three judges, of which his former associate in Congress, the Hon. Samuel Eddy, was chief.

In June, 1835, on the retirement of Mr. Eddy, he was chosen to succeed him; and continued to be appointed to the place of chief justice, by annual elections, during the existence of the government under the old charter, namely, to May, 1843. When the government was organized under the new constitution, he was again elected to the same responsible station, and continued in the discharge of its duties until the day of his death.

In less than three years after completing his collegiate course, he entered into the service of the state; and, with the exception of one period of four years, was employed, the remainder of his life, in one or other of the departments of her government. I need not dwell on the ability and integrity with which he discharged the various duties which thus devolved upon him, nor on the unwavering confidence which, in every situation, was reposed in him by the public. It is interesting to observe that his speech in Congress, in 1822, on the apportionment of representation, a question of much interest to this state, is marked by that broad comprehensiveness which is so prominent a feature in his subsequent productions.

But his services in the legislative halls of the state and nation, though highly creditable to him, appear unimportant when compared with those which, for fourteen successive years, he rendered on the bench.

The duties of a judge are, perhaps, the most important and delicate of any which are required to be performed in the operations of government. They demand the highest qualifications, intellectual and moral, aided by that practical wisdom which is the result of profound study, close observation, and mature reflection.

When the courts fail to perform their duties, the very foundation of society is destroyed. The bad are no longer restrained. The government no longer affords that protection which is the condition upon which the right of self-protection has been surrendered to it by the individuals of the compact, who, in such case, of necessity reässume that right. Much of the violence in our frontier settlements arises from the difficulties in obtaining redress for wrong through the judicial tribunals; and, even in the older states, we have seen juries sustained by public opinion in refusing to convict those guilty of the highest crimes, because, it was supposed, the laws provided no adequate redress for the injury which was the provocation to the offence; thus showing the prevalence of the sentiment, that, when the laws do not make such provision, the injured party may resort to violence, and take vengeance into his own hands.

These are terrible results of the absence of law, or of a lax and inefficient administration of its provisions, from which we may learn how highly we should appreciate the protection we derive from good government; but more especially do they indicate the necessity of competent and well-organized tribunals of justice. Destroy the courts, and society is, of necessity, dissolved into its original, uncombined elements, and strength and artifice have lawless sway. The case may be yet worse if the laws are badly administered; for this may give fraudful artifice a greater advantage over unsuspecting, uncalculating honesty, than it would derive from the total absence of law.

One step further in this downward progression,— let the courts be corrupt,— and we reach that most deplorable condition of society, in which the laws become but a weapon, and a most fearful weapon, in the hands of the wicked, for the purposes of oppression and destruction.

The judiciary, then, is the strong tie of society; and, in whatever aspect we view this essential element of government, its importance becomes more and more apparent. The judge must repress wrong, and protect every citizen, by administering the laws which the legislature constitutionally enacts for that purpose. He must also protect the citizen from any legislative infringement of the rights reserved or guaranteed to him in the fundamental law, which is the basis of the compact; so that, under our form of government, it may become the duty of a judge to interpose his authority between one citizen and all the rest of the community. It is not easy to conceive of a position requiring more firmness and independence of character.

The action of a judge must also often be based on abstruse principles, known or fully apprehended only by the learned. Both these causes have a tendency to place him further than any other officer from the control of the people.

They perceive the impolicy of holding to strict account one whom they wish should act independently, and the absurdity of attempting to judge of principles which they do not fully comprehend. They refrain from measuring by their own the judgments of one whom they have selected for the very reason that he is best able to judge of the questions presented for his official decision. This requires implicit faith in the ability and integrity of those who are invested with judicial authority.

The great importance of an independent judiciary has long been conceded, and is, indeed, very obvious. How it is best and most certainly obtained, is a difficult problem. It has generally been deemed necessary to provide large pecuniary compensation, and to make the incumbent independent of the appointing power, by being subject to removal from his office only by impeachment for official misdemeanor. This, though in the main working well, is not free from serious objections. The usefulness of a judge may be very much impaired by the loss of public confidence in his ability, or even in his integrity, in cases when he could not be successfully impeached. He may become superannuated at an age when a general rule excluding him, might, in other cases, deprive the state of the services of her most able jurists. The mere uncalculating consciousness of such security from the consequences of public disapprobation, may remove a wholesome check upon individual prepossession and prejudices, and, I may add, upon those sallies and caprices of judgment, which, in some men, otherwise unexceptionable, are engendered and encouraged by a sense of freedom from the usual restraints on mental activity, by being, as it were, removed from the jurisdiction of other minds. The person thus situated is liable, to some extent, to contract mental habits similar to those of the isolated thinker, unrestrained and uncorrected by collision and comparison with the thoughts of those around him. This is the extreme of independence, when it becomes an evil.

The system in this state is peculiar; and though, thus far, highly successful, cannot yet be considered as fully tested by experience. Whether we have permanently secured, in its full extent, the indispensable requisite of independence in our courts, and at the same time guarded against the evils of that system, which has generally been thought essential to this object, is still a problem, and one of no common interest to us, and to all interested in government. It is wisely provided in our constitution that the appointment of judges need not be made a subject of discussion in the legislature,—which is the appointing power,—except to fill a vacancy occasioned by death or resignation; thus, in effect, it requires some cause to be alleged as a reason for any such discussion. This, of itself, as compared with appointments at stated periods, has practically no little influence in making the office permanent; and, so long as our citizens are impressed with the importance of selecting suitable men to fill the bench, and of making the office secure to the incumbent while he discharges its duties with ability and fidelity, our system will undoubtedly do well.

Under any system, the first requisite to an independent

court is the selection of men of independent minds to constitute it. And this independence was a prominent characteristic of our late Chief Justice. The constant occupation of his mind, in the investigation of abstract truth, naturally led to habits of disinterested mental action; and no one can peruse his works without being struck with the intellectual intrepidity, swayed by no authority but reason, and restrained only by conscience, which is manifested in his every thought. With this first requisite he united, in an uncommon degree, other high qualifications for the station.

By some he has been thought deficient in juridical learning; but the information I have received from those better able to judge, and better informed than myself on this point, leads me to believe that this deficiency, if such it may be called, was only as to minute knowledge of adjudged causes. On the great mass of these, as mere authority, he seems to have set no great value. They are undoubtedly often a very *convenient* means of settling a new case by the application of an old one more or less like it, by a process of stretching and shortening, making the old one do, and thus saving the intellectual labor required to investigate and apply original principles to each particular cause.

Judge Durfee was not willing to risk the rights of parties on such uncertain ground; but he diligently examined the opinions of the great expounders of legal science, and attentively scanned the reasoning by which their opinions were sustained.

As, in philosophy, it was the habit of his mind to penetrate to the ultimate, to ascend to the cause of causes; so, in judicial investigations, he sought to go back to the law of laws, and to draw from the pure original fountains of abstract justice the general principles which should be applied to the particular case in question.

For this process he was eminently qualified, by the comprehensiveness of his views, and his peculiar powers of combination, of rigid analysis, and rational deduction.

Thus strongly armed by the reasoning faculties for the conquest of truth, he was hardly less strongly fortified against errors by his intuitive perceptions and moral attributes. His pure and elevated principles, his nice sense of right; in short, his enlightened conscientiousness, would do much to correct those errors in the processes of reasoning, to which the ablest logicians are liable, and would still more certainly prevent any practically injurious application of the erroneous results. The faculty which thus perceives, without reasoning to conclusions, is the sentinel of truth, guarding the mind against the wily approaches of error. It is the attribute on which the great mass of mankind rely, and without which a judge, whatever may be his intellectual endowments and legal attainments, will fail to command the highest confidence of the community. Without the nice moral sense, the pure conscientiousness, which gives sensibility and rectitude to this faculty, enabling it to discover truth and detect error, in advance of the logical power, and to sit in judgment on its processes, men will not fail to see that mere acuteness of intellect and juridical learning will sometimes enable a judge to make his way further in error, while they also give him the means of defending his position with plausible and ingenious reasons, and of fortifying it with learned authority.

Let it not then be overlooked, that, with talent and learning, a judge should possess independence of character, a mind trained to habits of disinterested thought, comprehensive views, elevated morality, pure and enlightened conscientiousness, and a high controlling sense of duty.

All these qualifications were concentrated in the mind and character of Judge Durfee; and who would have wished such a mind to look for light to the recorded decisions of inferior men — decisions often hastily made, imperfectly reported, and without such statement of the reasons for the opinions given as would admit the application of the rational test? The plan he pursued was dictated by a just sense of the responsibilities of his office, and shows, that even with the inactive disposition ascribed to him, he spared himself no labor which duty required.

In connection with the independence of the judiciary, there is another part of our system well worthy of consideration, and which appears, in a great measure, to neutralize all the evil which might arise from the dependence of our judges on the appointing power.

I allude to the small amount of compensation, which will always make the occupation of the bench, by one qualified for it, rather a matter of favor to the community, than of pecuniary advantage to the occupant.

He must take the place from other and higher considerations; from patriotic motives and a controlling sense of duty; and it is men, who act from such motives, who are especially wanted for this office. While, then, in the selection of a judge, the people tender the highest and most unequivocal proof of their confidence, and of their high estimate of the talents, wisdom, and virtue of the man they choose; they have, in the sacrifice to duty, which is involved in his acceptance, a guarantee that their estimate is correct, and their confidence well founded.

Such character on the bench is invaluable, and it is true

that it is better for us to pay any possible price, than not have it. If paying such price would insure an object of such immense importance, we ought not to hesitate; but all experience teaches that the hope of obtaining high qualifications, and especially high *moral* requisites, by the payment of large salaries, is illusive. When the pecuniary compensation is an object to mercenary office-seekers, the choice must, almost of necessity, be made from among them. They will crowd themselves upon the attention of the public, to the exclusion of modest merit, which is ambitious only to be useful.

We all know the mortifying fact, that offices of profit are too often filled, more with reference to claims for partisan service, or to apprehension of party injury, than to the fitness of the applicants; and we can hardly hope that even the sanctity of the judicial ermine would protect it from the desecrating touch of the irreverent, base and selfish, could they see any hope of profiting largely by its pollution.

Low salary, then, seems to be a necessary accompaniment of that part of our plan, which makes the tenure of this office uncertain. It perfects the system — introducing into it those checks and balances which are essential to its harmonious movement; and, in fact, makes our courts as completely independent as any mode yet devised.

It also brings with it the advantage of obliging the people to turn their attention to the subject, whenever, from death, resignation, or other cause, a place on the bench is vacant.

They must then *look* for a person to fill it; and, in the very difficulty thus created, they will learn properly to appreciate the rare endowments for which they are obliged to seek, and which, when thus obtained, they will not be prone to part with for slight cause.

But it may be urged, that, when the proper qualifications are found, the small compensation will be an obstacle to obtaining them. We reply, that then they are not yet found. The man who, to serve his fellow-citizens in this most important and most honorable of all official stations, would not forego the pursuit of wealth, and consent to live on an income, which, though moderate, is still much above the average allotment, does not possess the pure and disinterested patriotism, the chastened but exalted ambition, the noble purpose of soul, the self-sacrificing and fervid devotion to duty, which are the requisites for the station. He is not the man marked by Heaven; for morally he is not "higher than all the rest from his shoulders and upwards."

When the proper person is selected, there is little reason to fear that he will decline the proffered honor, for he is appointed in virtue of the high authority from which he has derived the talents which designate him for the office, — talents, which he will feel bound to use in obedience to the commands of Him who gave them. Besides, in our limited territory, men of even less elevated views of the duties which devolve on talent, might, in yielding their consent to the solicitations of the public, feel that they were but performing an act of kindness to their friends and neighbors; and thus the feelings of friendship, and local interests and attachments, would here reïnforce the more enlarged sentiments of patriotism and philanthropy. On this point we may derive encouragement from the past. It is true that under our present system we have had a very limited experience. Since its adoption, this is the first vacancy which has occurred on the bench.

But when we consider the peculiar mental character of

the late incumbent, the absorbing nature of those philosophical investigations which habitually occupied his mind, the rapturous delight he evidently derived from the contemplation of truth in her most ethereal realms, and see him cheerfully descending from this starry height, withdrawing his mind from the sublimest problems of spiritual science to settle the petty questions which arise in the ignoble strife and competition of ordinary human affairs, and that, in thus giving thought, he gave that which to him was beyond all price, we may well doubt whether the duties of the office will ever require greater individual sacrifices to public interest than have already been made.

Though these principles are most especially applicable to those offices which require the highest moral requisites, they apply with more or less force to all. That very moderate official compensation has always been a distinguishing feature in the system of this state, may have arisen, in part, from the limited resources of small territory; but it seems most probable that it sprung spontaneously from the truly democratic ideas which our ancestors incorporated in the very inception of our government. They deemed the souls of all men equally free; and from this root springs all other practicable equality. Hence it has here ever been the custom to allot to our senators, to the governor of the state who presides at their deliberations, and to the officer who sweeps their legislative hall, the same moderate *per diem* recompense.

This is practically illustrating the great principles of republicanism — practically teaching the momentous doctrine that the offices are for the benefit of the community, and not especially for that of the incumbents, and it is directly opposed to the doctrine, termed *democratic*, which has obtained in many of our sister states, that the salaries should be large, that the poor may be able to take office. This doctrine presupposes that the officers of government must, in virtue of their station, live in more expensive style than their neighbors. And this, we are gravely told, is to make the office respectable; as if in this Republican and Christian land respectability were measured by dollars and cents, or attached to fine linen and sumptuous fare!

Among the secondary principles which cluster around the leading idea of our state, I conceive there is none so important as the one we are considering — none fraught with such promise of great results to the nation and the world. If it were applied to the officers of the general government, from the president down, the power which official patronage confers would no longer threaten our institutions. The prætorian band of mercenary office-seekers would be dispersed, and make room for talent actuated by patriotism. We should practically enforce the great truth, just mentioned, that the offices are for the benefit of the community; and, if the same principle could be applied to our diplomatic corps, we should extend the moral influence of these views beyond ourselves. Our foreign ministers, living in the style demanded by this system, would illustrate republican equality and simplicity, instead of servilely pandering to a foreign state pageantry, which, however imposing and brilliant, is sustained at the expense of privation and suffering to the great mass of the governed.

This single principle, that official service is to be rendered from patriotic and philanthropic motives, has in it power, and, if faithfully maintained, will no doubt eventually shake the thrones of *civil*, as the gradual extension of our leading idea has already shaken those of *spiritual*, despotism. If any one is disposed to smile at the idea of our little state aspiring to the proud distinction of accomplishing such great results, let him recur to the time when, on its soil and near this very spot, a solitary persecuted man, cast out by his fellow-men, and exposed to privation and danger, still nurtured in his single soul the great idea of a state where there should be spiritual freedom. Let him contemplate the progress of this idea as it has become actualized in our state, has been incorporated in our national government, and has more or less influenced every civilized nation on the globe, relaxing bigotry, restraining persecution, restoring conscience to its rightful supremacy; and then let him judge whether it be idle in us to nurture, in the bosom of our *little state*, a principle promising such momentous consequences; and whether we may not trust for their accomplishment to that energy which is inherent in all truth, and especially in truth consecrated by the sacrifice of selfishness on the altar of duty.

These views also preclude the fallacy that good government can be obtained merely by the payment of sufficient money; a fallacy which leads many to suppose they are fulfilling their whole public duty when they contribute liberally to the pecuniary expenses of the social organization, and that they are thereby absolved from the more indispensable contributions of that personal thought and attention, without which the liberal use of money will, almost of necessity, produce evil instead of good results.

Such erroneous notions wither patriotism, and extinguish enthusiasm for country.

But the association of high compensation with official duty has yet a further reach, and causes many to suppose that, in withdrawing themselves from the cares of government, and yielding their claims to a share of the incidental emoluments, they practise a commendable generosity and self-denial. The effect of this is to throw the affairs of government into the hands of the mercenary, bringing official station into disrepute, and making a disregard of public duties a conventional virtue.

That the salaries in this state are now practically at the right point, or that, if so, circumstances may not require future changes, I do not presume to assert; but I am convinced that the principle is correct, and that we shall find no plan which insures so much respectability to office, or that will draw so much talent and moral character into the service of the state, as the one we have adopted, which brings into action higher motives than money can command.

The requisition which this system makes upon talent and virtue is in harmony with that precept of our religion which enjoins that those who have freely received should freely give; and may be regarded as a departure from the prevailing social organization, in which selfishness is almost exclusively relied upon as the stimulus to the performance of all duties. It is, so far, an approach to that higher and better system, in which the nobler sentiments of justice, benevolence and love, shall become the ruling principles of action.

There is a unity in all truth; and do we not find, in the harmony of this principle of low salaries and its consequences with the high truths of social science and revealed religion, assurance that it is itself a verity, and a verity which we should fondly cherish and vigilantly protect from the assaults of that common foe to all principle and virtue, temporary expediency?

Though, several times, Judge Durfee wished to retire, he was prevailed upon to continue in office, by those who saw the difficulty of another selection. He made the sacrifice cheerfully, for his love for his native state was ardent and constant. Patriotism in him was not, however, that limited sentiment which is circumscribed by geographical lines, and which, though sufficiently removed from selfishness to be esteemed a high virtue, is yet narrow, compared with that enlarged benevolence which knows no local boundaries. In Judge Durfee, the love of Rhode Island was but a concentrated modification of the intense interest he felt in the whole community.

In our little state he saw much of future hope to the whole race, and with her leading ideas of liberty for his lever, he made it the stand point from which he might, with whatever power was in him, move the world. Perhaps, in the glowing fervor of his attachment, he invested it with some of those ideal perfections which warmed his vivid fancy, and excited enthusiasm in his ardent mind. But under the influence of that calm spirit, which is the characteristic of a mind trained to high and ennobling conceptions, he saw our state trying the experiment of self-government under new circumstances, with the new element of soul-liberty incorporated in its whole system, and modifying all its institutions. From an element so obviously congenial to civil liberty, he argued even more than from the signal success of the experiment for two centuries. He saw in this first realization of a great idea, "a liberty which implied an emancipation of reason from the thraldom of arbitrary authority, and the full freedom of inquiry in all matters of speculative faith."

He saw that, in asserting that "Christ was king in his

own kingdom," our ancestors had virtually denied the legitimacy of all *pretenders* to spiritual thrones, and had thus proclaimed the downfall of religious despotism, and with it the most galling and hopeless form of civil thraldom and oppression. He traced the great central idea of our state, from its first feeble manifestations in the individual opposition of conscientious martyrs to the usurpers of spiritual authority, through the bold Waldenses, the heroic spirits of the reformation, and the devoted pilgrims of New England, until it became the acknowledged principle of government in Rhode Island; and there began, in a systematic manner to work out those practical results to which all true thought, however abstract, continually tends, as its remote but certain effect.

In view of the great importance of this principle, and the fidelity and vigilance with which it was guarded by our ancestors, it seemed to him a sacred trust which Heaven had confided to our care for the benefit of all future ages; and he delighted, in imagination, to trace its progressive influence on the happiness of the whole human race.

He saw, too, that with the Rhode Island notion of government engrafted on the principle of religious liberty, our ancestors had successfully guided the state between the two extremes of licentiousness and arbitrary authority, keeping on that safe ground of liberty, regulated by rational laws, which is equally removed from anarchy on the one hand, and from tyranny or unnecessary restraint on the other. And when, in his own time, he saw the state in danger of being driven from this middle ground by the influence of other notions of liberty, which, having obtained in our sister states, had gradually gained a foothold in this, he felt that a crisis had arrived, the event of which might very much retard the progress of rational liberty. The germ which had been so carefully protected and nurtured into vigorous growth, was about to be destroyed. He was aroused by the emergency, and, leaving his quiet home, repaired to the scene of agitation, and put forth all his energies to support the institutions of the state, and save it from anarchy and civil war.

This is not the proper time or place to question or defend his views on this subject, and I mention the circumstance only as indicating the intense interest he felt in all that concerned the welfare of the state; but more especially in the perpetuity of those leading ideas of her government, which he deemed so important to the progress of the world. This attachment to the state, and hope in her principles, are presented in his historical discourse, in language which must make every Rhode Island bosom glow with patriotic pride. The reader will there find that, while our state has, on all occasions, been the pioneer of freedom, she has also been foremost in those commercial and mechanical pursuits which have contributed so much to individual comfort and national prosperity.

She first asserted perfect *religious* freedom.

She passed the first legislative act, and struck the first blow for *civil* liberty.

She was the first to brave royalty in arms, and the first to cope with that navy whose prowess had made it the terror of the world.

And, when the great struggle for national existence was successfully terminated, she furnished, in her past history, the model of that constitution which was to cement the union and crown the triumph.

While, in Warwick and the Narraganset country, agriculture was pursued on a magnificent scale, Newport was early preëminent in commerce, and at a later period Providence led the way in manufacturing enterprises.

"In what, then," to use the language of the discourse alluded to, "in what, then, has Rhode Island fallen short of the high promise given by her fundamental idea? Is she not thus far first among the foremost in the great cause of Liberty and Law?"

Let Rhode Island men ponder on the glorious past, which they will find delineated in this noble discourse, till, from the fervid patriotism which inspired its author, and dictated its eloquent pages, they derive a kindred ardor, and firmly resolve, by being true to themselves, and to the great principles of the state, to retain the proud preëminence, which, by a firm and steadfast adherence to these principles, has always been achieved.

We may profit by other precepts and suggestions of the same work. We are there taught that we have a sure ground of hope in ourselves, and that we may rely on the sound maxims and practical good sense, which are the basis of the institutions by which we have been self-governed for two centuries; enjoying at once more perfect liberty, and more perfect security, than were ever before attained by any social organization.

And we are there warned, not to be led away from our own principles, by following the example of other states, in their wild pursuit of a social organization, in which there shall be liberty without restraint; the pursuit of an organization which shall be *no* organization. But let me repeat this lesson of practical wisdom, in his own words. He says, "It has been the fortune of Rhode Island, from her infancy to the present hour, to balance herself between liberty and law, to wage war, as occasion might require, with this or that class of ideas, and keep them within their appropriate bounds. And before certain other states, some of them not fairly out of their cradles, undertake to give her lessons of duty in relation to such ideas, let me tell them that they must have something of Rhode Island's experience, and have, like her, been self-governed for centuries." Shall such counsel be lost upon us? Shall we, recreant to our own honor, and to the high trust which has thus descended to us, desert the principles which have thus far made our career so glorious and so useful? Or shall we not rather resolve to cling to them, and, still pressing forward, continue to be the worthy pattern of other states, instead of their servile imitator? Both our longer experience in self-government, and our limited territory, favor our being the model state.

To be the model state, then, be our ambition, and, while looking with steadfast hope on the future, let us not be unmindful of the teachings or the glory of the past. From these we may derive wisdom to direct, and enthusiasm to give energy and noble purpose to our efforts.

For the means of taking a retrospective view of our past history, and the principles it inculcates, we are much indebted to the efforts of many of the members of this society; but no one has perhaps done so much to give our history and principles a popular and attractive form, as Judge Durfee has accomplished in his Whatcheer, and in his Historical Discourse.

One of his principal objects in writing the former of these works, as stated by himself, was to invest our history, and the principles and spirit of Roger Williams, with the interest which poetry can throw around its subject, and, through its potent influences, imprint them on the memory, and make them familiar to the popular mind. The same object is manifested in his prose writings, and especially in the discourse just mentioned.

The importance he attached to the preservation of these principles, and the institutions which had grown up under them, and the glowing fervor with which they inspired his ardent mind, are strikingly and eloquently portrayed in his official charge to the grand jury in March, 1842.

It has been remarked by intelligent observers, in other states, that Rhode Island is culpably regardless of her fame; and there is so much of dignity and of magnanimity to admire, in the willingness to perform great actions without levying approbation, or being solicitous for the renown which would follow them, that I can hardly find it in my heart to wish it otherwise.

But still a proper regard to the influence of those actions, as well as justice to those by whom they were performed, may prescribe the duty of making them known. This is strongly urged in the discourse alluded to.

Speaking of the "Rhode Island idea of government," he says: "I now ask you, fellow-citizens, whether there be not that in its history which is well worthy of our admiration; and that in it which is still big with destinies glorious and honorable? Shall the records which give this history still lie unknown and neglected in the cabinet of this society, for the want of funds for their publication? Will you leave one respected citizen to stand alone in generous contribution to this great cause? I ask ye, men and women of Rhode Island,—for all may share in the noble effort to rescue the history of an honored ancestry from oblivion,—I ask ye, will you allow the world longer to remain in ignorance of their names, their virtues, their deeds, their labors, and their sufferings, in the great cause of regulated liberty? Ay, what is tenfold worse, will your suffer your children to imbibe their knowledge of their forefathers from the libellous accounts of them given by the Hubbards, the Mortons, the Mathers, and their copyists? Will you allow their minds, in the germ of existence, to become contaminated with such exaggerations, and perversion of truth, and inspired with contempt for their progenitors, and for that state to which their forefathers' just conceptions of government gave birth? Citizens! — be ye native or adopted — I invite ye to come out from all minor associations for the coërcive development of minor ideas, and adopt the one great idea of your state, which gives centre to them all; and, by hastening it onward to its natural developments, you shall realize your fondest hopes. Let us form ourselves into one great association for the accomplishment of this end. Let the grand plan be at once struck out by a legislative enactment, making immediate and providing for future appropriations; let the present generation begin this work, and let succeeding ones, through all time, go on to fill up and perfect it. Let us begin, and let our posterity proceed to construct a monumental history, that shall, on every hill, and in every vale, consecrated by tradition to some memorable event, or to the memory of the worthy dead, reveal to our own eyes, to the eyes of our children, and to the admiration of the stranger, something of Rhode Island's glorious past. Let us forthwith begin, and let posterity go on to publish a documentary history of the state; a history that needs but to be revealed, and truly known, in order to be honored and respected by every human being capable of appreciating heroic worth. Let a history be provided for your schools, that shall teach childhood to love our institutions, and reverence the memory of its ancestry; and let myth and legend conspire with history truly to illustrate the character and genius of ages gone by, and make Rhode Island all one classic ground. Let a literary and scientific periodical be established, that shall breathe the true Rhode Island spirit, defend her institutions, her character, the memory of her honored dead from defamation, be it of the past or present time; and thus invite and concentrate the efforts of Rhode Island talent and genius, wherever they may be found. Let us encourage and patronize our literary institutions of all kinds, from the common school to the college; they are all equally necessary to make the Rhode Island mind what it must be, before it can fulfil its high destinies. Let this, or other more hopeful plan, be forthwith projected by legislative enactment, and be held up to the public mind for present and future execution, and we shall realize, by anticipation, even in the present age, many of the effects of its final accomplishment. It will fix in the common mind of the state an idea of its own perpetuity, and incite it to one continuous effort to realize its loftiest hopes."

"If Rhode Island cannot live over great space, she can live over much time, — past, present and to come, — and it is the peculiar duty of statesmen to keep this idea of her perpetuity constantly in the mind of all."

This is a strong appeal, fervidly urging us to perform an important duty. But I apprehend the deep interest in the preservation of our past history, which dictated it, may have led its author to overlook, for the moment, an object no less dear to him, and to recommend what might and very probably would lead to encroachment on our state principles. I allude to his appeal for aid from the legislature.

As a state, we have generally been careful that legislative action should not interfere with those matters which are more properly the subjects of individual duty. A liberal construction of our leading principle of soul-liberty covers this ground. We would give to conscience the freest possible scope. Let us not then narrow the limits for the performance of those actions which a conscientious conviction of duty demands. Let us not encroach on that sphere in which patriotism and philanthropy are nurtured, and in which they find their appropriate field for vigorous and invigorating activity.

When a people are accustomed to look to the government for the accomplishment of every desirable public object, the glowing sentiments which should animate them are lost in a soulless abstraction; public spirit degenerates to a mere state pride, and individual devotion to country, having no object for its practical application or development, becomes, in popular estimation, but a romantic absurdity.

These views are confirmed by analogies drawn from the system which divine wisdom has established. If the Supreme Governor of the world left no good to be performed, no difficulties to be surmounted by individual effort, how would virtue be developed, or find occasions for its exercise?

It may be said, that, when union is required, the government, being already organized and ready for efficient action, is a means at hand. But there is a wide difference in favor of the moral effects of a combination, in which every individual unites from a conscientious conviction that it is his duty to aid in the accomplishment of the contemplated object, and that in which the many find themselves accidentally and incidentally acting, without thought, interest, or volition; or, perhaps, with a feeling, that they act only by compulsion, against their judgment or their will.

The objection, that state interference prevents the development, or impairs the influence, of patriotic sentiment, applies even to objects universally admitted to be beneficial, but which could be as well accomplished by private action. If, however, it be a fact, — the hypothesis even seems a libel, — if it be a fact that there is not enough of public spirit among us to accomplish the object alluded to in the passage I have quoted, I am not prepared to say that it would not become the duty of the state, as such, to preserve that past history which is our common inheritance, and which it is our duty to transmit to succeeding generations. But, in thus assuming the guardianship of this portion of experimental knowledge, let it be careful not to encroach more directly on our principles, by becoming the propagators of speculative doctrines, political, philosophical, or religious. They are nearly related to each other. The political creed is engendered by speculative philosophy, which in its turn is nearly allied to theology.

Will it be said that it is the duty of a free state to sustain and propagate those views which insure its own perpetuity and its own stability? This is the plea of despotism, and the very foundation of the Church and State doctrine. A free government must conform to the progress of speculative ideas, as they become sufficiently firm for its foundation. Despotism, which does not thus conform, is liable to violent convulsions, and is stable only when there is no such progress.

Similar convulsions also attend premature efforts to change a government in advance of this progress of speculative ideas, or before they have been fully developed in the popular mind.

If any legislators suppose the power of government may be used to secure its own permanency, by directing this progress, let them first essay the more easy task, by legislative enactment to roll back Niagara's flood or arrest the thunderbolt; and, in the reflection that the latter has been accomplished by science, they may learn that, however important and beneficial in its appropriate sphere, the action of government is temporary and impotent, compared with that mighty current of ideas which has its sources in the abstract investigations of the philosopher, and the deep revolvings of the metaphysician.

In his Historical Discourse, Judge Durfee selected, as appropriate to the occasion, a purely Rhode Island theme. It was also one congenial to his feelings, and he here appears emphatically a Rhode Island man. But it is not as her statesman, her judge, her patriotic historian and enthusiastic eulogist, that we would choose to portray the great features of his mind; and we now come to the consideration of those works by which he extended himself beyond all local boundaries, and became a citizen of the world; or, in view of the almost boundless range of his thoughts, I might rather say of the Universe, and of that Universe which mind alone pervades.

His first appearance as an author was in the poem entitled Whatcheer,* taking for his subject the settlement of

* Since writing the above, I have learned that a poem of his, entitled "The Vision of Petrarch," recited before the United Brothers' Society of Brown University in 1814, was published at that time.

this state by Roger Williams. It is one of the few American poems which have been favorably noticed in the foreign reviews, and been republished in Europe. In the somewhat mechanical part of versification it is deficient. Its rhythm is not always smooth; but, tested by the true criterion of poetry, the power of bringing real or imaginary scenes vividly to the mental perception, and the consequent power of producing lively and intense emotion, it will be found to possess poetic merits of a very high order.

The subject well deserved to be immortalized in song; for history records few events fraught with more important results, than the successful establishment of a state based on religious freedom; and few acts more truly heroic, than that of its founder encountering, in the depth of winter, the perils and hardships of a journey through the pathless wilderness, and trusting to the favor of savage tribes, already irritated by the encroachments of the whites, rather than do violence to his conscience by renouncing his principles, or even refraining from propagating them. The adventures of his journey, and of his intercourse with the Indian tribes, are vividly depicted, and the reader will often find his interest wrought to a painful intensity. But the sentiment most powerfully excited by the whole work is that of admiration for the unconquerable spirit with which the hero of the poem adheres, in every adversity, to the noble and lofty purpose, to which, through life, he devoted all his energies. This appears to have been the author's principal object, and this, it seems to us, is most happily accomplished.

The next publication from his pen was an Oration before the Phi Beta Kappa Society of Brown University, delivered at the Commencement anniversary in 1843.

The leading idea of this work is, that the course of events

in this world is mainly determined by its deep thinkers, acting through the medium of scientific invention and discovery. It is presented with much force of argument and happy illustration, revealing one of the most consoling views which philosophy has ever presented to the popular mind. How encouraging to reflect that the errors of legislation, the folly of infatuated rulers, the miseries of war, the success of national fraud, and the supremacy of violence, are but temporary and local counter currents and eddies in the great tide of events, which, moved by the mighty impulses of thought, is still flowing resistlessly onward! And how inspiring to the philanthropist to find that his efforts to advance the happiness of his race, if directed by mature reflection, can only be very partially, and for a brief space, neutralized by the perverse action of thoughtless folly, vice, and ignorance!

His next and most important publication is entitled "Panidea, or the Omnipresent Reason, considered as the creative and sustaining Logos." The title has been thought unfortunate, but it probably conveys as correct an idea of the contents of the book as any which could be selected. It embodies his philosophical views, and is evidently the result of long and patient study and deep meditation.

It appears, indeed, to have been the final product of the floating thoughts of his meditative life, suddenly precipitated, as by some galvanic spark, and clustering in symmetrical order around his central idea, which combined all the infinitude of particulars into entireties, and which, in the last analysis, merges these entireties in the unity of Reason or Logos.

This converging of his ideas into a regular system was probably not long anticipated even by himself, and may be regarded as one of those delightful surprises which occasionally reward and cheer the solitary labors of the patient metaphysical inquirer, as the aloe, after its century of constant, but almost unobservable growth, suddenly matures the beautiful flower, which imparts comeliness and grace to its rugged strength. But his thoughts had evidently long tended to the formation of the system in which they eventually took order. His poem is slightly tinged with its peculiar doctrines, which in a more practical form are very observable in both the other prose works to which we have alluded. They dawned in his Commencement Oration, and their setting rays, reflected in his Historical Discourse, were the last his luminous mind shed upon our path.

In proceeding to the consideration of this work, allow me to dwell a moment on some objections which have been urged against it, and some charges to which it has exposed its author.

In the first place, it is said to be profoundly metaphysical, and therefore of no utility. We admit the charge, but we by no means concur in the inference. We are aware that to many the term metaphysics carries with it repulsive associations with all that is dark, intricate, and bewildering in thought.

There is much diversity in the definition of the term; but it is popularly applied to abstract investigations of the nature of existence and the causes of change, but more especially to the nature and phenomena of the ultimate efficient cause — *mind.* Why, then, this popular repulsion? Is there nothing in those faculties, by which we are distinguished as rational and intelligent beings, to stimulate our curiosity and induce examination? Nothing in those general abstract principles, which embrace all particular knowledge, to render their possession desirable? Is it nothing that such inquiries, at least, furnish a fair field for the healthful and invigorating exercise of the intellectual faculties? a retreat for the mind, from the annoyances, intrusions, and selfish influences of bustling life, to calm and disinterested thought, strengthening all its noble faculties, and nurturing all its holy aspirations for truthful acquisitions?

If, as it seems reasonable to suppose, the great object of the universe is to furnish a means, to discipline and improve the spirit, how imperfect the system without this provision for the study of its own nature and its mode of action! But, independent of the gratification and improvement of the individual student of metaphysics, it reveals to us important truths; many of them, as might be expected from spiritual science, nearly allied to the consolations of religion; and related to its divine revelations as the finite to the infinite mind. To what purpose are we told that the spirit is immortal, if we are to know nothing of its attributes, and its susceptibilities to pleasure or pain? From the dearth of such inquiry — the total absence of a proper infusion of metaphysical thought in the popular mind — it has ever, in its notions of a future state, fastened on a material heaven, and a material hell, as the ultimate of its conceptions of happiness and misery. It is this deficiency, which causes a religion to be popularly attractive in proportion as it addresses itself to the senses, and which makes the sensual paradise of the Mahometan more influential in producing consistency of belief and conduct, than the spiritual joy which is promised in the Christian's heaven.

We have already alluded to one very consoling and encouraging result of metaphysical research, as the subject of one of Judge Durfee's works; and, we may add that his definition of a State, so important in its practical application to the political rights and duties of governments and citizens, was a direct and immediate consequence of his abstract speculations on the doctrine of *entireties*, of which it is only a particular case. * So that, if metaphysics has not that peculiar utility which is intended by the objectors, it has still higher claims, and will no doubt be pursued while "the heart of him that hath understanding seeketh knowledge." But are such objectors aware of its direct and important connections with the immediate affairs of life? Do they consider that a great portion of all the honest persecution, which the world has endured, has arisen from a metaphysical error as to the relations between belief and the will? and that, next to the influences of religion, a comprehensive knowledge of the effects of vice on the mind would be the surest guaranty of virtue?

But the argument may be brought much closer to the utilitarian. Trace all the recent great mechanical improvements and discoveries to their source, and we shall find they manate from the abstract metaphysical thought which Bacon wrought out, or collected and embodied from the labors of more remote, and even more purely abstract, metaphysical thinkers. The metaphysician is, in this respect, the central point from which, when we advance beyond the instinctive, all action radiates. He is the necessary antecedent to the mere philosopher. Bacon furnished the key which enabled Newton to unfold the mysteries of the material universe, and he gave direction to Locke's inquiries into the spiritual nature. His metaphysical researches revealed a method,

* This definition has since been made the foundation of a very able argument, by a very able constitutional lawyer, in a cause before the Supreme Court of the United States.

and gave an impulse to material science, which, in its widening progress, has influenced all the efforts of mankind, from the philosopher to the simplest artificer and laborer.

Steamboats, railroads, and magnetic telegraphs, are but a portion of the grand result; and, when the whole ground is seen, I apprehend it will appear scarcely less absurd, in those who are benefited by these improvements, to question the utility of metaphysical inquiries, than for a man, eating bread, to ask the use of cultivating grain. Such people would have the improvements without the pre-requisite thought, the grain without sowing or reaping. They *may*, by some chance, find the one growing spontaneously, as the other may be discovered by accident, or unguided search. I conceive it would not be difficult to show that the power of England, disproportioned as it is to her area, is the result of the influence of her deep, abstract, metaphysical thinkers. Without them, her soil and climate might have produced strong bodies, but she would have wanted the animating soul which has made her what she is, and sustains her at a point from which, this wanting, she would precipitately fall.

The advancement of speculative philosophy, and of abstract science, must, of course, be but a progress of ideas. But these, in their developments, exert a practical influence on our thoughts, feelings, sentiments, habits, and actions; in short, on the moral, intellectual, and physical condition of the world. In the department of physical labor, they point the way to mechanical improvements, or, penetrating the political strata, when they are too strongly opposed by preëstablished institutions, revolutionize governments, or convulse nations. What was the political tragedy enacted in France near the commencement of this century, but a practical manifestation of ideas, which had advanced far enough to expose the evils of the government, but had not reached the construction of a better? At this point they but gave power to the blind instinct of revenge, without imparting the elevated feelings which a further progress will inspire. The masses caught some bright, transitory glimpses of the true objects of government; but the old notions that the glory of a nation was to be found on the battle-field, and that the bosoms of the millions should freely bleed to aggrandize a successful leader, had not yet been eradicated. A brave and chivalric people were subdued, the blaze of enthusiasm was extinguished in anarchy, and the aspirations and hopes of philanthropy were crushed beneath the iron heel of despotism. But the combined power of Europe has not been able for a moment to arrest that progress of ideas which, in this terrific struggle, with volcanic force shook it to the centre. The first convulsive throes of the pent-up elements are over, and, on the new soil which the eruption has thrown up from the murky abyss of superstitious ignorance, the verdure, the bloom, and more advanced stages of progressive thought, give promise that it will ripen in the consummation of those high hopes and lofty purposes, which mere physical force can only very feebly accelerate or retard.

The general principle involved in these views would, indeed, seem to be a necessary corollary to the obvious truth that intelligence is the only activity, the only efficient cause. Hence thought moves the world, and the energy of the changes, and the rapidity of the progress of any people, must find their limit in the energy of their thinkers In confirmation of these views we may remark that, where there is least speculative thought, there is also least progress even in the practical arts.

"Panidea" is also charged with being obscure. This, we apprehend, is inseparable from the subjects of which it treats. Its object is to extend our knowledge over a region as yet very imperfectly explored; a region lying on the outer confines of science, where conventional signs of thought are not yet established, and where the persevering and penetrating thinker must, consequently, construct a language as he advances. To make this language easily intelligible to others, is obviously a work of much difficulty, if, indeed, it be not wholly impossible. As well might we expect the first pioneer in a forèst to make an open highway as he travels through it, as the first explorer of new and remote metaphysical truth to construct a plain and definite language of communication with it. All that can be expected of either, is, that they will leave such traces of their progress that others may more easily follow in the same path, which will become plainer and plainer by use. But even this inevitable obscurity is not without its beneficial results in awakening thought, and causing more thorough investigation. That mankind should cluster on one plain, around some lofty structure, is no more in conformity with divine order in the mental than in the material sphere of human activity; and, whenever a metaphysical system is built of sufficient height to become an object of universal attraction to philosophers, this ambiguity of language is sure to divide and scatter them over the whole domain of thought, great portions of which might else remain waste and unexplored.

But another and a more serious charge has been brought against this work; and some, who, reiterating the charge of obscurity, would hardly claim to understand its metaphysical formulas, or to comprehend their various relations to some intricate and subtle questions of theology, are bold to assert its sceptical tendency.

On this point I might urge the known sentiments and piety of the writer; but I am aware that great and good men have sometimes advocated views, which, when carried out to their legitimate logical consequences, lead to erroneous and pernicious results which they did not perceive; and hence any argument drawn from the purity of their lives, though it might exculpate them from the suspicion of intentional wrong, would not prove that no error was involved in the doctrines they promulgated; which, therefore, must speak for themselves, and be judged without reference to the virtues with which they may thus be associated.

To these doctrines we confidently appeal, in the present instance, for a complete refutation of this charge. And what are these doctrines, as we find them recorded in Panidea, which, as we have before observed, embodies the philosophical creed of its author?

He does not, however, claim to have put forth in it much which is absolutely new in idea; but there is much of novelty, both in the combination and in the reasoning by which some of the ideas are supported, as also in the illustrations by which, with rare felicity, he reflects light into the profoundest depths of metaphysics.

It treats of some of the most difficult and interesting questions which have ever attracted the thought, or stimulated the curiosity, of mankind. The freedom of the will, the origin of our knowledge, the fact and the mode of communication between the finite and the infinite mind, the existence or non-existence of matter as a substance distinct from spirit, the relations of the material to the spiritual, and the mode of God's government of the universe, are among the subjects comprehended in its wide range of investigation.

In regard to the first of these, though in his "doctrine of entireties," and in representing the Omnipresent Reason not only as ever present in the human mind, but as controlling to a great extent the succession of its ideas, he seems only narrowly to escape necessity, yet, in his own view, he had clearly avoided it; for he distinctly states that his method does not disturb the identity, or mar the unity, into which material and spiritual natures are resolvable; and he repeatedly asserts the freedom of the human will. This is perhaps more fully explained in the passage, in which, after speaking of the Logos as spontaneously filling the mind with its own ideal imagery, he says: "I may *will* the *necessary conditions*, but the conditions *realized*, the imagery comes of a law *above* my will." In this view there is obviously still room for voluntary effort in producing the *necessary conditions*.

The origin of our knowledge he traces to the same Omnipresent Reason, ever present in the finite mind, spontaneously impressing it with some ideas, and ever ready, on certain conditions, to impart to it finite portions of its own universal knowledge. In regard to the mode of such communications, he seems to have held them to be as various as those by which finite spirits impart their ideas to each other. We do this by signs in the form of written or articulate language, by more perfect resemblances, as in painting, or other representations of the object, or by action. If to these we add the power of immediately communicating thoughts by mere volition, which is claimed by the advocates of animal magnetism, we shall perhaps have embraced all the conceivable modes of imparting our ideas. All these must, of course, be at the command of the Supreme Intelligence.

It is manifest that every phenomenon which is produced by the creative power, even in the material world, is the result of some antecedent or concomitant idea of the divine mind, and hence, let the question of the existence or non-existence of matter be decided as it may, in the observation of these phenomena we read the thoughts of God as he has himself chosen to express them. They are clothed in grandeur and beauty, and address themselves, with moving eloquence, to all that in our nature admires the good, venerates the holy, is elevated by the sublime, or awed by the powerful and terrific. In thus using material phenomena as one means of communicating his thoughts, and, consequently, a knowledge of his character to finite minds, the question very naturally arises, whether the Supreme Intelligence, in so doing, has called to his aid, or availed himself of the use of, some intermediate substance distinct from himself, and from all intelligence, and moulded his thoughts in it; or whether all the phenomena we term material are but the direct thought, the imagery of the mind of God, made palpable to our finite minds? It would manifestly be puerile to deny the possibility of this.

We can all of us, by mental effort, raise imaginary scenes in our own minds. We can close our eyes, and by an internal power, which is creative in the sphere of self, call into existence a landscape, with its hills and valleys, and forest and lawn; and vary the picture as fancy may dictate. Nothing external, then, is necessary to such imagery.

Suppose we possessed the power of transferring this imagery immediately to the mind of another person, who should thus behold the imagery of our mind, the same as he apprehends that of his own, but, being unable to vary it by his volitions, he would discover that it had an existence independent of himself; and this to him would constitute it *real*, as distinguished from the transitory imagery which he himself creates, and changes at will.

We have then only to suppose the Supreme Intelligence endowed with this power of directly imparting ideas and images to finite minds, to account for all the phenomena of the material universe, on the hypothesis that it is but the imagery of the Supreme Mind, the thought of God made palpable to us. It is obvious that it is only thought and sensation which we receive from it, and the phenomena of dreams are alone sufficient to show that no external substance is necessary to produce the same thoughts and sensations which we usually ascribe to the direct influence of what we term matter.

But it will be asked, by those who have not considered this point, if it be possible that all this material universe, which we can see and feel, is but a mere creation of the imagination, or a mere idea?

With the author of Panidea we would reply, that it is no mere creation of *our* imaginations; but that it certainly is the expression of a mere idea of the divine mind; and, supposing it to be only the imagery of the mind of God thus made permanent and palpable to us, it is still as *real* as any existence possibly can be. It exists independently of us, and resists, in greater or less degree, our efforts to change it; and hence, to us, is as real, as if it were a distinct substance existing independent of all intelligence.

A thought, thus petrified, is as solid as marble; ay, may be very marble itself, as a thought still varying in the infinite mind may constitute the heaving billow of the ocean, or the waving foliage of the forest.

That material phenomena are thus entirely the result of spiritual action is assumed, I cannot say I think it is demonstrated, in Panidea, though there is evidently much argument in its favor, as compared with the generally received opinion that they require or imply the existence of a distinct independent substance. All that comes under the observation of our own senses is as clearly explicable, or as darkly inexplicable, on the one hypothesis as the other. But, if in the present state of the question it would be premature to decide, we may remark, that the views adopted in Panidea are recommended by the greater simplicity which they presuppose in the plan of creation. By thus considering the material as but an *effect* of spiritual action, or a form of divine thought, all those difficult and embarrassing questions relative to the connection of soul and body, spirit and matter, are at once discarded, and we have only to consider the action of spirit on spirit, in producing those thoughts and sensations directly, which we usually conceive to be produced through the medium of a distinct material substance.

If any one is disposed to urge the almost universal conviction in opposition to the views adopted on this point in Panidea, let him reflect, that the same argument could once have been quite as strongly urged against the rotation of the earth, and that, if such argument is deemed conclusive, no error which has obtained general belief can ever be corrected. Or, if any one would apply a still more popular test, and supposes he can subvert this doctrine by knocking his head against a wall, let him try the experiment; and if he learns anything by his experience, it will not be that the wall, or even his head, has any such distinct existence as he supposes, but only that a foolish *mental* volition, growing out of an erroneous *mental* idea, has been followed by a painful *mental* sensation.

But the utilitarian may still inquire, if all the phenomena remain the same, and are equally explicable on either hypothesis, where is the use in laboring for a solution?

Such an inquirer would probably not admit that the improving exercise of the intellect, the pleasure of gratifying the curiosity, of ministering to the insatiable desire of knowledge, or the beauty of a completed system, nor perhaps even the unanticipated benefits which usually result from the acquisition of truth, would be sufficient inducement, to a rational mind, to engage in such arduous and difficult investigation. Less sensitive than Memnon's heart of stone, the dawning rays of truth awaken no music in his breast. Light, breaking through chaos upon a new and beautiful creation, kindles no transport in his bosom.

But, happily, there is a utility in the views we find here enforced, which even he will hardly fail to recognize. Though the solution of the problem would not in any wise alter the phenomena of the material universe, nor its effect in producing images or sensations in our minds, it might still materially change their influences on our spiritual nature.

The views adopted in Panidea are admirably calculated to give practical effect to our speculative belief in the Omnipresence of Deity; to make us feel that we are ever in his sight; that we may, at all times, commune directly with the living God, instead of being separated from him by the intervention of dead matter. There is, perhaps, no idea more calculated to ennoble man, than the thought that he is thus ever the immediate object of the attention and regard of the Supreme Being; and that he may at all times be the recipient of the teachings of perfect wisdom, communicated, even through the senses, in a language of which the purest and loftiest poetry is but a feeble imitation, or imparted in that purely spiritual mode, in which thought flows directly from mind to mind, and the chords of sense and passion, which respond so perfectly to the varying tones of nature, are hushed in a presence which fills the whole soul with unutterable harmony, awakening an elevated rapture which makes it feel that all the material apparatus, though so delicate and so potent, so seemingly perfect for instilling sentiment and kindling emotion, is but a feeble manifestation of the power which thus acts directly on the spiritual being.

The evidence of a strong, a controlling desire to reach the ultimate, and form a perfect system, is a prominent feature of the work. As, in the material universe, each subordinate system, though apparently complete in itself, is but an inconsiderable portion of a large, and again of a yet larger system, revolving around centres more and more remote, making a series to which the imagination assigns no limits; so, in the order of intelligence, every advance seems but to bring into view combinations more and more extensive, increasing the apparent distance of the ultimate, and discouraging all efforts to reach it through the successive steps of the progression.

In Panidea we have a vigorous effort to surmount difficulty; to reach at once the common centre of all material and mental phenomena, and to find a formula which shall express the sum of the infinite series of the progression leading to it.

That trait of mind which is restless and impatient of imperfection, and seeks completeness in its thoughts, is here strikingly displayed, while the comprehensiveness of the plan by which these results are sought, gives emphasis to our previous remarks on that characteristic of the author. It extends beyond the former boundary of science to an outer circle, which includes the heretofore ultimate principle of gravitation as one of its subordinate parts, and embraces under one law both spiritual and material phenomena. This higher and more comprehensive generalization he designates as the doctrine of assimilation.

This is in harmony with the effort made, in the first portions of the work, to reason from the material phenomena of vision to the abstractions of the intellect, and surmount the difficulty of the mind's extended action, by showing that extension itself is but a consequence of mental activity, that space is but a mere relation of ideas, necessarily arising in the mind, whenever material phenomena, or mental imagery, are the objects of its thoughts.

The difficulty of thus reasoning from material to mental phenomena will be appreciated by those, and perhaps only by those, who have themselves made the effort. How far it is possible to overcome this difficulty seems to depend on the solution of the great problem of the mode of matter's existence, which the acutest intellects have long attempted in vain; and we imagine the effort which is made in Panidea must rank with those which, though among the most successful, have merely enabled us better to apprehend the question itself without relieving us from its difficulties.

There is, however, displayed in the work so much profound thought, such acute and thorough investigation of the subjects of which it treats, and such logical ability, that, even when a demonstration appears inconclusive, we may well suspect that it may arise rather from our not fully understanding the argument, than from any deficiency in the reasoning, which others of the present or future time may more fully comprehend and appreciate.

But now we would ask, what is there, in these views, which teach that the Supreme Being is thus absolute in the physical creation, and ever present in every finite mind; that he is there "an ever present helper;" and that in him "we live and move, and have our being," which warrants the charge of sceptical tendency, in the sense in which that charge is intended? Is there aught in such views to impair our belief in the existence of God; to weaken our faith in any of his great attributes, or in the verity of his revelations? Or are not their tendencies rather as the author desired they might be, when, in the closing paragraph of Panidea, he says, "I leave these questions with the reader; and, whatever may be the conclusion to which he shall come, may it be such as shall strengthen his belief in the existence of God, in his omnipresence, omniscience, omnipotence, and benevolence; and such as shall inspire him with a new faith in an elevated destiny for man here, and with a fresh confidence in a continued existence hereafter."

It is true, the writer often seems to have ventured far upon that ocean of speculation, where, with no aid from the usual landmarks and charts of thought, "the soul goes sounding on its dim and perilous way," but the needle which guides his course is still true, ever pointing to the centre of eternal truth.

That such charges should formerly have been preferred against those who attempted any innovation in spiritual science, or any extension of its limits, does not appear very remarkable, when we reflect that ascendancy in spiritual matters then carried with it temporal authority, and that hence arose a select class, interested in perpetuating prevailing opinions, and especially in representing the Supreme Being as widely separated from humanity, occupying an imperial throne in the remotest confines of space, and there holding his august court, in which the great mass of mankind were permitted to appear only by attorney. It certainly was not strange that those, who arrogated to themselves the exclusive privilege of pleading in the tribunals of eternal justice, should denounce the doctrine of God's presence in the human soul, ready at all times to enlighten the honest inquirer, by immediate and direct communication to his finite spirit, as a heresy fraught with the most direful consequences; or that they should apply the most opprobrious epithets to such views, and to those who taught them. But in this enlightened age, and in this land of religious liberty, it would, I trust, be as unjust as it would be painful, to attribute this charge of sceptical tendency to such narrow views and such mercenary motives.

That such charges are still so commonly brought against all innovators in spiritual science, probably arises, in part, from a vague idea that every extension of the jurisdiction of the finite mind is an encroachment on the prerogative of the infinite. The same apprehension has occasionally been excited even by the progress of natural science, and Franklin seems to have been sometimes regarded as one, who with daring impiety entered the sanctuary of the Most High, and stole the thunderbolts of heaven.

Another reason, and probably that which has oftenest obtained in honest minds, against the doctrine of direct communication of the infinite with finite intelligence, or, in other words, against the doctrine of immediate inspiration, as the uniform or usual mode of Deity, is the apprehension that the truths admitted to have been thus revealed, and which are recorded in the Bible, will cease to be regarded as extraordinary manifestations of the divine power, and lose at once their miraculous character, and their hold on our faith and reverence. But this apprehension should vanish when we reflect that the evidence of their truth is, that they came from the unerring source of truth, and not that they were miraculously communicated. The first point established, nothing in the mode of communication could add to the certainty of the revelation; and, in this view, the advocate for the divine authority of the Scriptures would seem to gain no small advantage over the sceptic, by establishing that such revelations are a part of the great plan of an all-wise Creator. An eclipse of the sun or moon was once regarded as a miraculous interposition of Deity to change the established order of events, and he who had never witnessed one, might have argued from all experience against it, and have nurtured his incredulity on the impossibility of the sun's being obscured at midday. But, when advancing knowledge reveals that such apparent deviations are in reality but a part of the uniform plan of creation, all ground for such scepticism is entirely removed. And if it shall be demonstrated that divine revelations to man uniformly enter into the moral system of the universe, it would certainly be a very strange logic, which, from this demonstration, would argue a scepticism in such revelations.

But we must turn from this hasty and imperfect review

of his speculations, to make a few remarks on the individual characteristics of the author, which time admonishes us must be brief.

To common observation there was little in the appearance or deportment of Judge Durfee which was striking. The fire of poetic genius beamed not habitually in his eye, the intensity of philosophic thought was not written on his brow. Plain and unassuming in his manners, and unpretending in conversation, the character of his mind came gradually into view, and, like the symmetrical in art, or the grand in nature, required to be dwelt upon before it would be appreciated. But, though he did not seek to be brilliant, the scientific eye would not fail to discover the sterling gold, the existence of which the practical observer might have already suspected from the absence of the tinsel glitter.

He was thought taciturn, and for this opinion there was probably sufficient ground; but, when subjects in which he felt a deep interest were under discussion, this trait or habit was not observable. Touch upon the freedom of the will, the origin of evil, the mode of God's government of the material and spiritual, the mode of matter's existence, or any kindred problem, and his mind was aroused, his countenance brightened, and streams, sparkling with intelligence, flowed freely from the full fountains of thought which had been silently accumulated.

He was also thought to be of indolent disposition; perhaps, in the estimation of some of the busy world, an idler, wasting time on useless theories, and aimless reveries; but there have been few who could so

"Justly in return
Esteem that *busy world* an *idler* too."

He was not easily excited by the ordinary motives to exertion. Accustomed, in his speculations, to contemplate the grand, the entire, and the ultimate, the particular incidents of life, on the magnificent scale of his thoughts, must have shrunk into comparative insignificance, and hence lost much of their exciting influence on voluntary action.

But the desire of knowledge, and that love of truth, which were so prominent in his character, imparted vigorous impulse to those powers which heeded not the ordinary inducements to effort.

It certainly was not wonderful that one thus habitually elevated in thought above the purposes of mere organic existence, and the pursuits of the bustling crowd, should not enter with ardor into their puny competitions for wealth and place. Nor should we marvel that a mind, comprehensive and profound, bearing on its broad expanse, the wealth of earth's remotest realms, while it reflected in its own tranquil depths the grandeur of a supernal sphere, was not easily

> "Into tempest wrought
> To waft a feather, or to drown a fly."

But where do we find the evidence of greater and more persevering efforts, and efforts directed to the most noble and elevated pursuit, than are evinced in his arduous, truth-seeking investigations? Verily, if his disposition was indolent, he has displayed a wonderful industry and energy in overcoming its natural tendencies.

Had Panidea been his only work, we might have inferred from it that his mind was wholly absorbed by the reasoning faculty, and hence possessed, in a remarkable degree, the power of erecting lofty logical structures, and of penetrating by rational formulas to those misty realms where, to feebler minds, truth itself yet appears in undefined nebulous confusion.

But when from it we turn to "Whatcheer," we find that these logical powers were united with poetic talents, which, with equal cultivation, might have become his most prominent characteristic; that, while, with resistless demonstration, he could convince the judgment, and dictate to the intellect, he could also sway the affections, and touch the heart with poetic fervor. Though these powers are, perhaps, not so incompatible as has often been supposed, yet the combination of them, with both in a high degree of perfection, is still very rare, and indicates great intellectual ability and versatility of genius.

The fact that the poetic and reasoning faculties are respectively adapted to each of the two principal modes of mental operation,— the one to the *direct* examination of realities, material or spiritual; the other, to the investigation of the relations of these same realities, through the medium of substituted terms, and the consideration of the mutual aid they render, and the reciprocal protection which they render to each other against the intrusions of error, — may enable us better to appreciate the strength and beauty of that mind in which these faculties were blended in such full measure, and in such harmonious proportions.

In Judge Durfee these were happily united with that ardent love of truth and exalted philanthropy, which made him feel it to be at once the happiness and the duty of his life to devote them to the advancement of knowledge, and the elevation of his race.

But his labors in this sublunary sphere are closed forever. For such change, however sudden, the wise and good seem ever prepared; and, as if anticipating his destiny, he had already, by his last public effort, completed for himself a mausoleum in our past history, where his memory is embalmed, and in the future inscription of which our children will learn to appreciate his talents and admire his virtues. There is a consoling though mournful interest in contemplating his views in connection with the closing scene of his life. They were already so spiritual that we hardly associate the accustomed idea of great and sudden transition with his departure to the world of spirits. It seems as if his soul had only gone forth to mingle with those vast manifestations of creative energy with which, in his system of thought, it was even here completely assimilated, and with whose author it was so closely allied by such numerous and interesting relations. All existence had, in his mind, assumed a form so ethereal that we hardly conceive that throwing off its mortal coil could have suddenly imparted new spirituality to its conceptions. For him the material universe had already been rolled together as a scroll, and had fulfilled its great purpose of conducting thought through the transitory objects of sense to the immutable forms of abstract truth, and to the contemplation of that higher mode of existence which is eternal and imperishable. Thus, partially anticipated in its high office of awakening the soul to a life purely spiritual, death to him could have no terrors, and to us seems robbed of half its circumstance. Animated by the rational and cheering hope shed upon the future, by a life thus marked by a true progress of soul, and in which, as he simply expressed it, he had "endeavored to do right," with calm composure he saw the stern messenger of fate opening the portals for his entrance to a new and untried state of existence, and died without fear and without ostentation.

SPEECH OF MR. HAZARD,

IN THE RHODE ISLAND LEGISLATURE, FEBRUARY, 1855.*

MR. SPEAKER: I heartily concur with the gentleman from Warren (Mr. Gammell) as to the importance of the objects for which the petitioners ask aid; for Rhode Island has a glory in the past which must not be lost. Of successful achievement in the domain of the material, in the peaceful triumphs of skill and industry, or in the stern conflicts which nations wage to assert their rights or avenge their wrongs, she may justly claim a full share; but it is our proudest boast, that her brightest laurels have been won in that triumph of eternal, immutable principles, which forever improve and elevate the condition of mankind. I would that the record of this triumph should be made as enduring as the principles it established, and that the self-sacrificing devotion, the stern, uncompromising virtues of those who achieved it, should be known and appreciated, wherever the

* This speech was made in defence of a principle which belongs peculiarly to Rhode Island. That the state should interfere as little as possible with the sphere of individual duty, is one of its original, fundamental ideas. The Historical Society asked the legislature for aid. Mr. Hazard, though a member of the society, and earnestly desiring the preservation of everything connected with our history, opposed the petition, because, as he supposed, it interfered with this old established policy.

thrones of tyranny have been shaken by the great ideas which our ancestors asserted, and maintained in defiance of all the despotisms of the earth. And I would that every member of this legislature, every constituent, every son of Rhode Island, should know and feel how much the glory of our future depends upon our preserving from oblivion the renown of our past. To illustrate this, suppose a thoughtful man, standing on the ridge line of the present, were asked whether he would prefer that the past on the one hand should be obliterated, or that the future on the other should be forever sealed against him. He would pause — from the abhorred vacuum on the one side, he turns to one no less abhorred on the other. Great problems rise before him; possibly, in some aspects, he feels himself as more or less a product of that past, in which he has lived, seen, felt, thought, and part of which he was; and fears that the annihilation of the effect will be involved in that of the cause. Perhaps, in view of the popular but unphilosophical belief that death cuts us off from the past, he may in some sort be said to decide the question whether he prefers to live rather than to die. However sterile his past may have been in virtuous efforts or good results, he still clings to whatever of wisdom its experience may have taught, and to whatever of pleasant memories its incidents and its vicissitudes may have supplied. That experience is to be his guide, and those memories are the foundation of his hopes in the future. Without the past, his future would appear desolate; without the future his past would have been in vain. Thus intimately are they related and dependent. These considerations are even more applicable to a state. This exists by virtue of an organism in the past that guides and directs its course on the ocean of time, as a ship is guided and directed by the rudder behind it. Destroy that past, and for it there is no rational future; at best it floats an undirected chaotic mass. To preserve this past has ever been the allotted work of gifted men. Harpers and minstrels, poets and historians, painters and sculptors, by song and ballad, by myth and legend, by glowing narrative and graphic delineation, have infused the ideas and the spirit of the past into the present. And we have our gifted men ready for this work. But things are changed. The people, stimulated by commercial enterprise and mechanical improvements, have become busy. The harper can no longer gather the multitude around him, and pour heroic song and legendary tale directly into the popular mind, and in return partake the frugal fare and the simple raiment, proffered with a liberality which he himself inspired, and by those whom he delighted and instructed, whose hearts he warmed with patriotic ardor, whose affections he purified, and whose sentiments and feelings he elevated and refined. The printing-press, with its paper and type, has intervened, and its aid must be invoked with gold.

Fully agreeing with the petitioners in the importance of the object, I must say, if money is essential to its accomplishment, let it be had; to withhold it would be as bad economy as for a farmer to withhold seed corn from the soil ready prepared to receive it, and which would be cultivated by skilful hands at free cost. But I differ from the petitioners as to the best means of obtaining it. Much as I would value the *history* of Rhode Island character, important as I deem a faithful *record* of its principles, I *value that character and those principles more.*

With the petitioners I would that our past should be presented to us in thoughts which glow and words that burn, that we may be moved to emulate the virtues of our ancestors, and catch something of the spirit and the zeal with which they were animated. Sir, when I contemplate their elevated thoughts, their lofty principles and self-sacrificing devotion to truth and duty, in contrast with the sordid and grovelling calculations which rule the hour, I am ready to exclaim,

> "O, rise some other such,
> Or all that we have left is empty talk
> Of old achievement and despair of new."

When I see the state controlled by the weak, the reckless, and the unprincipled,—low cunning, party management, intrigue, and even direct bribery, substituted for those appeals to great questions of right or policy which here once swayed the popular mind,—I feel how necessary it is that we should derive higher motives and purer incentives from the conduct and principles of the past. But, sir, my fear is, that the plan proposed accords not with that conduct, and that it is a departure from those principles; for I hold it to be the true Rhode Island idea that government should interfere as little as possible with the sphere of individual duty. Every encroachment upon this takes from the citizen opportunities for cultivating some virtue by its practical exercise. Let all the charities of life be dispensed, and all noble enterprises be prosecuted by the state, and you destroy private benevolence and public spirit; the individual, dwarfed and shriveled, from want of that practical exercise of virtue which strengthens and liberalizes his nature, grudgingly pays what the law exacts from him, without thought of its application. He neither knows nor cares whether it is used to found a college or to erect a gallows. I fear that we have already in many instances widely departed from the principle of our forefathers; but yonder venerated institution, which crowns this fair city, is at once a noble monument to this principle, and a proud tribute to its practical wisdom. Brown University has never had one dollar from the state treasury, and I trust will never condescend to ask it. It was founded and endowed by private munificence, and, a few years since, when it needed one hundred and twenty thousand dollars in addition, individuals freely gave more than it asked; and, if it should again need pecuniary aid, I trust it would again be freely given, rather than that the money should be wrung from the unwilling and the reluctant by the tax-gatherer. I would say then to the petitioners, rely upon this truly Rhode Island sentiment; if it has become sluggish, arouse it by such appeals as you, above all others, can make. Sound the notes of patriotic eloquence; touch the strings of patriotic pride; let the alarum be heard above the buzz of spindles and the rattling of shuttles. Startle the men of trade with an electric gleam of something brighter than their gold; thrill them with the ecstatic thought of an investment which, dating far back in the past, will be surely cumulative of mighty interests through all the future; make them feel that however useful and honorable their usual avocations, they should be mingled with higher and more liberalizing pursuits. Show them that, while they are providing for a few years of the present, centuries of a past existence are escaping; that while they would add a few dollars to the legacy of their children, that noble patrimony, the virtue, the wisdom, the glory of the past, is being irretrievably lost to them; and you will thus warm with generous purpose, and kindle a patriotic pride and enthusiasm in the breast of many a man, who, if the state performed all good and noble deeds, would never have known any higher incentive to effort than the necessities of food, raiment, and shelter; and in whom the innate, inextinguishable and irrepressible desire of progress would have found no higher sphere for its development than vain show, empty pomp, or objectless accumulation. Let us beware of all such encroachment. If we act truly upon right principles we may safely trust the consequences. What boots it now to the craven Greek, that his native land was once renowned for all that was beautiful in art, lofty in thought, refined in sentiment, and glorious in achievement? Had the *spirit* of ancient Greece been as well preserved as its *history*, her sons might have been exterminated, but could never have been enslaved. My feelings are all with the petitioners; with them I would that every relic and fragment of our past should be preserved; that the birthplace of their mighty ideas, which with resistless power have broken the chains, and bid captive humanity go free, should find a historian worthy such majestic theme; and that its fame might become coëxtensive and commensurate with the benefits it has conferred upon mankind; that in every clime it may be reverenced as the natal place of freedom, and, at each return of its epiphany, the thoughts of the wise and good, throughout the world, be turned to the spot where the star of liberty suddenly shone out with such miraculous effulgence; that, to the devotee of every nation, tongue, and sect, this should be all consecrated ground — to the Christian the Palestine, to the Mahometan the Mecca of freedom. But I would not that, when the future pilgrim shall visit this hallowed shrine, he should ask, Where are now the great ideas and the immutable principles of your illustrious founders and apostles? Where the wisdom you manifested when, in counsel, your Ellerys, and Hopkinses, your Burrills and Hunters, and Burgesses, stood forth the representatives of these ideas and the advocates of these principles? Where is now the brave spirit you displayed, when, in the hands of your Greenes, your Varneys, your Olneys, your Bartons, and your Perrys, your flag was boldly unfurled on every wave, and borne in triumph from many a battle-field? I would not that he should despairingly repeat the question, Where are they, where? and, from a moral waste around him, nothing but an echo answer, Where?

I would that we should have a history which, within our borders, upon every hill and headland, in valley, nook, and glen, should embalm every spot memorable for noble deed, or hallowed by the memory of the illustrious dead, and make Rhode Island all one classic land. But I would *not* that some gifted traveller, visiting these classic scenes, looking upon our lovely bay, the shores with which it is so beautifully fringed, and the islands with which it is so brightly gemmed, should doubtingly ask, Is this the spot where Roger Williams, bearing his noble thoughts in his breast, met a Heaven-sent welcome? This the land which the lofty soul of Clarke elevated, enlightened, and liberalized? This the air, and this the scenery, which invigorated the acute mind of Berkley? That the beach upon which Channing inhaled inspiration, and yonder the glen where the sturdy mind of Durfee was attuned to harmony, where he matured his profound thought, and breathed life into his noble, and ennobling conceptions? And turning again, and with a poet's eye to the natural scenery, still serene and lovely in its beauty, and with a poet's heart feeling all its hallowing associations, in view of a race debased in spirit, forgetful of the ideas and recreant to the principles of their sires, sorrowfully repeat the line,

"'T is Greece, but living Greece no more."

Mr. Speaker, on such a question I could have met the opponents of Rhode Island ideas and Rhode Island principles with a determined, unflinching, defiant spirit of resistance; but I know that these petitioners are the friends of Rhode Island ideas and Rhode Island principles. As such they are my friends, and my friends too by the ties of association to preserve these ideas and principles; many of them my friends by the ties of social relations. I respect and esteem them all; it is painful for me to differ from them. I know the rectitude of their intentions; I value their opinions and respect *their* judgment; but I should not be a true Rhode Island man if, on such a point, I yielded my *own* to aught but conviction. Mr. Speaker, in mentioning these circumstances, and in looking at the objects proposed, I feel the power of resistance waning within me. I almost would that the views and arguments which I have deemed it my duty to present, should be proved fallacious or futile. The promptings of my own heart tell me how feeble is any logic which can be arrayed against them, and how equal the conflict they maintain even with mighty principles; and in view of the noble purposes of the petitioners, and the great interests they have at heart, I am willing even to hope that your convictions may differ from mine, and to say that if you think, if you feel, that you can grant this petition without sapping the foundation of those principles of government, which our ancestors maintained at all hazards, and at every sacrifice of temporary expediency; without desecrating the shrines at which they worshipped; then, by your love of country, by your patriotic pride and devotion, by your interest in the universal humanity, I conjure you to yield to the noble impulses of your hearts, and do it. I cannot.

CAUSES OF THE DECLINE OF POLITICAL MORALITY.*

In the selection of a topic for this occasion, I have chosen "The Causes of the Decline of Political and National Morality," not because it is one with which I am very familiar, or on which I could expect to shed much new light; but simply because it seemed to be that which, at this juncture, could be most usefully brought into notice. Of political discussion, it is true, there has recently been no lack; but, from those rancorous contests which arise from the excited feelings of partisans engaged in a violent contest for political supremacy, little good is to be expected. Under such circumstances, arguments are but too often used to obtain power, rather than to ascertain or exhibit truth. General principles are seldom well settled by arguments employed to answer a temporary purpose.

The conflict which still agitates the whole country has fully developed this attribute of partisan warfare. Angry feelings, or interested motives, have been so prominent as to cause many honest men to doubt whether the love of country and the love of truth have embarked in the controversy

* A lecture delivered in Rhode Island, immediately after the election of General Harrison.

on *either* side. The arguments resorted to have almost exclusively been such as address themselves to the pecuniary interests, and call into action some of the lowest impulses of our nature. The means employed have been, to say the least of them, far from elevating; and to the thoughtful observer the result, even if favorable to his views, can hardly reconcile him to their permanent adoption, or blind him to the danger which may attend their use for improper purposes. Nor can even the most complete success prevent a poignant regret in every patriotic mind, that his countrymen should be more moved by thoughtless hurrahs, tumultuous parade, and volatile songs, than by the most urgent and sensible appeals to their understandings; or that those familiarizing epithets, which seem to sink the individual to whom they are applied to every man's level, should conduce more to his popularity, than the most dignified deportment, combined with all the cardinal virtues, could effect. There is manifest danger in such a condition of the popular mind. If it can be wrought upon by such means it may almost as easily be excited to wrong as prompted to right. Self-government is a grave business; and if, as in a former lecture I had occasion to remark, *despotism leads to volatility in the people under it*, the converse of the proposition is still more obvious. Their levity, their want of sober thought, and just examination, will be taken advantage of by designing men for the increase of their own power. With these views I deem it proper to seize the first moment of calm, even though it be but the "breathless interval betwixt the flash and thunder," and endeavor, while the public mind is still alive to the subject, to direct its attention to the necessity of higher and more elevating modes of conducting our political contests.

The safety, the perpetuity of our free institutions depends upon it. The government and the governed act and react upon each other; so that corruption in either tends to corruption in both. In this discussion I would wish not only to be impartial, but to avoid unnecessary censure of any party; but, when I observe the change which has been wrought in the last twelve years, a period almost entirely free from war, I am forced to the conclusion that all the other elements of national corruption have been in action. For this it is fair to hold that party most responsible who have possessed the most power to control our destinies; while at the same time there is much reason to apprehend that the minority have not always exercised that conservative influence, which a dignified and honest resistance to bad measures, and a steady and persevering adherence to correct principles, might have effected. The progress of the individual in moral degeneracy, however rapid, is generally by steps so regularly progressive as to be almost imperceptible to himself. No sudden shock arouses or alarms him; he glides gradually into crime, until the commission of enormities, at the idea of which he would once have shuddered, no longer costs him a struggle or a pang; and it is only when some portentous event recalls the ever-cherished recollections of early youth, and he recurs to the generous feelings, the untarnished honor, the spotless purity, which then ennobled him, and contrasts his then calm or buoyant spirits, and the joys of innocence, with his present perturbed and troubled breast, that he realizes the change which has come over his spirits, and mourns the loss of that virtue which at other times he is scarcely conscious that he ever possessed. It is the same with a nation. Our views of national justice and national honor accommodate themselves, if possible, with even more pliancy to the existing state of things. Every downward step prepares us for another, until the most gross and palpable violations of right call forth no censure, the most dishonorable transactions arouse no patriotic pride, and the most flagrant abuses of power fail to excite our indignation.

Nor does it argue much in favor of our national elevation that, while in these matters we accommodate ourselves with such pliant facility, we are sensibly alive and sufficiently earnest in regard to all measures affecting our pecuniary interests. Important as such measures are, in their *immediate* operation upon the results of industry and the comforts of life, they sink into insignificance when compared with the influence which they, in common with other legislation, exert on the public morals. That we may better note the change which has taken place in this respect, let us recur to some period of the past, and compare it with the present. I will not go back to our national birth or infancy. Could I depict the virtue and purity of those times, I fear it would now appear too much like the fictions of the poet, for the practical illustrations I seek. Nor will I resort to those traditions, which, if they recorded aught of our ancestors but their virtues, would not be accredited.

I fear it is but too unnecessary to go so far back. The last twenty years furnish a contrast only too striking. Within that time the breath of suspicion sullied for a moment the fair fame of a statesman, then and now occupying a prominent position before the country. It was sufficient; it blasted his bright prospects. The American people then said, by their acts, "He to whose guidance we commit our destinies, he whom we would elevate to the highest political rank, must be not only pure, but above all suspicion of base motives."

And of what was he suspected? Of having bargained away his vote for his personal aggrandizement. Such was then the state of moral sensibility that the people were aroused by this suspicion, and indignantly hurled the parties to the supposed contract from the offices they had obtained. How would it be now? Would indignation be thus excited by such a bargain, if actually entered into and consummated? or would it not be looked upon as a common, every-day occurrence, a fair political transaction? What are the facts? Mutual and combined support, on the part of the officers of government, for joint and private benefit, is openly avowed, and unblushingly advocated. The executive has proclaimed, by his acts, that those who vote for and support him may expect place and emolument, while all hope is denied to his opponents; and the public are deprived of their services, however valuable they might be. It is true, and there is encouragement in the fact, that the people have risen in their strength — I wish I could say they have risen in their majesty — to displace the party who have sanctioned such enormities. But is it for these enormities that they have been rebuked? Some use has been made of them, and no doubt with some effect on honest minds; but they have been so far from the prominent causes of complaint, that their condemnation will hardly appear to be a result of the national decision.

Among the early causes of the change we are commenting on, the unfortunate expression of the then chief magistrate deserves notice. When General Jackson said, "I take the responsibility," he gave the sanction of the highest official station to lawless feelings, which are ever engendered in the worthless portion of a free country, and which are the most dangerous elements necessarily involved in free institutions, under which, obedience to the laws, and reverence for the order they establish, are of vital importance, and require to be preserved and nurtured with vigilance and care.

The sentiment thus boldly, and no doubt honestly avowed by the head of the government, was readily adopted by inferiors in office, who were under less moral restraint, and has pervaded the whole community with a spirit of lawlessness. Swartwout, and a host of other defaulters, *took the responsibility;* bank presidents, directors, and cashiers; merchants, clerks, speculators, and porters, all *take the responsibility*, till there is no safety for property, and, in some portions of the country, little regard for the laws for personal protection. "I take the responsibility." These were words of awful import. To the future philosopher and historian they may appear but as the first decided and marked expressions of a popular tendency which was already sapping the foundation of our government.

That such assumed power was honestly and beneficially exerted, but increases the danger. Much of the power by which tyrants have oppressed and cursed our race has been first fostered by temporary utility, and permitted to encroach on rights because of the palpable benefits immediately conferred.

Another thing, attended with most pernicious and widespread consequences, is the venality of the public press. In this country, where newspapers reach every hamlet, and are read by almost every individual, they might, if properly conducted, be made the vehicle of instruction and elevation to a greater extent than any other means under the control of human intelligence. But, perverted, they become almost equally efficient in propagating error and debasing the public mind. The effect could not fail to be very injurious, if merely one-sided views and partial statements were generally circulated through this medium; but when, as there is too much reason to believe is the case, statements are constantly made for the purpose of deceiving the readers and preventing their reaching the truth, and, in many instances, absolute falsehood is resorted to for party purposes, the evil is increased to a degree which becomes truly alarming. The streams of intelligence are polluted. If the people drink, they are poisoned; if they refrain, they are cut off, individually and collectively, from information of vital importance.

Unfortunately, our newspapers are considered merely as a portion of the machinery of party tactics, and their editors as having no personal responsibility, no private conscience, and no right to any higher principle of action than devotion to the cause they stand pledged to advocate, right or wrong. Thus that pride of character, which would make an editor feel a blemish on his page as a stain upon himself, is wholly lost in truckling to party spirit or popular prejudice. And the political character of our newspapers has fallen so low, that we hardly look for anything better than partial statements from them. I wish it were confined to them; but the same mercenary spirit has occasionally manifested itself in some works from which we should have expected a higher tone. The great Reviews, for instance, should watch over public sentiment, and impartially canvass every opinion, to expose error and give prominence to truth. Yet some of them indicate, by their very names, that they are devoted to particular systems; and it is not long since one of them, having a higher place than has been accorded to any other periodical in this country, gave notice that its pages would thereafter be devoted to a particular interest, and would advocate a system in opposition to the conclusions of many of the most profound investigators of the subject.

Is this our boasted freedom of the press? It is true the press is still free — still subject only to the law itself imposes. But it seems to have determined to use its freedom in its full extent for evil, and to restrict the freedom of inquiry necessary to the pursuit of truth and happiness.

The public press should be conducted solely with a view to give correct information of facts, and to disseminate truth in all its forms. And, in performing this office, some regard should be had not only to decency and propriety, but to elegance. Our newspapers, and other periodicals, should contain nothing having a tendency to lower the standard of morality, or to vitiate the taste and feelings of the community. They should not lend or let themselves to deception, in any of its multifarious forms. The attempts of the venders of lottery tickets and patent medicines, or others, to impose on the ignorant by false representations, should not be countenanced, much less encouraged, by them.

Some attention should be paid even to the style of the ordinary business advertisements. Low and inelegant expressions, arising from ignorance or want of elevation in the advertiser, should be discarded, or at least discouraged. In short, they should exhibit pure motives and dignified and chaste expression. I have been thus minute on this subject from a conviction that attention, even to minor matters, in the preparation of what constitutes so large a portion of the daily food of the public mind, would be attended with great and beneficial results upon its health and purity.

Another cause which, within the last few years, has been influential for evil, is the prodigality of our citizens. We have been spendthrifts. Instead of devoting ourselves to regular industry, the whole nation has been gambling in stocks, wild lands, and resorting to every conceivable means of sustaining luxury without labor. We have squandered millions of the accumulations of patient industry, and loaded ourselves with a foreign debt, of which we are already tempted to rid ourselves by a sacrifice of national honor.

The admission of many erroneous principles has accelerated the decline of political morality. Among others, I would mention the increased and increasing concessions to the will of the majority. Under our institutions, practically, the majority must govern; but there are limits which they cannot with propriety transcend. Even they should be obedient to the laws until they are constitutionally altered; otherwise the right of the majority becomes but a revolutionary right—the right of the strongest. But, even when this power is kept within constitutional limits, it should not be forgotten that there is often a wide distinction between the right to exercise a power, and the exercise of an acknowledged power rightly. To any erroneous principle involved in the wrong doing of the majority, the minority should never assent. Every individual who has a clear perception of the wrong should protest against it, nor (if the occasion is of sufficient importance) cease to express his opinion, and to enforce it with all his power of argument and skill in illustration, until that portion of truth which seldom fails to enter into an honest opinion is elicited, and produces its proper effect in modifying popular sentiment.

Rotation in office is another principle which has obtained almost universal assent, but appears to me to be fraught with injurious consequences of no inconsiderable importance. It seems to have been deemed republican to divide the offices as equally as practicable among the people, that as many as possible may enjoy the honors and emoluments which are derived from them. The plausibility of this view has probably given the maxim its general currency. This error would not be so important in itself, but that it necessarily involves another and a more mischievous principle, as it presupposes that the offices are for the benefit of the incumbents, rather than for the good of the people generally. The true principle obviously is, to procure for every office the man who, in filling it, can and will best promote the general interest. By making their situations permanent, so long as they do this, there will be greater inducements for suitable men to accept them; more encouragement and more opportunity for them to qualify themselves for the particular duties which devolve on them, and to discharge these duties with skill and fidelity; and less temptation to sacrifice reputation, by seizing the opportunities thus offered to make them the means of great immediate gain. Subject only to be removed for want of ability or integrity, they would have more and more independence and pride of character; the standard of thought and action would almost of necessity be higher, and they would no longer be the pliant tools of any party which happened to be in power.

The principle of rotation also enables the ruling party to retain a host of greedy expectants, who hang upon the hope that their turn is coming. We may form some idea of the addition which the adoption of this principle makes to the power of executive patronage, from the fact that, on one occasion, there were fifteen hundred applicants for the office of marshal in one of our judicial districts. Those who hold office, added to those who expect them, with the numerous relations and friends of both, who are induced to act with them, make a very large combination of voters, influenced by selfish or private motives, rather than by those considerations of public benefit which should always determine a man's political actions.

It is true that this effort, so far as party influence is concerned, is in part neutralized by the party out of power, taking upon themselves to promise to their adherents all the offices in the possession of their opponents; but both causes unite in degrading the expectants, and destroying political morality. It is putting up all the offices of the country to be scrambled for once every four years. The dignity of self-government is thus destroyed, and the generous impulses of freedom converted into sordid calculations of personal interest.

If men were dismissed from office only because the public good required it, there would be an end of these several causes of political degeneracy. The officers of the government would be relieved from the suspicion of interested motives in advocating the political opinions of those who have the disposal of the places they occupy; and suspicion has of itself an influence on the integrity of men, which few have the moral courage to resist.

If in any officer there is such a concentration of power or patronage, that his continuance in office might enable him to obtain the mastery of the people, frequent changes will in such a case be necessary to obviate such danger.

The party now expected to come into power will apparently be strong enough to do right, and even to be generous; and though the previous appointment of mere partisans may render it both expedient and just that many changes be made, it is to be hoped it will very soon adopt the principle, that no man is to be proscribed for his opinions, or displaced merely to make room for another, no better qualified than himself; and thus discard this fruitful source of corruption.

The bold and shameless assertion of corrupt principles, especially when attended by their free exhibition as actually carried out in practice, is often fraught with more immediate evil to the morals of a community, than the mere covert employment of similar means. When such assertion does not shock, it makes a lodgment in the public mind, and the general sentiment is degraded. In this view, the open and unblushing avowal of a combination of the office-holders, to effect the elections, by appropriations of money from their salaries, is perhaps the most direct attack which has been made on the morals of the country, for it is the most outrageous and flagrant attempt to destroy the purity of elections.

But, great as is this pernicious influence on the minds of the community, generally, it is still greater upon the individuals of the combination. What more natural, than that they should look upon offices, thus obtained, as bought and paid for, for their individual use and benefit; and what more probable than that they will feel a sort of right so to use them, and to make up by peculation the sum they have contributed, or even to make the account lean to the winning side? For them a more corrupting system could hardly be devised, and through them it must extend itself very widely in every direction. That they have a right, and may properly exercise the right, to express and vote their honest opinions, will not be denied; but their having, in the present arrangement of parties, a personal interest in the result, should make them modest in pressing those opinions. It is also to be apprehended that, swayed by this personal interest, they are led to devote a portion of the attention necessary for the discharge of their official duties, to electioneering purposes; thus using that time for which they are paid to serve the public, in propagating their private opinions for private benefit. Their combining, and using money at the elections, needs no comment.

The narrow and one-sided views, growing out of sectional interests and party prejudices, present us with another important element in the decline of national character. As a people, we are proverbially obnoxious to sectional feeling. We have no common appellative, under which to appear as one and indivisible; no name for pride of country and patriotic feeling to rally under; none around which the poet can gather the deeds of valor, and give us one inspiration and one inheritance in the heroic virtues of our ancestors; none around which he can associate all those emotions, which kindle enthusiasm and inspire devotion to country, and which render a poetic name so influential on national character. Ours answers none of these purposes. It must ever remind us that, though united, we are still *states*,—separate and distinct states, with separate and distinct interests. It is perhaps well that we should always be thus reminded of this fact. It will have its influence in preventing the encroachments of the general government. It will resist the establishment of a standing army, and aid in preserving all the rights of the states. But the benefits of this distinction bring with them the evil of local jealousies, and lead the members of our national councils, too often, to consider themselves as the champions of *particular portions*, rather than as legislators for the *whole* country. This obscures and contracts those grand and enlarged views of national feeling, which a more elevated course would illustrate and expand.

It has also become too common to exact pledges from the candidates in office. This degrades the individual selected to a machine. He acts under no moral responsibility. He goes into the national councils, not to exert his own talents, to exercise his own judgment for the common benefit; but simply to vote the will, or advocate the views, of others; not to learn the condition and provide for the wants of the whole country, but simply to do what he has promised or been required to do, by a small fraction of it. We might almost as well send a representative made of "wood and wire, and sole leather," as of flesh and blood, with a mind trammelled, and not at liberty to think or to decide for itself. Would it not be obviously better to select good men, whose ability and integrity can be relied upon, and leave them to act as, upon consultation with the representatives of other sections, may seem to them most for the general benefit? To the views of their constituents they would add other means of information. Their thoughts would be more concentrated upon the subject, and more correct results might reasonably be expected. In any event, with good men at the head of our affairs, we should incur the least danger from bad measures. Requiring pledges lessens the chance of a selection of such men in two ways. In the first place, many of the best men will not accept office with such conditions; and, in the second place, it apparently enables the people to dispense with character and talents of a high order; for neither are absolutely required to reiterate their sentiments, or vote as instructed. It holds up a false appearance of protection from political dishonesty. Honesty, being no longer requisite, is superseded and banished. Character is no longer deemed of that importance which is its due; and is not guarded with that scrupulous care which a higher appreciation of its value would induce. Hence, the practice of requiring pledges is another cause of political turpitude.

But, of all the causes which tend to deteriorate our national character, there is probably none more efficient than the influence of party discipline in restraining the freedom of individual thought, and the candid expression of individual sentiments and opinions. By this agency, a large proportion of the thought of the country is annihilated. The community, organized and drilled under two sets of partisans, implicitly follows as they dictate, and either does not think at all, or, if its thoughts lead it to conclusions at variance with those of the party, they are wholly nugatory; they neither impress them on others, nor act in conformity to them themselves. For our political regeneration there is perhaps no element more needed than free thought, and an honest, earnest, and fearless expression of its results. We need individuality of character, that men should separate themselves from the conglomerated masses, and think and act under the feelings of individual responsibility, with truth for their only object; that they should have the moral courage, singly, if necessary, to judge of public men and public measures by their intrinsic merits, without reference to the party with which they are associated, and freely to express their opinions. There would be even more hope of a people who thought wrongly, than of one who did not think at all. It may be objected to this individuality of action, that union is necessary to strength, and that no important political results can be reached without it. This objection would not apply to any case where only one question was pending at a time, nor perhaps to any case whatever, except the selection of an officer whose duty it might be to decide a number of questions. In this case, the better way would generally be to select the individual best qualified for that duty, and trust the decisions to him. This would obviously be the safest mode, if questions unknown at the time were liable to arise for his decision, as is generally the fact.

If, however, the candidate were previously pledged to particular measures, the man who had thought for himself would, of course, support the one whose pledges most nearly coincided with his own conclusions, or who, according to his views, would best subserve the public interests. For this task he would certainly be as well qualified as those who acted without having thought of the merits of the questions involved. If such men should sometimes appear to injure the party with whom they more generally united, by opposing their measures, they would more frequently be able to obtain a candid hearing from their opponents, by which they might at other times more than compensate for any loss thus occasioned to their friends. Such men would not, except in times of national difficulty, be likely to be called upon to assume the cares of office; but they would at all times have the satisfaction of rendering essential service to their country, by instilling correct principles, and encouraging action from honest motives. Thus they would neutralize the violence of factious spirits, and break up the rigid lines of party divisions. This would prevent those extremes in legislation, which are almost equally injurious to whichever side they oscillate. One party is displaced, and another coming into power, pledged to an opposite course, changes the policy with a rapidity scarcely less detrimental to the country than a perseverance in bad measures.

In the change of administration now expected, as in all similar cases, it is to be apprehended that alterations will be made merely to preserve the appearance of consistency in the victorious party, or to justify the censure so liberally heaped upon most of the measures of those heretofore in power. It would be well if legislators, instructed by an ancient apothegm, would, in their innovations, take a lesson from that greatest of all innovators, *time;* which changes so slowly as to mock the senses. This, so far as the action of the government is concerned, would prevent those sudden changes of value, which lessen the security of the industrious in the product of their own labor, and often transfer it to the idle capitalist, without any just equivalent. In regard to the business of the country, the great evil has been, not so much in the mode of government interference, as in its interfering with it at all. The laws of commercial intercourse being once established, nothing more is required in that department of legislation, except to perfect those laws by such alterations or additions as experience may direct.

Our system of revenues necessarily brings the government in contact with our business pursuits, and, in this particular, I believe nearly all parties have become satisfied, by numerous experiments, that sudden changes are prejudicial even to the apparently favored class.

As a young and vigorous nation, we are bold, I might almost say reckless, in trying new projects. We keep other countries in a state of continual astonishment. They seem to be always saying, What will, or what will not those Yankees try next? But, after a period of success which made us the envy and admiration of the world, we have met the common fate of excessive enterprise, and are now held up to exhibit the folly of deviating from the established modes of business, and running wild in new experiments. It is to be hoped that we shall ourselves learn wisdom, and grow more cautious, as we grow older. We are in no danger of going into the extreme in this direction. Our free political institutions must always generate an elastic spirit, which will exhibit itself in free action, bold and probably excessive enterprise. This, if an evil, is the minor one, and must be borne.

We have now adverted to what we deem the principal causes of the decline of national morality. To recapitulate: the degrading influence of the means resorted to in our political contests; the general want of elevated thought and character; the spirit of lawlessness encouraged by the expression, "I take the responsibility;" abuse of the press; public and individual prodigality; rotation in office, increasing the power of executive patronage, and multiplying the number of those who act from private, instead of public considerations; the combination of office-holders to influence the elections by personal effort and contributions of money; the influence of sectional interests and party views, making legislators mere champions for measures of local or partial utility; the requiring of pledges from candidates for office, and making those pledges a substitute for the better guarantee of character; the want of individuality of character, of free thought, and of earnest and fearless expression of its results, unswayed by private interest, and untrammelled by party; too sudden changes of policy, discouraging regular industry, and stimulating inordinate speculations; the unnecessary interference of the government with the business of the country; an excessive enterprise, inducing reckless experiment and bold adventure.

The remedy for this formidable array of evils I apprehend is to be found only in the improvement of the moral and intellectual condition of the whole people. And, yet, I fear too much reliance has been placed on the general diffusion of mere knowledge, by means of common schools. This is a necessary step, but it is only a step. It is not only necessary that we should be educated, but that we should be *elevated.* A people, to govern themselves well, must have elevation of thought, liberal and comprehensive views, and lofty and inspiring sentiments. To this, as the main object, every well-wisher of his country should direct his efforts. The talents of the country and the power of the press should be united in it. Let us be an elevated people, and our institutions are safe. Without such elevation we may sink into anarchy, or fall into the arms of despotism, at any moment.

But allow me here to recur to our state provision for general education. I blush to say that the lottery system is still resorted to, as a means of obtaining a portion of the funds applied to that object; that it is procured by legalizing a system of gambling, fraught with perhaps more evil consequences than attach to it in any other form; thus demoralizing the people that they may be taught to read and write. Why is this still permitted? Have our legislators never reflected that it is easier to educate an ignorant, than to elevate a degenerated people; or, that, if we must choose between the two, ignorance with innocence is infinitely preferable to knowledge with vice? And, as a gift for the benefit of the poor, to what does this provision amount? It is a well-known fact that lottery tickets are sold most extensively to that class; stimulated by the hope of acquisition, to which they see no other path open to them — ignorant of the calculation of chances, and duped by the ingenious allurements of the venders, they too often invest their little savings in this way. It is equally notorious that a very small portion of the tax, actually paid in this mode, is available for the objects for which the lottery grant is made. By far the greater part is usually absorbed by the expenses and the profits of the managers. It is clear, then, that, for the sum appropriated to the education of the poor from this source, they themselves pay a much larger amount. Instead of a *gift* to the poor, it should be termed a *fraud* upon them. This is peculiarly unfortunate in our state, whose institutions especially demand that legislation should be liberal to that class; that their interests should be kept steadily in view, and every reasonable concession made to them; that, in fact, the government should be to them a better one (as I believe it has been in many respects), than if they participated in its powers.* The appropriation, however, even in this mode, indicates a determination to furnish the means of general education at any cost, and there probably was a time when a more direct tax for that purpose would not have been submitted to. I hope that more just and liberal views now prevail, and that the honor of our state will not long be tarnished by the foul system of raising revenue by dishonest means from those who are least able to pay it.†

* This discourse was made before the alteration in the constitution of Rhode Island, which extended suffrage. — Ed.

† The lottery system was abolished soon after the delivery of this lecture.

If I have dwelt on the evils of our system of government, and have not portrayed its better features, its manifold virtues and benefits, I assure you it is not that I regard them lightly, but rather from an earnest desire to see them perfected and perpetuated; to see this grand experiment of free political and religious institutions successfully carried out, and forever stand as a monument of the ability of man for self-government. I have spoken under a firm conviction that this is not a time for flattering speech; that the crisis demands that we should have a full knowledge of what is necessary to be done, and that we should press forward to its accomplishment with a determined spirit. Vigilance and activity are among the conditions of self-government. When we relax from the constant effort which it requires, others assume the office for us, and despotism commences. The public ought never to suffer themselves to be lulled into a state of false security, or watchless repose.

The recent contest, though exhibiting a great want of elevation, has been marked by an intensity of interest, and a devotion to the cause espoused, which shows that the people are everywhere alive to the importance of the subject. It only remains to direct their feelings by rational means to rational ends, to ensure a government as perfect as the condition of humanity will permit. Let us be elevated, and a glorious destiny is ours. If we sink into corruption, our fall will be but the more signal for having aspired so high.

PUBLIC SCHOOLS.

THE grand element, the essential condition of human happiness, is progress, and we hail with joyful feeling whatever accelerates it.

It is cause of gratulation that the means of individual improvement are extending, and that, through them, our community, our country, and our race, are advancing; and it is a cheering thought that to this progress there is no limit; that success in removing one impediment but nerves us with victorious energy to encounter another; that every advance but brings us in view of some higher position to be attained, while the horizon of perfection remains at the same apparent distance, or recedes as we rise into a purer atmosphere. In this way obstacle after obstacle has been overcome, and one stage of our progress after another accomplished, until we have now arrived at the subject of universal education. In conformity with that universality, which is a characteristic of this age, it is proposed to provide the means of literary instruction for the whole people. Obvious as is the importance of the measure to bare investigation, we are not proceeding on mere theoretical grounds. We have witnessed its results in portions of this, and in other states.

It is not long since our legislature employed a competent person to make a geological and agricultural survey of our, territory. A spirit of inquiry was thus induced, and much valuable information disseminated, the good effects of which are already so obvious, in improved and more economical modes of cultivation, that I think I should be within bounds in saying that the expense of that survey has already been repaid an hundred fold. With such results of an experiment in one portion of science, it is not surprising that the state should extend its views and its efforts to its other departments; that it should adopt measures to diffuse information, awaken interest, and increase the desire for the extension of knowledge generally, with liberal provision for its accomplishment; and thus, embracing the whole subject at once, secure its numerous advantages as early as practicable.

For this purpose an agent has been engaged to coöperate with the citizens, and give them the aid of his experience and mature thought in the important work of reforming the schools. The wisdom of this course is apparent; and it is gratifying to find that those on whom the expense principally falls are most zealous in advocating, and most assiduous in their efforts to promote, its accomplishment.

This is honorable to our state, and particularly so as this zeal and assiduity manifestly arise, not from any sordid calculations of interest, but from noble and philanthropic feelings. To a people actuated by such high and disinterested motives it would be worse than useless to hold up any lower inducements; but I may here remark that in this, as in other cases, generous action, based on liberal and correct principles, secures those minor advantages which are the ultimate and exclusive objects of a grovelling, narrow policy; for, leaving out of the account all the delightful anticipations of increased comfort, virtue, and happiness, and all the benevolent satisfaction of being useful in the world, the man who appropriates a portion of his wealth to the diffusion of knowledge is still making an investment for which, even in a pecuniary view, he will be amply repaid. Go where we will, we find the value of property very much depending on the intelligence of the community where it is located — an obvious consequence of the fact that intelligence is necessary to make property productive. It develops all the resources of a neighborhood, and applies them in the best manner. Besides this, it brings the advantages of superior society — of good literary, moral, and religious instruction, and various benefits which a union of intelligent persons may easily command, but which no one individual, however talented, or however wealthy, could so effectually compass; and these all make the real property of such a community more desirable, and, of course, more valuable.

It also enables men better to discharge the duties of legislators, judges, and jurors. General education, then, will enhance the nominal and intrinsic value of property, while it also renders it more secure.

How far it is expedient to make popular education the subject of legislation is an important question. In Prussia an amiable king, disposed to exercise the despotic power with which he is vested, in a paternal care of his subjects, has furnished the means of instruction to all; and, by penal enactments, made it obligatory on parents and guardians to send their children to the schools he has established.

Such legislation would be worse than useless here. It would be repugnant to our feelings, and in opposition to the spirit of all our institutions. In some minor matters regarding schools imperative legislation has failed even in states where the people are more accustomed than we are to the interference of legislative authority with the sphere of individual duty.

I apprehend that, in proportion as a state assumes the task of regulating the mode of instruction, parents will feel themselves absolved from its responsibilities; and it is the care and thought of parents, in educating their children, which forms the foundation, or a very large portion, both of parental and filial virtues, the destruction of which would annihilate all that is most beautiful and holy in the social fabric.

Air, light, and partial warmth, are all that a wise Providence has bestowed on us without some efforts of our own; but, having furnished these prerequisites of life and activity, it has made the rest dependent on that thought and labor which are also necessary to develop the energies of body and mind. Let a state then provide the money essential to the existence of public schools, adopt means to enlighten the public mind on the subject, and to warm it into effort, adding such suggestions and recommendations as, on such a subject, may very properly come from its selected talent and wisdom, and leave the rest to the free thought and voluntary action of the community.

The immediate connection of education with the interests and the condition of mankind is too obvious to have been entirely overlooked by any but the most barbarous tribes; and yet, in its present aspect, it may be said to be new. Though pursued by many with higher views, education has too often been sought merely for the selfish advantages which the instructed derived from it in competition with the uneducated — advantages which its general diffusion would destroy. Hence, at one time, the learned sought to express themselves in a manner unintelligible to any but the initiated; and the clergy, by the exclusive advantage of superior knowledge, gaining the ascendency of the political and military power, established an ecclesiastical despotism which, with the most tyrannical insolence, dictated to nations; and, arrogating to themselves the powers of darkness, and scarcely less infernal powers of earth, by the combined terrors of hell and the tortures of the inquisition, destroyed every vestige of freedom, and left scarcely a ray of hope to humanity. It was fraud monopolizing knowledge to subdue the ignorant and prostrate their minds in a bondage the most cruel and the most direful that history records. The institutions of Lycurgus embraced a system of general education. Under them the Spartan youth were trained to endure privation, fatigue, and pain, and habituated to the use of arms, that they might more effectually serve their country in war, and were taught to steal that they might be prepared for its stratagems.

But, to increase the general happiness, and secure the freedom of man by a system of education which shall impart useful knowledge, intellectual power, and moral elevation to the *whole* people, is an idea of our own times.

That the period for the practical development of this idea has arrived, is manifest from the unanimity of public sentiment in its favor. I may almost say that none deny its importance, or doubt its utility, though there may be some diversity of opinion as to the mode of its accomplishment. To devise and bring into action the best means in our power for this purpose, is the object of this Association. I need not labor to secure your interest in its favor, by dwelling on the beneficial results which may be expected from the success of the enterprise; for I cannot believe that any one who has at all reflected upon the influence of increased thought, and the extension of knowledge upon individual happiness and progress, upon national prosperity and national honor, upon our intellectual and moral condition, and upon our political and social relations, can contemplate with indifference the efforts now making in this country in behalf of education.

I wish I could claim a more active participation in them. But I must confess myself one of those whose time and thoughts have been too much tasked by business pursuits, to permit me to render as much personal aid to this important movement as I desired, or so much as my views of duty to the community dictated. But I have observed with deep interest the noble efforts of those gentlemen whose labors in this cause have laid us under high obligation, and claim our warmest gratitude and sincerest thanks. It is gratifying to find that they have sanguine hopes of success. They do not, however, expect to escape the difficulties, or to avoid the obstacles, which ever beset the path of the pioneer in social improvement. They know that popular prejudices are to be dispelled; that the iron grasp of avarice is to be relaxed, and supineness stimulated, by a sense of duty which they must awaken in the public mind. They know that the reformer requires industry, zeal, energy, and perseverance. By the intelligent exercise of these qualities they have already accomplished more than was anticipated in the time, and there is now much to cheer us all to effort, to animate and exalt our hopes, and inspire us with lofty and generous purpose; and it is a work in which the aid of all is required. The object we aim at is nothing less than a system — a better system for the improvement of man. If, in such a cause, the people are inert, it will be in vain that legislators pass acts, and make liberal appropriations of money. If parents do not take an interest in it, and perform their duties, the labor of those philanthropists who have made it an object of earnest investigation and deep solicitude, and sought to inspire others with a kindred interest, will be fruitless. Properly to sustain and carry forward such a movement, the whole people must unite in it, heart and hand, thought and action. They must think, and think justly and liberally. They must act, and act with the energy of excited interest.

We must not content ourselves with dreaming over the prospect, however encouraging. I know it is delightful to regale the imagination with visions of an intelligent and happy people, under a wise and beneficent government, such as may be anticipated from the general diffusion of knowledge; and to indulge in all the luxury of benevolent feelings, amid those congenial scenes of felicity and virtue, which a prophetic fancy may here so vividly portray. And it is allowable, it is useful, thus to warm ourselves to effort, by dwelling in imagination, on the intended, the probable results of our labors.

But we must not stop here. We sow the seed in hope and faith, but we must bestow the careful vigilance, the laborious attention of actual business, before we can expect to gather the fruit. Money may be freely appropriated, and yet not a single spring necessary to the success of the movement be put in action. The plan may be wisely conceived, and put forth with all the attractions of eloquence, and illustrated and enforced by all the powers of argument, and yet little be done towards its practical accomplishment.

But I do not fear that the interest now manifested is the mere effervescence of popular enthusiasm, or that it is such an excitement as dissipates its fervor in idle imaginings. I am persuaded that it is the result of deliberate thought, terminating in the firm conviction of the importance, the necessity of earnest attention to the objects for which we are now assembled. That object has already been stated to be the improvement and extension of the means of education; an object, the beneficial tendencies of which are manifest and manifold in every aspect of the subject — so manifest that one can hardly speak of them without uttering truisms.

It is a trite remark, that the success and stability of a popular government depend on the intelligence and virtue of the people. It is obvious that these qualities are no less essential to individual happiness than to national prosperity or national security.

In despotic governments the object of education is to make the people good *subjects*. On us devolves the higher task of so educating them that they may become good *sovereigns*. And, to the inducements growing out of these considerations, I may add, what under our institutions seems the grand desideratum, that there is nothing which has so great an influence in lessening and neutralizing the inequalities of society, as a system of education which embraces all in its provisions. It opens to all a common source of enjoyment and aggrandizement. The rich and the poor here meet on common ground. Seated side by side, the heir of wealth finds that the circumstances of birth afford no advantages in the competition for intellectual superiority; while the child of poverty also learns that his advancement depends on his own efforts, and on his own conduct. Give him the key to the stores of learning and the treasures of thought, and he may complacently smile at the little glittering pile, on which the merely rich man rests his title to consequence. He may look with scorn on the miserable ambition, or with pity on the folly, which contents itself with those accidental advantages, which an accident may destroy, to the exclusion of those benefits which, becoming identified with mind, can only be lost by the destruction of the spiritual being.

The great object of education is, not to give those who receive its benefits an advantage over others in the competition for wealth or place, but to increase their rational enjoyments and their usefulness, in whatever circumstances their lot may be cast;—if wealthy, to use their wealth with intelligent and noble purpose; if poor, to apply a like intelligence to the economical management of their concerns; if in retired life, gracefully to perform the duties of a private citizen, and shed a right and happy influence in their sphere; or, if called by their country to official station, to perform its duties with credit to themselves, and benefit to the public; but, more especially, to enable them to enjoy the happiness which arises from a consciousness of the performance of every duty, and of progress in the scale of being. In short, to make them more happy in themselves, and more useful to others.

To fulfil these purposes in the highest degree, requires strong and active minds, and pure hearts with cultivated affections, in sound bodies. Hence, education, in reference to these objects, must embrace the physical, intellectual, and moral nature. Our part now has reference more especially to the intellectual, but, in attending to this, we need not, we do not intend wholly to neglect the other departments. In regard to the physical, something may be done by the erection of suitable buildings, and, by care, to protect the inmates from unhealthy influences. And, in regard to the moral, much may be done, by good regulations, by the selection of teachers, who, to proper intellectual endowments, unite purity of heart, elevated sentiments, and refined feelings, rendered more attractive by modest, manly deportment and winning manners; and, when practicable, by locating school-houses in situations where the natural scenery will instil beauty into the soul, and bring it under those harmonizing and elevating influences, with which a wise and beneficent Creator has imbued his works. Let them stand aloof from the turmoil of business, and elevated above its cares, where the orient sun will inspire hope, and his setting hues gild a glorious futurity. Let them be where verdant fields and flowery groves, made vocal by the melody of birds, will regale the senses and refresh the imagination; where extensive prospects will awaken the sense of the sublime, inspire lofty aspirations, and mature all the infinite tendencies of the immortal spirit. Place them where, in some sanctuary of nature, the crystal fountain sends forth the refreshing stream, in which the infant soul may baptize itself in purity, and from its murmuring waters catch the hallowed voice of song. And, when this is impracticable, let the same intention be fulfilled, as far as possible, by artificial means — by paintings and statuary, by poetry and music. Let the whole arrangement be such as will gladden the heart, and make the future recollections of the spring-time of existence, and all its associations, a celestial vision, blending its tranquillizing and holy influences with the cares and asperities of life, and gilding with poetic gleams its stern realities.

Procuring suitable teachers is, perhaps, the most important and the most difficult portion of the work. Properly to fill that station requires the highest order of talent, and the most exalted character. But can we expect men of high talent and character to devote themselves to a pursuit, in which the honors and emoluments are so far from being commensurate with the labor and responsibilities? A high sense of duty impels some persons thus to devote themselves; but, in the present state of public feeling, we cannot rely on this inducement for a sufficient number to fill any considerable portion of our schools. In this state we are very deficient in this particular. Preparation for such an office has neither been a duty, a trade, nor a profession, and we have of course to rely much upon our neighbors. I do not object to this, for the reason sometimes urged against it — that it gives our school-funds to the citizens of other states. The argument on that point is wholly involved in the mooted question of free trade and protection. There may be some advantages in the circulation of intelligence, which is produced by this employment of instructors from other sections, and their continual change from place to place; but I apprehend they are trifling in comparison with the disadvantages.

In this state, I believe, our sound and liberal political and religious institutions have laid, in the free thought and mental vigor of the people, a broader and firmer basis for education than has elsewhere been found, and I would that the superstructure should be raised by those who are familiar with these institutions and have profited by them; by those whose thoughts have never been circumscribed by authority, and whose souls have never been narrowed by bigotry or debased by superstition. In these views, I believe, I am influenced by no merely sectional feeling. I know there are many in other states who, in this particular, will well compare with the best in ours. But I do not think that their institutions and acquired habits of thought are so favorable to the development of this character, or that it is so universal among them. But there are other considerations which I deem more conclusive on this point. In the present mode of engaging a teacher for a few months, with only a mere chance of his being reëmployed in the same district, he cannot be expected to feel the same interest in the affairs of the community, or even in the progress of his pupils, as if he were permanently located among them, and expected to see the fruit of the seed he planted.

Such is now the general neglect in visiting his school, and in extending to him even the civilities of society, that in an ordinary term he will hardly become acquainted with the parents at all, unless he "boards round;" which, by the way, is the only recommendation of that system which occurs to me.

Now, every man with improved mind, cultivated tastes, and elevated morality, exerts a great and happy influence on the community in which he resides, and those requisites should be indispensable to all the teachers of our schools. They will, in some respects, be better situated to exert this influence than most other citizens. They will receive no fees for their opinions; and not having to encounter the suspicions of interested motives, and the feelings of rivalry which the competitions of business so often engender, their approval of right and reprobation of wrong will have all the weight of intelligence, character, and impartial judgment. The influence of such men, permanently located in all our districts, their interests and feelings all blending with those of the community, could not fail to elevate the moral standard, and strengthen all the ties which bind society. As they advanced in years, and their pupils came into active life around them, this influence would assume a paternal character, and be to the whole community what that of a long settled and venerated minister of religion is to his congregation. Perhaps, too, there would be a more grateful feeling for the moral influences which the teacher has insinuated into the mind with science, than for even greater benefits, in the same way, from one who imparted them in the fulfilment of duties, which, in virtue of his office and his salary, he was bound to perform.

To secure these benefits, and remedy in part the difficulties alluded to, it is proposed to establish, within the state, normal schools for the education of teachers of both sexes. I will not enter into the details of this plan further than to say that it is the intention of the projectors of it to rely on voluntary subscriptions for the funds necessary to carry it into effect.

Some years must elapse before we can realize the full benefits expected from this source, but, in the mean time, much may be done by vigilance in procuring the best teachers which circumstances permit, and by encouragement and aid in their efforts to become better qualified for their responsible station. The association of teachers, already formed in this county, for the purpose of mutual improvement, gives promise of much usefulness, and reflects credit on its members.

While, however, the rate of compensation is so low, it is to be apprehended that men of talent will only make school-keeping a stepping-stone to some more lucrative occupation. This presents a very serious difficulty, and I confess I have been alarmed by the consideration that our best lawyers, who devote themselves to their profession, realize two, three, and even five thousand dollars per annum, and that education requires talents not inferior to theirs — *not inferior to any*. I endeavored to flatter myself, that, when the importance of the subject was justly appreciated, we would be willing to pay as much to the man who performs so important a part in training the minds of our children, as to the man who ever so ably and successfully defends our purse, or even our personal rights.

But, when, entering into figures, I found that this would require certainly more than ten, perhaps more than twenty times the amount now appropriated by the state, I despaired of its early accomplishment, and sought relief in another aspect of the subject, which I think presents some encouragement. I find this encouragement in the fact that most men do not labor exclusively for money. The number who have so wofully misconceived the ends of existence, as to make the mere accumulation of wealth, or even a wholly selfish application of it, their ultimate object, is very small. Now, those who, for the purposes of rapid acquisition, devote themselves to active, laborious pursuits, involving anxiety, perplexity, and mental vigilance, have almost always one or more of three objects in view — the pursuit of agriculture, of literature, or of benevolence.

I know that some may doubt these premises, and, as they are important in themselves, and essential to the cheering conclusion I aim to deduce from them, I will trust to your indulgence to dwell a moment upon them.

The very general desire of men to escape, from the anxieties and perplexities of hazardous and intricate business, to the green fields, the golden harvests, the home-felt joys and sober certainties of agricultural life, is matter of every-day observation and experience; nor will it be doubted, that, with many, the calm pursuits of literature and science are looked to as an evening haven from the storms of a bustling life; but I am aware that.

on the last point, the popular mind inclines to a belief of the engrossing selfishness of business men. They see them pursuing wealth with an energy so intense and an interest so absorbing, that they may well suppose that with them it is the final and exclusive object of existence. The uninterested and superficial observer does not suspect that they are goaded on by a consciousness that the great work of life is still before them; that they are yet far from home; that night is approaching, and they have not entered even into the territory of their abiding place. But it may be urged, that, even when successful, they are slow to apply their wealth to benevolent purposes. This is very often the case, and yet, paradoxical as it may appear, it does not argue that this is not the purposed object for which they are acquiring it. They overrate the value of money as a benevolent power. They measure it by its cost; and this, when every energy of body and mind has been engrossed in its acquisition, they can hardly over-estimate. Though holding in theory to their early impressions of its omnipotence, their business experience and judgment enable them practically to perceive, in every attempt to apply it, that money in itself is a very low order of power, and requires the aid of as much thought and labor to make it effective as an agent of good, as it does to make it productive in business. They hope, however, for an opportunity of applying it with those magnificent and certain results, the imagination of which has lured them to its exclusive pursuit, and it is not till they have exhausted this hope that they yield to less inducements.

They are then only carrying into the application of their wealth the rules by which it has been acquired, and are loth to part with it at less than the original cost, or to invest it, where, in the absence of their own supervision, they have not what they deem sufficient security that it will be judiciously applied. Those habits of saving money, and of parting with it only upon the expectation of a larger return in kind, and which are generally necessary to enable them to commence accumulating, may at first militate against their giving freely for any other purpose; but, when they have once learned to look to humane objects as a return for investment, their acquired boldness in parting with large sums, in confident anticipation of profitable results, comes to the aid of their benevolent feelings, and perhaps goes far to supply the want of enthusiasm, which is the effect of the vividness of the imagination having become obscured in matter-of-fact calculations, and the engrossments of reality.

The recent subscription of business men for the erection in this state of an asylum for the insane,— carrying into effect the original design of one of their own number, whose generous aid throughout his life to literary and benevolent objects, might, of itself, go far to disabuse the public mind on this point,— shows how cheerfully they will give, when, in their opinion, the object warrants it. And the very liberal donation of one individual, who, perhaps for the very reasons I have suggested, set a high value on money, shows how freely he can bestow it, when his judgment is convinced of the utility of the application. He is now animated by a new impulse. His life is no longer objectless. The cheering thought that all his labor has not been in vain attends him. He is inspired with a fresh hope, for he has found an opportunity of investing the proceeds of his toil and anxiety in a manner which evidently affords him more satisfaction than he ever felt in the acquisition of a like sum. The sagacity by which he at once secured the present coöperation of the community, and ascertained that their feelings were sufficiently interested in the object of the gift to warrant the expectation that it would continue to receive the attention from them essential to its usefulness, is a striking illustration of the thoughtful prudence of business men, under circumstances which might have dazzled the imagination and misled the judgment of those having less practical habits and experience.

Having touched upon this subject, it may not be out of place here to remark, that the improved treatment of the insane, and the education of the deaf and dumb and the blind, are among the most glorious triumphs of knowledge, and that education has raised her proudest trophy in the midst of that intellectual and moral illumination and holy joy, which she has carried into the recesses of mind, from which, by combination of the two latter maladies, every ray of light or hope was formerly excluded. Who would not rather have been the first who triumphantly planted the standard of intelligence and hope within the apparently impregnable ramparts of that dark and dreary citadel, than to have victoriously borne away the martial banners from the fields of Arbela and Waterloo?

But to return. The facts I have mentioned go far to confirm my premises, and I think warrant the assertion, that, so far as the prospects of this life are concerned, agriculture, literature, and benevolence, may generally be regarded as the *ultimate objects of busy men.* The intelligent farmer may well be content; for he already occupies one of the positions which so many are toiling to obtain, and one in which constant observation of the liberality of nature must imbue his mind with generous feeling, and thus eminently fit him for the enjoyment of another of the *ultimate objects.*

The office of the teacher also embraces two of these objects, the pursuit of literature, and the gratification of benevolent feelings.

If the farmer may look with delight on the green fields in which he has made two spears of grass grow where only one grew before, with what higher rapture may the teacher look on the beaming countenance, which attests that another idea, another truth, has been successfully engrafted on an immortal mind! If the farmer, when he plants, may look forward with pleasant anticipation to the refreshing fruit or shade, with what more holy hope and joy may the latter reflect that the germs he is nurturing will grow through eternity!

A man imbued with benevolent feelings, and a passion for knowledge, may find, in the office of a public instructor, that pleasurable occupation and exhilarating exercise of his faculties and feelings, which will induce him to pursue it for a moderate compensation, that will ensure him a comfortable subsistence through life. And the very causes which induce this willingness ensure, at the same time, the highest qualifications, and most devoted zeal in their application. In the adaptation of the office to the gratification of these high tastes, and the peculiar necessity of these same tastes to the office, we may recognize one of those beautiful provisions of Providence by which the supply of all our essential wants is brought within the reach of reasonable effort and moderate ability.

But there is one other condition, without which even these high gratifications will fail of their inducements. We must elevate the profession to its proper rank. We must render it respectable and honorable. We must make its credentials a passport to the best society. If those who now fill its ranks have not always the grace of manner, or even the good breeding and the power of rendering themselves agreeable and instructive in conversation, requisite to make them welcome at our tables and our firesides, the more shame on us that we have inflicted such instructors upon our children, and the greater need, if we would not have them grow up rude, clownish, awkward, and vulgar, that we give their teachers the best means of learning the courtesies of life, and of acquiring the grace and elevation of polished society, which their respective locations can furnish. None more require the sustaining power of society, and by none will it be better repaid. In elevating them, we elevate our children. An examination of facts may further confirm the views I have taken in regard to compensation. Men, whose business obliges them to endure the anxieties attending the risks of fluctuating markets, and the perplexities consequent on extended operations and intricate combinations, and are thus in a great measure debarred the tranquillity of mind and the leisure necessary to the pursuits I have designated as the *ultimate objects of busy men*, must be sustained by the hope of large compensation. The lawyer whose time is fully occupied, and his mind overtasked with important and intricate cases, is in this class, with the additional aggravation that his professional intercourse with mankind is little calculated to gratify benevolent feelings.

The lawyer who is less occupied, and has time and opportunity for some, or all, of the *ultimate objects*, is satisfied with moderate compensation; while, among the clergy, whose vocation embraces literary and benevolent pursuits, we find talents of high order engaged at very moderate salaries. A similar rule, with some modifications, will apply to physicians. The pecuniary remuneration for official services in this state is very small; but I am much mistaken if there is any one in the Union more faithfully, or more efficiently served, or in which the public officers have a larger share of public confidence. Look, too, at our numerous banks, whose presidents have no salaries. Has the large compensation, paid in many other places, procured more ability, or more character, or better administration in any respect?

But the lords of the soil, the professors of law, medicine, and divinity, governors, judges, legislators, and bank presidents, hold honorable places in society. Let us, then, from the high considerations of justice, as well as from those of interest, admit the professors of education to their proper position.* Make their fraternity honorable, and it will soon be crowded by talent, competing for moderate compensation. This proposed elevation will be but justice to the teachers; and it will be expedient, in the first place, to render them more capable of doing us service, and, in the second place, that they may be thus induced to perform these services at a price which will meet the popular views of public ability. In this way, too, we may procure greater advantages than money can command. Money cannot produce so much elevation as honorable place and consideration in society can do. It cannot excite the same interest and kindle the same zeal which literary taste and benevolent feelings can inspire. Besides, if a compensation in money were the only inducement, impostors would rise up, we should be overrun by a host of mercenary office-seekers, generally,

* These remarks are of course made in reference to our district schools. The high character and social position of those engaged in the more elevated institutions leave little cause of complaint, so far as they are concerned, and furnish another illustration in point.

of all men the least fitted for the stations, the emoluments of which they covet.

In its conection with schools, the proper government of children is a very important problem, and one replete with difficulty, in both the theoretical and practical department. There is great diversity of opinion on the subject, and, not feeling myself competent to its full development, I will venture only a few remarks in regard to it.

In the first place, a teacher should be able properly to govern himself. All punishment, inflicted under the influence of anger, is to the child but an example of violence. If he does not perceive its propriety and justice, it is to him but tyranny and oppression. He feels himself overpowered by mere physical strength, to which it would be in vain to oppose his feeble frame; and either rises above it in a feeling of resolute defiance, or, sinking under it, seeks relief in that low exercise of the intellect which develops itself in cunning and falsehood. Violence and fraud naturally produce and reproduce each other. Again, a child should be punished only for what is wrong in himself, and not for doing what is merely inconvenient to its caretakers. The opposite course confounds his ideas of moral right with what is only expedient, destroys the nice sense of justice, which is always found in the infant mind, and sets an example of selfishness which cannot but be prejudicial to the child, and to the proper authority of its guardians.

In regard to the supposed necessity for corporal punishment, I believe it arises more from a want of moral power and moral purity in parents and teachers, than from anything inherent in human nature. The child may be degraded by ignominious punishment, and debased by fear. It is true he may, by these means, also, be restrained from practical wrong, and thus preserved from acquiring bad habits; but I doubt if a single virtuous impulse was ever thus imparted. Most children soon learn to disregard the anger of their parents, but there are few whose better feelings are not touched by seeing them grieved by their conduct, or who can resist the united influence of parental solicitude and parental sacrifices of comfort and convenience on their account. Force is the lowest form of power, love is the highest, and it is the latter which inspires virtuous resolution and noble action. But force appears to be the shortest mode of enforcing obedience, and the parent thinks he has not time, or perhaps that it is not his place, to appeal to the reason and the feelings of the child. He sadly mistakes his duty, as well as the true economy of the subject. The rod has its influence while the pain lasts; but when the feelings are touched, and the understanding is convinced, the work is done, and well done, forever. A restraining power and a virtuous impulse are thereby fixed in the child's own mind, which attend him as guardian angels wherever he goes.

The authority of the parent, if founded on fear, has no existence beyond the acts of which he may become cognizant. At school the child escapes this jurisdiction, and a similar authority is there to be established. We may very naturally suppose that it will be effected by the same means. For if parents, with their greater interest, reinforced by natural affection, found *their* engagements did not allow them time to resort to the moral means of love and reason, when the mind was tender and open to such influences, how can we expect the teacher, charged with the literary instruction of a number of pupils, to find time to act upon the more obdurate material, now presented to him, through the medium of the moral feelings or the moral judgment? He, too, must adopt more summary means, and violence must go on reproducing itself.

I am aware that my opinions on this subject have not the authority of experience, but it does appear to me, that, so long as corporal punishment is deemed essential to school discipline, teachers cannot rise to their proper place in public estimation. So long as they are hired to whip, their vocation will be more or less associated with that of a public executioner; and in our school government we shall be committing the gross absurdity of uniting the offices of a supreme judge and a Jack Ketch in the same person.

If this is necessary I despair of the dignity of the profession. The remedy must begin with the parents. I know that they have not an exclusive and infallible control of the characters of their children, but we all know that much may be done by them in its formation, and especially by the mother. If necessary, then, let the father increase his efforts, and submit to greater privations, that this most important maternal duty may not be neglected, that his children may not want a mother's care, and that holy influence which she can exert on their destiny. But how are they more generally to become properly qualified for the performance of these high duties? The natural affection of mothers does not require to be excited or increased, but to be enlightened by knowledge, and made more discriminating by well-directed thought; and, rude and inadequate as the means now appear to such a delicate and important result, I apprehend it must be commenced in our district schools. Than this there can be no higher consideration to stimulate our efforts to improve these schools. If a boy, when first shown the letter A, could form even a faint conception of the knowledge and science to which it is made the first step, with what burning curiosity would he gaze upon it, and with what persevering assiduity would he apply himself to obtain the key to those vast stores of the intellect! And if here, at the threshold of this movement, we could bring ourselves to realize that by it these treasures are to be made accessible to the whole rising and to future generations, and as a yet higher result, parents, through it, be qualified to instruct their children in all the proprieties of life, and properly to cultivate their intellectual and moral attributes, and thus, by this simple and natural means, regenerate a nation, and make a people virtuous and happy, with what kindling zeal should we contemplate the result, and with what intensity should we apply ourselves to the A B C portion of the work in which we are now engaged!

In regard to physical power, it may be remarked, that it does not comparatively occupy the high place which was assigned to it in a less scientific age. It decreases in popular estimation with the advance of the arts and civilization. It was deified in all the ancient mythologies. It gave preeminence among barbarians. Though in newly settled countries, where its benefits in subduing the forest are felt, it still holds a high place in public estimation, the scientific progress of the age has so far lessened the apparent necessity for it, that there is now reason to fear it will be too much neglected. The supremacy of the laws has dispensed with it as a means of individual personal protection. The invention of gunpowder has made science the efficient defender of civilization, and thus dispensed with the necessity of muscular power to cope with barbarian strength.

By the improvement in machinery, the steam-engine and water-wheel are made to supply a very large portion of that mere automaton strength which was once necessary to provide clothing and prepare food for mankind, and intelligence, being more required to direct these new powers, has become the most valuable element even of labor. It is this which is raising the value of voluntary labor more and more above slave labor. It is the elastic, free thought and diffused intelligence of New England which now enables us successfully to compete, on common ground, with the low wages, low rate of interest, and other advantages possessed by the manufacturers of Great Britain. Nor is agriculture less indebted to science. The saving of labor arising from improved implements, a knowledge of the proper application of manures, rotation of crops and mixture of soils, is vast, and, being more universal, will well compare with improvements in manufacturing machinery, if, indeed, they are not the more important.

In these and other great advances in physical science, we everywhere recognize the truth of the Baconian apothegm, "Knowledge is power."

But we have gone further. More recent discovery, the honor which, I am proud to say, belongs, through one of her distinguished citizens, to this state, has shown, that notwithstanding the edicts of kings, the parade of invincible armies, the valor and skill of military commanders, the arts of superficial statesmen and diplomatists, the bustle of shallow politicians, and the ceaseless turmoil of the multitude, it is still the abstruse philosophers, the deep thinkers, who control the great current of human events and determine their succession; that, in short, profound thought moves the world.*

* This view was first distinctly put forth in an oration, by the Hon. Job Durfee, delivered before the Phi Beta Kappa Society of Brown University, in 1843.

This cheering truth is teeming with great results. It has crowned thought with a new diadem, and invested it with new powers, before which despotism, in every form, already trembles in anticipation of its death-warrant. It raises us from knowledge, to the creative power of knowledge; and if, when the competition was between physical force and science, the Baconian maxim was apposite, we may now, when we wish to carry this competition into the higher departments of intellect, say, with at least equal propriety, "thought is power," from which another step will advance us to the philosophical truth, that mind — intelligence—spirit in its finite and infinite conditions, is the only real and efficient power.

Hence, physical perfection is now to be desired, not as formerly, for its direct use in providing for the subsistence and safety of the individual, and to make him an able defender of the state, but principally to minister to that continuous and energetic mental activity, by which he can render infinitely more essential service to himself and to his race, than the strength of a Samson or Hercules could effect. In this view, the healthful action of the organic system becomes of incalculable importance; and education should not be unmindful of the foundation upon which she is to build, much less should she do aught to weaken or impair it. Disease, in many of its forms, lessens or destroys a man's capacity for thought, and hence, in this age, makes him comparatively powerless; and I apprehend that much disease has its origin in crowded, unventilated, badly warmed school-rooms.

In constructing school-houses, this evil should be carefully guarded against. In another view, this is also very important. Some may think that, if the instruction is given, it cannot matter much what sort of a house it is given in; and I may add that this idea is a very natural one, to persons whose occupations are of an active character and principally in the open air. But we all know that in a crowded, close room, and especially if too warm, the mind soon loses its power of attention; and if in this state it can be roused from its listlessness and excited to effort, it is a painful spasmodic action productive of no good effects.

Under such circumstances, children not only do not and cannot learn, but they soon become disgusted with school, and all their associations with it are of an unpleasant character. Similar effects are sometimes produced by keeping children too long confined, without that muscular exercise which is so particularly essential to them, and often without anything to interest or employ their thoughts. This is painful to them, and productive of bad effects to both body and mind. We have all observed how a brisk walk in the open air restores the mind to its activity, when it has been rendered torpid by too long confinement in a close room; how, instead of having to urge it to exertion, it springs forward with an elastic energy of its own, and the danger is, that we will be lost or entangled in the exuberant profusion of thought through which it hurries us, whether we will or not.

Children are universally fond of acquiring knowledge. They have an insatiable curiosity, which demands gratification from this source. Witness the glowing countenance of a child when the light of a new idea suddenly bursts upon him; the thrill of pleasure, when for the first time he has mastered the intricacies of some ingenious and conclusive argument, and comprehends the truth it demonstrates. I cannot but believe that it must be by some great error that what is thus naturally so congenial to the infant mind should so generally be made distasteful to it. Not that I think learning is attainable without laborious effort, or that it is desirable that it should be, for this would destroy one of its prime benefits as a mental discipline, but only that by proper means a child might be so interested in its acquisition as to pursue it with interest and avidity. You will perceive that the improved modes of instruction tend to this object. A supply of proper apparatus will very much facilitate this result. The machinery of the school-room has been as much improved as that of the cotton-mill, and the consequent saving of labor to teachers and pupils by the one is almost as great as that to the spinners and weavers by the other. The want of economy in retaining the old plans, in either case, is obvious. The proper selection of books is important, and has claimed the attention of the Association. A committee, appointed for that purpose, are investigating the subject, and will report the result. It is desirable, not only to procure the best elementary treatises, but also to secure uniformity, by which much time will be saved to teachers and pupils, and the extra expense of continual change avoided.

In passing to the consideration of the intellectual and moral, I will first remark, that, even independent of moral results, there is a wide difference between a learned man, and one whose intellect has been properly educated. A man may have a vast memory, fully stored with facts drawn from every department of science, and yet be profoundly, stupidly ignorant of all their relations to reality. Such men are in the predicament of a school-boy who can repeat all the descriptions in his geography, and point out the position of every name on the globe or map, and yet does not know that the descriptions, globe and map, have any relation to the earth's surface. If such knowledge as this ever was power, for any other practical purpose than to dazzle the ignorant, and inflate or bewilder its possessor, that time has passed away. This age yields the mastery only to thought.

Now the human mind is not a mere warehouse, of given dimensions, in which you may, with careful stowage, put package after package, of ever so great value, and, when it is full, say its use is accomplished, it is now paying its maximum profit; but it is a living agent, which must masticate, digest, and assimilate its nutriment; and is susceptible, with proper aliment, of never-ending growth, and an unlimited enlargement of its capacities. The acquisition of the small number of facts which can usually be taught in the schoolroom, however useful in life, constitutes a very inconsiderable portion of the benefits of education. Its chief object should be to impart such habits of thought as will enable the student to continually build upon what he there acquired. Those facts are but as the seed of knowledge. Give him this, and the implements, with instructions for its cultivation, and he may ever after add to his store the accumulated harvests of active thought and intelligent observation.

In furtherance of this object, it is proposed to establish circulating libraries in connection with the district schools; and arrangements are already made for trying the experiment, which I deem a very important one. Without some such aid, our efforts may only result in making a larger market for the works of Paul D'Kock and other writers of the same stamp, or a channel for the more general dissemination of the bad taste and worse principles, with which a mercenary press is flooding the country. Let the laborer, when he seeks relief from toil, have proper mental recreation at his command. Furnish him with a choice of agreeable and instructive books, which will elevate his tastes, inform his understanding, and strengthen his moral feelings, and he will no longer be "food for cannon," or material for demagogues.

This will be extending the benefits of intellectual education through life, and at the same time giving a moral direction to the increased powers of thought which it will develop. It will be ministering to that progress which is essential to happiness. This moral elevation does not necessarily follow from mere intellectual culture. All we can say of this or that point is, that the faculties, being made more acute, will more readily and clearly perceive the infallible connection between interest and duty, and that, by opening to the mind higher and purer sources of gratification, the influence of low and degrading passions will be diminished. Let a man become absorbed in any scientific pursuit, even of those most allied to earth, the object of his devotion is truth. For it he cherishes a pure disinterested love, and this elevates all his sentiments and refines all his affections. Let him advance a step further, and, in the province of the fine arts, learn the power of genius and the ennobling and refining influence of the sentiment of the beautiful; or, rising above our own little sphere, let him attempt to grasp in thought the wonders of the universe as revealed in the modern astronomy. Let him first direct his attention to the sun, to the uninformed eye apparently only a little dazzling spot in the blue concave; let him reflect that it is a million times larger than this earth, and some thirty times larger than a sphere whose diameter would reach from us to the moon; and when, by the aid of such comparisons, he has formed some faint conception of the magnitude and splendor of this august central mass, let him observe the wondrous mechanism, by which world after world is made to revolve around him in harmonious movement, with velocities so great, and occupying a space so immense, as to defy all his powers of conception. Then let him turn to the fixed stars, and, by the united aid of facts and analogy, see in every one of them a sun, similar to our own, each of which imagination invests with a like courtly train of planetary worlds and their attending satellites, while, by the powers of an infallible geometry, he demonstrates that their distance is inconceivably greater than that of the furthest planet from our sun; that a cannon-ball, projected from this earth, must travel with its usual velocity hundreds of thousands of years, before it could reach the nearest of them; and that in all probability there are a great number of such consecutive distances between the centre and outer verge of our starry system; and yet that all these, embracing such inconceivable, such incalculable distances in space, are but one cluster — one nebula, such as the telescope reveals to us still far beyond, appearing to occupy only a span in immensity. With instrumental aid let him wander amid these nebulæ, until his eye rests on one which is incomplete, and there learn that creative power is not yet exhausted; there observe nature in her laboratory; the materials for new systems, the uncombined star-dust scattered around her; or, turning to another, mark it crumbling in the decay of age, and ponder on the time which has elapsed since the morning of its existence. But, alas! time has no telescope through which even the eye of fancy can reach an epoch so remote.

Next let him note the beautiful grandeur and harmony which pervade the whole of this stupendous combination. How each minor orb comprised in a system revolves round its appropriate centre — how, in turn, each of these systems, with its central luminary, revolves round some more distant centre, the less continually merging in the greater arrangement, which each successive reach of the telescope or of imagination discloses, until the mind is overpowered in the splendor and magnificence of this mighty display of creative energy. Think you that from these lofty speculations — these vast and overpowering conceptions — he will descend to this little orb to act an ignoble part in its petty concerns? Will he tarnish the brightness, or sully the purity of that intellect by which he is enabled to soar to such commanding thoughts and such ecstatic views?

But as yet he is made acquainted only with the lower department of knowledge; and, however magnificent the development he has just witnessed, it is but a magnificent materialism. Let him rise above this materialism, and, on the confines of spiritual science, in the pure mathematics, learn the pleasure of disinterested thought, and acquire the habit of pursuing truth with concentrated attention, and without the disturbing elements of prejudice, passion, or selfishness. Let him there become familiar with universal truths, which, being beyond the province of experience and of the senses, are apprehended only by the pure reason. Let him enter the domains of metaphysical research, and thus be introduced — ay, introduced — to his own spiritual nature, and, with emotions of surprise and awe, realize the presence of the divinity within him. There let him contemplate the great problems, and ponder on the mysteries of his spiritual being; and, thence ascending to the loftiest regions of human intelligence, let him partake of the inspirations of poetry, and commune with the spirit of prophecy, till his rapt spirit forgets its earthly thralls, and wings its way through realms of light beyond the finite bounds of space or time.

Think you that, descending from the empyrean height to this mundane sphere, he will enter into its competitions with other than the most exalted feelings and the noblest motives? No! Selfishness will be eradicated, and all that is sordid and mean will have given place to liberal and lofty sentiments. The almighty dollar will have lost its omnipotence, and the high places of worldly honor will have dwindled into insignificance. The glittering shrines of wealth, and the gorgeous thrones of power, will have no attractions for him, except as they minister to the sublimity of his soul, or enable him to impart a kindred elevation to others.

Such, at least, is the apparent, perhaps I may also add, the natural and the general tendency of such pursuits; and this is much needed to neutralize the material, comfort-seeking propensities of the age. But experience teaches us that there are those who make use of these high attainments only for the immediate personal enjoyments they command; to minister to the gratification of a fine taste, an acute understanding, and a vivid imagination, while the heart is untouched, its propensities unchastened, and its affections unrefined; and who, by the power of intellect, can even subdue the moral sensibilities, and compel them to contribute to this engrossing selfishness; men who, while they indulge in the raptures of benevolent imaginings, and in fancy delight to dwell on romantic visions of virtuous distress nobly relieved, never lend a helping hand to actual suffering — never whisper a word of consoling sympathy to the afflicted; but, in the complacent confidence and security of intellectual superiority, look with cold indifference on the sorrows, and with scorn on the follies of mankind, while they turn with disgust from misery, in all its forms of repulsive reality. But, as if to complete the evidence that intellectual supremacy is not the highest condition of humanity, we have striking examples of men who have still further perverted high intellectual attributes, and made them the mere panders of a gross sensuality or degrading avarice. If the elevation of the intellect may make the objects of crime appear contemptible, it is through the cultivation of the moral and religious sentiments that crime itself must be made odious, and a sensitiveness awakened which spontaneously shrinks from wrong, and feels every lodgment of temptation as a stain on its purity. If the pride of intellect has made the objects of humanity appear insignificant, and its sufferings repulsive, the optics of a high morality will restore them to their true importance, and make the sorrows, the weaknesses, the errors, and even the follies and the crimes of our fellow-beings, the objects of benevolent thought, and philanthropic action.

If, by fostering the intellectual, we can attain the sublime, the improvement of the moral, coöperating with the religious sentiments, will elevate us to the holy. This moral cultivation may be commenced very early in life. Before the child has left its mother's arms, its affections and its sensibilities may be the objects of her successful care; and, while prattling on the father's knee, it may learn to abhor the gilded crimes by which the vaunted heroes of history have ascended thrones, and to idolize the unpretending virtues which have led martyrs to the scaffold and the stake.

The mind of a child is a very delicate and intricate subject to act upon; and, when we reflect on the influence of early impressions and early circumstances on the formation of character, we may well feel a disposition to shrink from the responsibilities of meddling with it, even while most impressed with the necessity of attending to its development. It is a solemn duty, the proper performance of which requires much patient thought and sleepless care.

How few people reflect on the injury they may do by introducing an unpleasant or gross perception into the mind! If we are induced to believe what is merely injurious by being false, we may detect the error in fact or argument, and the evil is entirely effaced from the understanding; but an impression made on the imagination, or through the medium of association, cannot be thus eradicated. This principle, so obviously liable to abuse, may as obviously be applied to great advantage in moral training. As one application of it, I would have for the use of the children in every school a few portraits of great and good men, and a few representations of virtuous and heroic conduct, the influence of which would blend with their expanding thoughts, and become incorporated in all their anticipations and plans of future life. Who can estimate the effect which the recollection of a sunny childhood, spent amidst pleasant associations and benign influences, under the guiding care of those we respected and loved, and whom, to our more mature judgment, memory ever depicts as worthy to be esteemed and revered, will exert on the whole character and destiny? The sheen of such sunny years will never fade. Its light will ever blend with our purest and highest enjoyment, and memory will often recur to it, to relieve the wearisome toil and gladden the gloomy scenes of life; while, even amid crime and sorrow, it will continually remind us of the better and brighter elements of human existence, with which we were then so familiar. To the moral culture all other cultivation should be subservient.

By attending only to the physical, we may nourish giant frames; but perhaps only for the purposes of ferocity and violence. By exclusive care of the intellectual, we may nurture mighty powers of thought, for good or for ill, and we may give great acuteness to the faculties; but perhaps only for the purposes of fraud, the subversion of the rights, and the destruction of the happiness, of others. In either case, we proceed at the risk of sacrificing all that is most estimable and most holy in human character. Indeed, I can conceive of no worse condition of society than that in which great physical energies should be combined with lawless, brutal, and malignant passions; and great intellectual strength and acuteness with low propensities, selfish motives, and sordid dispositions. It is upon the supremacy of the moral powers that we must rely to give a proper direction to the physical and intellectual energies; and, without their controlling influences, all other cultivation may be worse than useless. Why, then, it may be asked, is this movement directed more particularly to the intellectual? Why not immediately to the higher and more important work of moral improvement? It is true, we rank the moral above the intellectual. We also rank the intellectual above the physical; but, if a man were starving, we would not give him a treatise on geometry or logic for his relief. The highest wants of man may not be the most urgent or most imperative. To have an intellectually great man, there must be a living man; to be morally great, and good, and useful, presupposes a being with capacities for knowing, and with discriminating judgment; and the improvement of these attributes is our present object.

It may be further remarked, that in early life the moral training is most appropriately allotted to parental care, and that for general moral and religious instruction society is already organized, and does not admit or feel the necessity of any material change. There is also a certain equilibrium to be observed between the intellectual and moral progress. They mutually aid and sustain each other, and cannot be widely separated. As the moral becomes more pure, the intellectual sees further, and, clearly discerning the obstacle to further progress, dictates the proper remedy. We have just taken an important step in morals, and the temperance reformation has probably opened the way for the improvement of our district schools. Before the success of that enterprise, the public mind would hardly have entertained the subject of universal education. Intemperance was then an evil too pressing and vital to admit of such slow remedy.

There are some striking analogies between the two movements. Getting drunk seems once to have been thought a manly exploit, and men of high standing gloried in it. So, when the competition commenced between knowledge and physical power, men of renown gloried in their ignorance, thought learning derogatory to them, and useful only to priests and scribes. The sentiment, attributed by Scott to Douglass, represents the feeling of that time.

> "Thanks to saint Bothan, son of mine,
> Save Gawain, ne'er could pen a line;
> So swore I, and I swear it still,
> Let my boy-bishop fret his fill."

The individual advantages of temperance, as of learning, were next observed, and then that the intemperance or ignorance of any was a public calamity, and that public policy, no less than enlarged benevolence, required that all should be made temperate, and that all should be educated by the united efforts of the whole community. At each step, in both instances, there was something to be known, before further progress. Let us again cultivate the knowing faculties, and perchance they will then reveal to us, and bring within our reach, some other moral object. Possibly one of its first results will be to reünite in public estimation individual and political honesty, the separation of which is now so threatening. The deception practised by a partisan seems to be regarded by his fellows as a pious fraud, and, as such, praiseworthy if successful, and at least harmless, so long as it does no injury to their party. When we reflect on the influence of fraud to contaminate and destroy all it touches, and upon its still more immediate tendency to provoke violence, we may well tremble for our institutions, and seek a remedy in some means of elevating the moral sentiments. Possibly another effect of the dissemination of knowledge will be to destroy sectarian feeling, and even without producing unanimity of belief, which I do not think is ever desirable, to unite the public sentiment in favor of some more universal system of moral and religious instruction. But perhaps it is useless to anticipate. It is sufficient for us to know that a better system of education is now necessary to our progress, and that it is our duty to labor for it. This is our mission. Let us in a proper spirit press forward to its accomplishment by all proper means, and leave the result to the Great Disposer of events, with our prayers that the benefits of our efforts may descend to our children, and enable them better to perform their duties, and to fulfil their mission, whatever it may be.

INTEMPERANCE.

On this day, the anniversary of our national birth, our thoughts instinctively turn to that great era in history, and, unbidden, dwell on those events of thrilling interest — those deeds of heroism, and those manifestations of virtue — which marked our entrance into the family of nations, and opened for us the pathway to that high place among them, which it has been our happy destiny to achieve.

Nor is it the day alone which now invokes these associations. We are here emphatically in the great temple of Liberty.* Amid the sublime and beautiful of nature's scenery, she has ever had her truest worshippers; and here, under the blue dome of her sanctuary, the heart, in sympathy with the powers around, spontaneously does homage at her shrine. Here the free and playful zephyrs — those clouds which soar to heaven, or roam through space, unenthralled by earth or sky — the graceful waving of the forest foliage, and yonder fetterless waterfalls, bounding on their way to meet the untrammelled waves of ocean — awaken in our breasts the sentiment of freedom; while the serene empyrean imparts that purity which inspired, and these granite rocks

* This address was made to an assembly in a beautiful grove near the Falls of the Pawcatuck River, July 4th, 1843.

seem ready to lend us that firmness which sustained her votaries in the crisis which on this day we are accustomed to commemorate.

It is an honorable pride which swells the bosom of every American, as he contemplates the conduct of our ancestors in that memorable struggle for political freedom. Their calm, but firm resolve, their dauntless energy of purpose, their disinterested devotion to principle, their lofty patriotism, the wisdom they evinced in council, and their valor in the tented field, have been the chosen themes of the historian's rhapsodies, and the poet's praise. It is their just meed; but if moral revolutions should have allotted to them in history that place to which their importance properly entitles them, whether that importance be measured by the progress they communicated to our race, by their influence on individual happiness and virtue, or by their effects on national strength and national glory, or even by their agency in changing the political condition of the world, some of them would appear on its pages with an effulgence which would pale the brilliant exploits of statesmen and soldiers who have brought political revolutions to a successful issue; and, among these, the temperance reformation of our own times would occupy a proud position. This great movement, commenced within twenty years by a few individuals of this country, has, by the exercise of *moral power*, been extended throughout Christendom, and, in some instances, beyond its confines, though *there*, strange to say, its influence was generally less needed. The enterprise was attended with great difficulties — difficulties of which, now that its benefits have become so obvious, it is not easy to form a just estimate. The habit of drinking was then a vigorous graft upon the social system. To drink together was not only the test of good fellowly feeling, but was even made the pledge of the high sentiment of friendship. He who declined the goblet, when tendered, did it at the risk of giving offence; and he who refused to offer it rendered himself obnoxious to the charge of being morose or mean. This, though not the universal, was the generally diffused feeling; and hence at once the necessity and the apology for a combination to revoke by agreement what by common consent had passed into a law of society. It had become necessary, by some action to legitimate sobriety, to make it not uncivil to refuse the cup ourselves, or to refrain from urging it upon others. Our successors will find it difficult to believe that such laws could ever have become so deeply rooted in the usages of civilized, intelligent, and Christian communities. They will not easily comprehend how depriving a companion of his sense of propriety, and rendering him temporarily insane, could ever have been deemed the trophy of hospitality, and the evidence of friendship and regard; and hence they will be unable to appreciate the efforts which have been put forth to overcome this *one* obstacle to the cause of temperance.

The opposition of those engaged in producing and distributing intoxicating liquors was another impediment of no small magnitude. These availed themselves of the long established habits of society, and of the opinion, then very prevalent, that alcoholic stimulants were, within moderate limits, useful; and that intemperance was but the *abuse* of what in itself was good and beneficial.

This argument was fairly met by the advocates of total abstinence, and the results of their investigations embody a mass of facts and opinions, derived from those having the best opportunities for observing their influence, which clearly show that such stimulants are always injurious to those in health; and that, though like many other poisons, they may sometimes be efficacious as a remedy in disease, yet that even these instances are rare, and that their general use can no more be warranted on the ground of utility, than the propriety of an habitual and general administration of prussic acid, or arsenic, can be inferred from their occasional sanative influence. The distiller of liquors, and the wholesale dealer in them, were not brought into such immediate contact with the wretchedness they produced, as those who dispensed it directly to the consumers. It was, therefore, reasonable to suppose that they would not so readily be impressed with the pernicious consequences of their pursuits; and the first decided effect of the temperance movement, upon those interested in the traffic, was probably upon the better disposed portion of the retailers. Many of these had been engaged in it almost from childhood, had seen it sanctioned by public opinion, and even by legislative authority, and had become so confirmed in their position, by education and habit, that, though daily witnessing scenes of poignant misery, it hardly occurred to them that it was not the natural and necessary condition of humanity, or that they were performing any other part than that properly allotted to them in the theatre of human action, where life itself was made a woful tragedy.

These required only to have their attention directed to the fact that they were the voluntary instruments in producing so much distress; and, this done, they soon resolved to abandon a business which, seen in the new light shed upon it, appeared burdened with guilt and sorrow. I believe many such left it with feelings which ripened into disgust, and produced a mingled emotion of surprise and horror that their moral vision had been so obscured, or their sensibilities so blunted by the influence of their own habits and the sanction of others, and that under such influences they had so long continued to minister to the degradation and destruction of their fellow-beings. That such men *did* so continue, is a striking illustration of the power of public opinion; which, however, is scarcely less forcibly exhibited in the fact that, by its influence, some retailers, who never knew any sympathy for suffering humanity, — who never evinced any regard for the welfare of their fellow-men, nor any feeling for the miserable victims of their cupidity, — were induced to relinquish the objectionable portion of their business. We see in this how emphatically public opinion is a power for good or for evil. It sustained well-disposed men in doing wrong, and it made bad men refrain.

There was, however, yet another class engaged in this demoralizing traffic, whose consciences were seared against all appeals to their sense of right, — who were destitute of humane feeling and human sympathies, — who, sunk in depravity, and alike regardless of the good opinion of themselves and of others, defied the moral power of public sentiment, and contemned the good example of many of their brother dealers.

They had found, or expected to find, the selling of liquors a money-making pursuit. It seemed to them the ready means of transferring the property of the spendthrift, and the wages of the laborer, to their own possession.

These resisted any encroachment upon their "natural right" to scatter ruin, and pestilence, and famine, among their neighbors, with as much pertinacity as the inhabitants of a certain seaboard district opposed the removal of the rocks, and the erection of a lighthouse on their coast, by which, they indignantly asserted, the philanthropists were about to destroy their business of plundering wrecks, in which it had been their privilege to make an *honest* livelihood from time immemorial.

Some of this class still continue to infest our country, and to keep up the necessity for vigilance on the part of the friends of temperance. Many of them are noisy politicians, professing to believe that the very salvation of the country depends on the ascendency of a particular party, yet ready at all times to unite with any other, for the promise of a license; thus, in effect saying, you may ruin the whole country if you will only give me the privilege of destroying and plundering a very small portion of it.

I have looked upon such men with mingled feelings, which it would be difficult to analyze or describe. I feel *pity* for the man who, knowing no higher incentive to action than sordid gain, for a paltry sum relinquishes all the delight of a clear conscience, all the ennobling aspirations of a well-directed ambition, and all the honorable efforts by which he might exalt himself in doing good to others. I feel *contempt* for the man who, for a like paltry sum, consents to become the pander to the lowest appetites, the habitual companion of the most beastly and disgusting of the human family, and the scorn of all good men.

And my *indignation* is excited against the man who, for the same paltry sum, or who, for *any* recompense, however great, becomes the voluntary instrument of such utter ruin to a fellow-being, and the immediate cause of reducing him from a state of hope, happiness, virtue and usefulness, to the lowest stages of vice, misery, worthlessness and despair. I say, my indignation is excited against the man who, unmoved, can witness these effects of his own acts, nor feel any horror of himself, nor any compunctious aspirations for a better life, nor any determination to attain it. But when, as has sometimes been the case, in addition to the appalling and disgusting exhibition of the immediate victims of his combined cupidity and turpitude, there is also brought to his attention the distress and destitution of the delicate wife, and the sufferings of the helpless children, in terms and circumstances so eloquent and so touching, that we would almost expect them to waken feeling beneath the polish of the marble sculptured in man's form, and I find him turning from the picture with apathy, or even a constrained indifference, my indignation gives place to horror and astonishment. I seem to see something bearing externally the shape and lineaments, and having the locomotion of a man, yet destitute of all those inherent feelings which distinguish the race. I confess that I do not understand such beings, and hence, perhaps, I ought not to have spoken of them, except to elicit general inquiry, or to ask, for my own information, what sort of bipeds they can be; whether they are *spurious men*, or altogether of some other class of animals.

To men, generally, it is an obvious truth that it cannot be right for a man voluntarily to do that which he knows will inflict great and irreparable loss upon his neighbor; and the tendency of the arguments adduced by those who persist in selling intoxicating liquors is rather to show that they themselves believe it to be wrong, than to convince others that it is right. As such, it is hardly necessary now to notice them, and I will mention only one of the most prominent. The rum-seller says, "If *I* refuse, others will consent to sell, and thus the same injury be done to the drunkard, without any pecuniary gain accruing to me." The analogies by which this argument has been successfully parried, and its fallacies exposed, are obvious. They have been sufficiently urged, and I now recur to it, merely to remark, that it covers only half the ground it assumes. If the seller should also say, if I do not sell to this man, I shall, as a consequence of my refusal, yield to the temptation to sell to another, and thus do equal wrong and equal violence to my own conscience, he would open the whole question, and present a much fuller view of the moral relations in which he stands to the buyer.

It is obvious, that, in preserving the purity of his own conscience, he would also protect his neighbor from injury.

In connection with the obstacles opposed to the society, and growing out of interested motives, I may here mention the argument raised in behalf of the growers of grain; for whom it was asserted the distilleries made an important market, which could not be dispensed with without great injury to the agriculturist. It certainly requires no very deep insight into the science of political economy, and no very comprehensive benevolence, to see that mankind could derive no benefit from the destruction of wholesome food to make unwholesome drinks; but the argument gained something in effect from a fallacy then prevailing, and which is not yet eradicated from the popular mind. This fallacy, in common with the argument alluded to, presupposes that it is meritorious for us to contrive to make work for one another. The man of wealth, who is so liberal in providing for his personal luxuries as to use up a hundred fold what his own labor produces, is still not unfrequently deemed a general benefactor. It is time that this opinion gave place to the more rational view, that one great object of society is to enable all to enjoy as much as possible from the same amount of effort; and that he who diverts labor into unprofitable channels, or destroys its valuable results, or wastes them in luxurious extravagance, diminishes the general stock of the comforts of the world, and lessens the chance that each and every individual will get that portion which it is just and proper should be allotted to him, or even that share which may be necessary to save him from the pangs of hunger and cold.

If it were here proper, it would not be difficult to show that the theoretical fallacy which lies at the bottom of this objection to the temperance enterprise, has been productive of an immense amount of practical suffering; and from it may also be deduced an easy explanation of the fact that where there is most luxurious expenditure in one class, there is also most poverty and want in another. The acquisition and retention of money may accumulate a power for future good or evil; but no harm is done to the community in the process of hoarding it, unless it is carried to such an extent as to produce appreciable fluctuation in the values which it is used to measure. It is idleness and waste of labor, and of its products, which produces or increases want. In the remedy of these evils, the temperance society has certainly contributed in no small measure; and, in the very reasoning thus directed against them, do we find a sound argument in their favor.

It is pleasant, in this connection, to observe how all these fears of injury to the agricultural interest have vanished. The surplus produce of our western granaries is, by the aid of chemical science, now made to cheer with light the homes of the people, instead of spreading a cloud of moral darkness over the land.

Another ground of objection to the society, less palpable and less commented upon, but more subtle and pervading in its influence than those already alluded to, has grown out of our ill-defined notions of civil liberty, in connection with a prevalent idea that the temperance society curtailed it, and that it at the same time encroached on the province of free agency. Both these subjects have their metaphysical difficulties, even after science has done all she can accomplish to simplify their elements and reduce them to order; and we shall be very liable to error, whenever we attempt to found any connected and rational argument upon the crude notions of them which have a popular currency. With some, it is an improper restriction of liberty to prevent a man's hanging himself, and an unjustifiable interference with free agency to restrain him from the destruction of his intellectual powers, and the perversion of his moral nature. Hence, the retailer insisted upon his "*natural right*" to sell, and the buyer upon his "*natural right*" to get drunk, whenever he chose to do so. These vague notions of principles, so deeply rooted in our nature, were the very elements for the arts of sophistry, and also furnished the materials from which interest and inclination could draw as many doubts as were necessary to prevent a decision against them in the tribunals of conscience. But, though society may have no natural or conventional right to interfere in those acts which affect only the individual, except by argument or persuasion, yet it has a right to compel from him, by all proper means, the performance of all his social duties; and, incidental to this, must be the right to restrain him, by such means, from *dis*qualifying himself for the performance of those duties.

It is seldom, however, that we find a popular sentiment, however vague, which has not substantial truth for its basis. If the sentiment is right, it is an intuitive inference from that truth; if wrong, it is an accidental perversion, growing out of the want of a full and clear perception of it. The objection to the temperance society, which we are now considering, had its origin in the sublimest verities of our being.

To do good, or to resist evil, from an internal conviction of duty, and by an internal moral power, is the highest prerogative of intelligent natures. It is the attribute of individual sovereignty; and to yield this sovereign right, to substitute for this free vital activity any external agreement, law, or force, would be the greatest sacrifice which pride, dignity, and self-respect could make upon the altar of humanity. Allied to this is the conviction that whenever society, in the form of government, or in subordinate associations, by the authority of law or the power of union, compels an individual to a course of action, even such as he approves, yet not originating in his own convictions of duty, they take from him the merit of voluntary performance, and rob him of the cheerful influence of self-approval. They deprive him of some of the opportunities for that exercise of virtue, in resisting evil, by which his moral strength is increased. In every attempt, then, to curtail the limits of this field for the exercise of individual virtue by combinations, the question must arise, whether the injury thus done is more than compensated by the benefits arising from the association; and, if so, how far the power of union may advantageously be substituted for that of individuals, and of pledges for unaided self-restraint or control.

It was in reference to *these* views that I spoke not only of the necessity, but of the *apology* which existed for the formation of the temperance society. Their collision with the principle of free agency was, perhaps, more apparent than real; but the remarks I have made will serve to show how deep-rooted in human nature was the opposition which grew out of them. I say the collision was, perhaps, more apparent than real, for the society appears to have felt the importance of interfering as little as possible with personal freedom. In confirmation of this, I may remark, that, though the injury arising from intemperance is by no means confined to the victim of it, or even to his own family, yet they have wisely abstained from resorting to the authority of the civil government for penal laws against it. For its cure they have relied upon moral power alone, and the result has conclusively shown the wisdom of their course. The pledge they required of their members was little more than a corollary from their resolution to do all in their power, by precept and example, to redeem the nation from a pestilence which was already preying upon its vitality.

In one class of men the vague notions of interference with liberty and free agency were but the welcome allies of interest and inclination. Another class, more or perhaps wholly disinterested, felt their influence without analyzing their feelings. In portions of both these classes these obscure perceptions of important truths were the occasions of that bravado spirit which induced those under its influence to drink, that they might satisfy themselves or convince others that they really were independent, but which conclusively proved that they had no self-reliance, nor any true dignity of character.

To those who seriously reflected upon the subject, it must have become apparent that individual liberty is of *necessity* modified by the conditions of society, and that the real question was, whether they would be more useful by becoming members of the association; and if a submission to its requirements, being still a voluntary yielding to the convictions of duty, would not lessen the merit of performance, or the gratification arising from it. To such considerations the national jealousy of freedom, and the individual pride of personality, in some measure yielded. But the great subduing argument against all these subtle theories, vague speculations, deep-rooted, and in some instances perverted feelings, has been the palpable practical good continually manifested by the progress of the society in the achievement, and even in the extension of its original designs.

Its success has outstripped the anticipations of its warmest friends, and the predictions of its most zealous advocates. The good it has already accomplished has entirely allayed the fears of the cautious, removed the doubts of sceptics, and silenced the cavils of interested opponents. Those who still oppose it make no pretension to any higher motive than selfishness; and, even in some of these, better feelings are sometimes aroused, better motives imparted, and better actions induced.

At the time of the formation of the society, and for some years after, the principal object and hope of its members appear to have been, to preserve the temperate, and, perhaps, reclaim some of those who had just passed within the outer verge of the fatal whirlpool. In a report, so late as 1831, they expressly say, "No sooner is a person brought within the power of intoxicating liquors, than he seems to be proof against the influence of all the means of reformation. If at any time the truth gains access to his mind, and impresses his heart, by a few draughts of the fatal poison the impression is almost sure to be effaced. Hence, the notorious and alarming fact, that a person addicted to this vice is seldom renewed in the temper of his mind, or even reformed as to his outward character."

Still, what they proposed was in itself a magnificent undertaking, and one which might then well bound their utmost hope. To arrest the evil where it was, and thus, in one generation, free the earth from this great scourge, was then, to all appearance, a work so vast as to appal any but heroic minds. They expected but to stand between the dead and the living, and that the plague would be stayed. But the incense which arose from the sacrifices, by which they consecrated themselves to the cause of humanity, had even more efficacy than that which Aaron took from the altar. It not only preserved the living, but it reclaimed the dead. Little room, indeed, was there for the members of the society to hope for such a result, when they commenced their arduous work. Then, by many sober and well-meaning persons, they were deemed wild or visionary enthusiasts, who might possibly do *some* good, but would never materially affect the deep-rooted evils of society. But some of the seed fell on better ground, and sprang up in pure thought, lofty purpose, and energetic action; and, on these vigorous germs, the blossoms of hope matured to a rational enthusiasm. And when was enthusiasm in a good cause successfully and permanently resisted? The annals of our race afford few such instances. And what in a good cause will it not accomplish? Witness its astonishing effects in the cause of temperance! Let the association of reformed inebriates reply. For them the voice of enthusiasm carried the cheering promises of hope to the lowest depths of degradation and despair; the offcasts of society and the self-abandoned gathered a new inspiration and awoke to a new life.

It is here that the moral grandeur of the temperance enterprise is manifested in its full splendor.

Thus to impart fresh feeling and noble sentiment to a fellow-being so totally crushed and despised; to rekindle in him a new sense of the majesty of his nature; to exalt him with fresh hopes; to plant an aspiring energy in his bosom, and stimulate him with a new ambition; to restore to him the pure and gentle affections and social influences; to recall to his mind the sense of the beautiful; to reöpen to his soul the avenues of religion, and pour upon his troubled spirit the consolations of piety, — is the grandest achievement of humanity. In witnessing its accomplishment, we cannot but feel that we partake on earth of that joy, which, in heaven, is greater over one sinner that repenteth, than over ninety and nine just persons.

Well may the society which has been the instrument in this glorious work say, "We never know what we may do by wise, united, and persevering efforts in a good cause, until we try."

An investigation of the causes of their success might elicit some useful truths.

What strikes us as a prominent one is the disinterested desire of doing good, which actuated the members, and formed the basis of the liberality and freedom from party and sectarian prejudices, which have marked their progress.

Honest differences of opinion have arisen among them, but, being honest, the discussions they provoked had truth for their only object, and have been beneficial, as are all discussions upon real questions, when free from selfishness and bigotry. They engrafted no speculative problems upon their original design, and made no mystery of the means of doing good. They trusted to every man to select his own mode, merely aiding him with knowledge, and encouraging him by word and example.

Let narrow reformers take from them a lesson, and learn, by separating union from authority and its dogmas, to make it a means of calling out free individual action. The mighty torrent, with all its force and grandeur of movement, does very little to fertilize the soil, compared with its elements, when diffused in rain and dew. Let each drop nurture a spear of grass, or refresh a flower, and the whole earth will be covered with verdure and beauty. Thus beautiful is individual moral action, and thus on every field has temperance shed its refreshing dew. Where is the abode of that man who cannot see its beneficial effects around him? In every part of our country the dwellings of the poor (if that term can with propriety be applied to any class where all have such plenty) have assumed a style of comfort; the grounds about them are better cultivated. The garden manifests the husband's careful provision for his family; the wife finds time to indulge the innocent and elevating luxury of taste, in the cultivation of shrubs and flowers; their children are seen decently clad, in frolicksome mood, going to and from the village schools. An air of content brightens every countenance; hope, and cheerfulness, and social intercourse, lighten their week-day toil; and, when the Sabbath brings its season of rest, and its hallowing impressions, they flock with grateful hearts to the numerous sanctuaries for the worship of God, and there perform their part in appropriate solemnities. How different from the scenes so common among the same class but a few years ago! Then their families were often, from the mere want of decent clothing, debarred the advantages of society, and of literary and religious instruction. Intemperance banished peace and comfort from their dreary homes. Approaching their miserable abodes, you might often hear the sounds of maddened revelry, or of brutal and excited passions in harsh discord, drowning the plaint of wife and child; or, entering the hut, you would there witness, in all its interior arrangements, the evidences of squalid poverty and destitution, and on the countenances of its inmates, the unchanging expression of hopeless woe. Perhaps, too, we might there sometimes recognize in her, who now mingled the tears of bitterness and sorrow with the milk which nurtured the infant at her breast, the altered features of one, whom, but a few years before, we had seen in the buoyancy of youth, when her cheek was blooming with health and animation, and her eye brightened with hope and intelligence, while a maidenly pride manifested itself in personal decoration, and imparted grace to her agile step, now sunk in despondency, the very wreck of her former self; her cheeks sunken and pale with care and want; her eye dimmed by anguish and despair, and her pride crushed even to abjectness, by cruel disappointment and her hopeless fate. You have already anticipated her history. He, to whose plighted troth she had trusted, had become the victim of intemperance. She had long continued to hope, but despondency was now legibly marked upon her brow, and her gentle spirit, subdued and broken, seemed to have no tie to earth, except in those who claimed from her a mother's care. Yet amid such scenes were sometimes exhibited the noblest qualities which exalt our race. Here did woman put forth all the power of gentleness, and all the force of principle; and, sadly defaced and mutilated as humanity was, she still, by a steadfast adherence to her high nature, presented some of its best features in all their original beauty. Here she manifested her faithful devotion, her calm fortitude, her patient endurance; and, with no friendly hand to aid, no approving eye to encourage, no sympathetic voice to cheer and enlighten her toil, — with no high hope to inspire her arduous efforts, and no solace but her piety,— she yet, with a noble spirit, sustained herself amid all the hardships and privations of her lot, and still strove to fulfil all the duties of her station. And nobly did she perform those of wife and mother. Often, in calm remonstrance, would she urge upon the cause of her misfortunes, the degradation he was bringing upon himself and family, and, with throbbing breast and tearful eyes, beseech him to avert from them a fate which was fast destroying all the present happiness and future promises of life. And then, won by her gentle persuasions, and looking upon his children, clad in comfort, and still made happy by her care, he made those resolves and promises which gladdened her heart, and brought hope again to her despairing bosom. And this hope brightened with that change in his life which she fondly trusted would be permanent. Alas! it was but a short reprieve. He was again absent from his home. The setting sun and succeeding twilight had not witnessed his return. The anxious wife felt that all her hopes were hanging upon that hour. Overcoming the timidity of her nature, she ventured to the scene of his former revels. Her fears were but too fully realized. He, who with hallowed rite had promised to protect and cherish her till death dissolved the sacred tie, was before her in a state too torpid to be roused, even by the unseemly and unmanly jeers her appearance called forth from his comrades. By him her frantic entreaties were met only with the dull, stupid stare of mental inanity, and by others with contumely. From this trying scene she retired with feelings, which words cannot express, and imagination but feebly depict. Hope now fled from her bosom, but the great principle of duty remained. A mother's love still animated her, and though her physical powers were tasked to a state of exhaustion, yet often, as she divided among her children the scanty earnings of her unremitted toil, did she impress on their tender minds the principles of virtue, and endeavor to inspire them with religious faith and reverence.

Her trials, her fortitude, and her virtues, are written in no earthly history, but they are recorded in heaven. Her heroic deeds have had no poet, but they have not died. They live in the memory of many a virtuous daughter, inheriting her maternal worth. They inspire the breast of many a worthy son, whose amen to his mother's tearful prayer for his preservation was a firm resolve never to drink from the fatal bowl. Some of these are now ornaments of this society, and to them is due a full share of the glory of its success. They were eminently fitted to take part in the vital concerns of the association, and brought with them much of that patient zeal, practical activity, sturdy endurance, and sympathy for the sufferers, so essential to success in the early stages of its career. At the fireside altars of their early homes they had vowed eternal enmity to intemperance. And O! if my feeble description of that home has enabled you to call up in imagination any adequate conception of the tender and stirring influences which there wrought upon them, you will feel no surprise at the alacrity with which they obeyed the first call, and came forward ready armed, and earnest to do battle in the good cause; and that in zeal and efficiency they often outstripped those whose sensibilities had been carefully fostered in the lap of refinement, informed in the halls of science, and matured and disciplined in scenes where taste, elegance, and liberality, lent their attractions to the performance of all the practical charities of life. And you may cease to wonder that in the virgin soil of their unsophisticated natures enthusiasm, whose seed is sown from heaven, struck deep its roots, and acquired a luxuriance and vigor which it seldom attains in more cultivated minds; or that, under the influence of its inspiration, the ungifted suddenly became full of wisdom and energy, and that they, who before were slow and rude of speech, could now, in the fluent utterance of their burning thoughts and vehement feelings, command from language all its graces of diction, and all its powers of persuasion. I have already endeavored to exhibit, though in faint delineation, some of the misery in which the family of the drunkard is of necessity involved. I felt the impotence of any language at *my* command to express their sufferings. What power, then, can I summon to depict his own wretchedness? For, however he may blunt his sensibilities, and shield himself in stupor, remorse will find occasions to inflict its bitter pangs, and his distresses will receive from virtue no mitigation of their acuteness. His *own* aspect, and his *own* acts, most eloquently tell his sufferings. What mental rack has so broken every noble principle, and distorted every moral feeling of his nature, that the despair and want of wife and child have no power to move his compassion, or to arouse his energies? What withering influence has so destroyed the vitality of his mind, that it gives signs of life only in the convulsive movements of frenzy or madness? What has made his life so dark a picture, and covered all his future prospects with such dread anticipations, that he seeks to shut out all thoughts of past.

present and future, in a guilty delirium, or annihilating stupor? By what intensity of agony have the strong energies of the soul been crushed, every nerve and fibre wrung, and the whole man wilted, rived, and shattered in *delirium tremens?* What subtle fiend, in his alchemical search for sublimated tortures, invented *mania à potu?* What malicious and remorseless demon summons before his victim the dreadful phantasms, which wring from him such shrieks of horror, or fix on his countenance such diabolical contortions?

And has humanity no power to save him from these infuriate spirits of darkness? Alas! the hell he suffers is in his own breast. He has made it a portion of himself. Yet, even at this desperate stage, has the evil been arrested, and the victim restored to the rank of a moral being, elevated to self-respect, and made a useful citizen. The difficulty of reforming such men was, as I have before observed, fully appreciated by the early members of the temperance associations. This difficulty, in part, grew out of that prostration of their moral energies, the complete paralysis of the powers of the will, which is caused by intemperance. It is not sufficient that you make the drunkard willing. His will, if he can be said to have any, is the slave of his appetite, and has little or no efficacy against it. Hence it is that his reclamation peculiarly requires a sustaining power from *without* himself. He needs to be warned against temptation, and to be aided by others in a self-restraint for which his own weakened energies are insufficient. He must be encouraged to regard himself, and to hope for the regard of others. Society must give him an opportunity of being useful and respectable.

Until recently such means were not resorted to. The

drunkard was looked upon as an incurable leper, cut off from the sympathy and companionship of his fellow-men, an object of universal aversion and disgust. Hence it was that so very few were reclaimed. Their own palsied faculties made but feeble efforts, and these were repelled by the scorn or contempt of the world. The energy of the will reëstablished, and a sense of self-respect and of ability for usefulness confirmed, the reformed inebriate is well fitted for further moral improvement. In rising from so low a depth, he has gained the great idea of moral progress; and the energy which he has put forth in his redemption has taught him the benefit of moral effort; and moral effort, with a view to moral improvement, embraces the whole science of moral culture.

Though the temperance association has done so much to relieve the physical distress of the drunkard, and those dependent upon him, and in reclaiming his moral nature, it is by no means to them alone that the benefit of its efforts has been confined. It has been the means of bringing into salutary connection men of all stations and grades in society, of all sects in religion, and of all parties in politics. It has united them by the ties of a common object. They have met each other with honest purposes of mutual aid, and good and liberal feeling has been the natural result of pure and elevated motives. They have thus become better acquainted with each other, and learned that these artificial divisions, accidental differences, and theoretical or verbal distinctions, have little influence on the real characters and practical tendencies of men. This has softened the asperities of party and sectarian prejudices, and made men not only appear better to each other, but caused an absolute improvement in their characters.

The society has also contributed, more than any other means, to bring the great mass of men into activity upon that moral stage, where before there were only a few performers. The evil to be remedied was at every man's door, and afforded to all an opportunity of being useful in eradicating it. Many a man who, until aroused by its efforts, had seldom extended his benevolence in thought or action much beyond his own threshold, or indulged any idea of being useful to the world, except in his business occupations, nor, perhaps, looked upon drunkards with any higher feeling than that of thankfulness to God that he was not like unto them, now awoke from his lethargy, and began to exert himself for their improvement. He soon witnessed the effects of his efforts, and found in himself capabilities for good, of which, till then, he had been ignorant. With this discovery he felt a new inspiration. His heart glowed with philanthropy. He acted with energy, and, kindling with pure and elevated feeling, spoke with a fervor which lighted the flame of humanity in other breasts; and with every effort he felt himself grow stronger, and every good action but made him the more ready for another; and, from this fervor, and this active benevolence, he learned the value of pure motives, and fitted himself for the highest duties. In this we realize a beautiful truth, which the illustrious Channing has embodied in the simple expression, "We catch virtue from ourselves as well as from others." *

The illustrious Channing! —since the last anniversary

* This apothegm is from a letter of Dr. Channing to the author. I deem it a gem worthy a place even in the rich casket he has bequeathed to us.

this society has lost in him one of its warmest friends and ablest supporters! With it, all the high interests of humanity deplore his loss.

If I felt competent to the work, it would be a grateful task here to offer to his memory the mingled tribute of public regard and individual affection and reverence. But I shrink from it, under the conviction that this hallowed ground would be desecrated by my uninspired intrusion upon it. Yet in humble phrase may I speak to you of the irreparable loss we have sustained; for, to my mind, nothing has been said — in my apprehension nothing can be said — which conveys a fuller idea of the magnitude of that loss, than the mere announcement of it. Nothing has ever enabled me better to realize it, than the simple expression, "*Channing is dead.*" Who that knew him (and who that speaks our language did not know him?) but felt these words thrill through him, and vibrate with solemn harmony on chords, in the deep recesses of his soul, which till then had never responded to any emotion of awe or sorrow? Were not our faculties overpowered by the sudden and unexpected intelligence? Did not our thoughts, for the moment, lose their hold on the realities of sense, and, as thus entranced we saw his spirit ascend to the mansions of the eternal, did we not rather feel that we had gained a friend in heaven, than that we had lost one on earth? that the mind, which here filled the infinity of our thoughts, had but extended itself to that infinity which our thoughts cannot compass? The announcement of his death was unexpected, because that, which in him absorbed our attention, seemed to be — was — immortal. But as the echo of the words, which thus wrought upon us, came back upon the recovering sense, did we not, in the spirit-like return of the sound, "Channing is dead," awaken to the reality that he still lived, though the vesture which he here wore had been returned to its native earth? May we not imagine, ay, believe, that one, who on earth was marked by such expansion and universality, will not, in heaven, be excluded from the sphere in which he shone with such celestial purity and splendor? And may we not, without irreverence, suppose him now conscious of our labors in a cause which, while visible among us, he had so much at heart, and that, by the mysterious power of the higher intelligences, his spirit here mingles with us and encourages our efforts? But I am trespassing on ground I intended should be sacred, and I feel that silence is the best expression of those emotions to which words can give only such feeble utterance.

In the double action of the temperance society, upon themselves and upon others, which we were just considering, we get a glimpse of one of those beautiful combinations by which honest and disinterested efforts in a good cause are made to extend and multiply their good effects. It also unfolds to us one of those high and extensive bearings which the efforts of a few individuals may have upon the destiny of the nation and the world.

The multitude of men, who have been trained to moral effort in the temperance enterprise, are as a standing army, ready for the protection of our national morality; ready to resist the introduction of any new vice, to eradicate existing evils, and garrison the strongholds of virtue.

The want of such protection seems now particularly needed, by the decline of political and commercial morality, which has reached a point threatening even the stability of our government. The temperance reformation seems to have come in at the very hour of our need to arrest these evils, and, by increasing the moral power, intelligence, and virtue among us, counteract the tendency of this decline to destroy our civil institutions.

It is fitting, then, that on this, the birthday of these institutions, we should mingle, in our commemorations of the political revolution which ushered them into existence, some tribute, also, to that moral revolution, which has done so much to sustain them, and to brighten the hope of their perpetuity.

HISTORY.

Prescott.

HISTORY OF THE REIGN OF PHILIP II.

By William H. Prescott. With Portraits, Maps, Plates, &c. Two volumes, 8vo. Price, in muslin, $2 per volume.

The reign of *Philip the Second*, embracing the last half of the sixteenth century, is one of the most important as well as interesting portions of modern history. It is necessary to glance only at some of the principal events. The War of the Netherlands — the model, so to say, of our own glorious War of the Revolution — the Siege of Malta, and its memorable defence by the Knights of St. John; the brilliant career of Don John of Austria, the hero of Lepanto; the Quixotic adventures of Don Sebastian of Portugal; the conquest of that kingdom by the Duke of Alba; Philip's union with Mary of England, and his wars with Elizabeth, with the story of the Invincible Armada; the Inquisition, with its train of woes; the rebellion of the Moriscos, and the cruel manner in which it was avenged — these form some of the prominent topics in the foreground of the picture, which presents a crowd of subordinate details of great interest in regard to the character and court of Philip, and to the institutions of Spain, then in the palmy days of her prosperity. The materials for this vast theme were to be gathered from every part of Europe, and the author has for many years been collecting them from the archives of different capitals. The archives of Simancas, in particular, until very lately closed against even the native historian, have been opened to his researches; and his collection has been further enriched by MSS. from some of the principal houses in Spain, the descendants of the great men of the sixteenth century. Such a collection of original documents has never before been made for the illustration of this period.

The two volumes now published bring down the story to the execution of Counts Egmont and Hoorn in 1568, and to the imprisonment and death of Don Carlos, whose mysterious fate, so long the subject of speculation, is now first explored by the light of the authentic records of Simancas.

HISTORY OF THE REIGN OF FERDINAND AND ISABELLA, The Catholic.

By W. H. Prescott. With Portraits. Three volumes, 8vo. Price, in muslin, $2 per volume.

"Mr. Prescott's merit chiefly consists in the skilful arrangement of his materials, in the spirit of philosophy which animates the work, and in a clear and elegant style that charms and interests the reader. His book is one of the most successful historical productions of our time. The inhabitant of another world, he seems to have shaken off the prejudices of ours. In a word, he has, in every respect, made a most valuable addition to our historical literature." — *Edinburgh Review.*

HISTORY OF THE CONQUEST OF MEXICO,

With the Life of the Conqueror, Fernando Cortez, and a View of the Ancient Mexican Civilization. By W. H. Prescott. With Portrait and Maps. Three volumes, 8vo. Price, in muslin, $2 per volume.

"The more closely we examine Mr. Prescott's work the more do we find cause to commend his diligent research. His vivacity of manner and discursive observations scattered through notes as well as text, furnish countless proofs of his matchless industry. In point of style, too, he ranks with the ablest English historians; and paragraphs may be found in his volumes in which the grace and eloquence of Addison are combined with Robertson's majestic cadence and Gibbon's brilliancy." — *Athenæum.*

HISTORY OF THE CONQUEST OF PERU;

With a Preliminary View of the Civilization of the Incas. By W. H. Prescott. With Portraits, Maps, &c. Two vols., 8vo. Price, in muslin, $2 per volume.

"The world's history contains no chapter more striking and attractive than that comprising the narrative of Spanish conquest in the Americas. Teeming with interest to the historian and philosopher, to the lover of daring enterprise and marvellous adventure, it is full of fascination. A clear head and a sound judgment, great industry and a skilful pen, are needed to do justice to the subject. These necessary qualities have been found united in the person of an accomplished American author. Already favorably known by his histories of the eventful and chivalrous reign of Ferdinand and Isabella, and of the exploits of the Great Marquis and his iron followers, Mr. Prescott has added to his well-merited reputation by his narrative of the Conquest of Peru." — *Blackwood.*

Mr. Prescott's works are also bound in more elaborate styles, — half calf, half turkey, full calf, and turkey antique.

Barry.

THE HISTORY OF MASSACHUSETTS,

By Rev. John Stetson Barry. To be comprised in three volumes, octavo. Volume I. embracing the Colonial Period, down to 1692, now ready. Volumes II. and III. in active preparation. Price, in muslin, $2 per volume.

Extracts from a Letter from Mr. Prescott, the Historian.

BOSTON, June 8, 1855.

Messrs. Phillips, Sampson, & Co.

Gentlemen, — The History is based on solid foundations, as a glance at the authorities will show.

The author has well exhibited the elements of the Puritan character, which he has evidently studied with much care. His style is perspicuous and manly, free from affectation; and he merits the praise of a conscientious endeavor to be impartial.

The volume must be found to make a valuable addition to our stores of colonial history.

Truly yours,
WILLIAM H. PRESCOTT.

Hume.

THE HISTORY OF ENGLAND,

From the Invasion of Julius Cæsar to the Abdication of James II., 1688. By David Hume, Esq. A new edition, with the author's last corrections and improvements; to which is prefixed a short account of his life, written by himself. Six volumes, with Portrait. Black muslin, 40 cents per volume; in red muslin, 50 cents; half binding, or library style, 50 cents per volume; half calf, extra, $1.25 per volume.

The merits of this history are too well known to need comment. Despite the author's predilections in favor of the House of Stuart, he is the historian most respected, and most generally read. Even the brilliant *Macaulay*, though seeking to establish an antagonistic theory with respect to the royal prerogative, did not choose to enter the lists with *Hume*, but after a few chapters by way of cursory review, began his history where his great predecessor had left off.

No work in the language can take the place of this, at least for the present century. And nowhere can it be found accessible to the general reader for any thing like the price at which this handsome issue is furnished.

These standard histories, Hume, Gibbon, Macaulay, and Lingard, are known as the *Boston Library Edition*. For uniformity of style and durability of binding, quality of paper and printing, they are the cheapest books ever offered to the American public, and the best and most convenient editions published in this country.

Macaulay.

THE HISTORY OF ENGLAND,

From the Accession of James II. By Thomas Babington Macaulay. Four volumes, 12mo., with Portrait. Black muslin, 40 cents per volume; red muslin, 50 cents; library style and half binding, 50 cents; calf, extra, $1.25.

"The all-accomplished Mr. Macaulay, the most brilliant and captivating of English writers of our own day, seems to have been born for the sole purpose of making English history as fascinating as one of Scott's romances." — *North American Review.*

"The great work of the age. While every page affords evidence of great research and unwearied labor, giving a most impressive view of the period, it has all the interest of an historical romance." — *Baltimore Patriot.*

Gibbon.

THE HISTORY OF THE DECLINE AND FALL OF THE ROMAN EMPIRE,

By Edward Gibbon, Esq. With Notes by Rev. H. H. Milman. A new Edition. To which is added a complete Index of the whole work. Six volumes, with Portrait. 12mo., muslin, 40 cents per volume; red muslin, 50 cents; half binding, or library style, 50 cents per volume; half calf, extra, $1.25.

"We commend it as the best library edition extant." — *Boston Transcript.*

"The publishers are now doing an essential service to the rising generation in placing within their reach a work of such acknowledged merit, and so absolutely indispensable." — *Baltimore American.*

"Such an edition of this English classic has long been wanted; it is at once convenient, economical, and elegant." — *Home Journal.*

Lingard.

A HISTORY OF ENGLAND,

From the first Invasion by the Romans to the Accession of William and Mary in 1688. By John Lingard, D. D. From the last revised London edition. In thirteen volumes; illustrated title pages, and portrait of the author. 12mo., muslin. Price, 75 cents per volume.

"This history has taken its place among the classics of the English language." — *Lowell Courier.*

"It is infinitely superior to Hume, and there is no comparison between it and Macaulay's romance. Whoever has not access to the original monuments will find Dr. Lingard's work the best one he can consult." — *Brownson's Review.*

"Lingard's history has been long known as the best history of England ever written; but hitherto the price has been such as deprived all but the most wealthy readers of any chance of possessing it. Now, however, its publication has been commenced in a beautiful style, and at such a price that no student of history need fail of its acquisition." — *Albany Transcript.*

Lamartine.

HISTORY OF THE FRENCH REVOLUTION OF 1848,

By Alphonse de Lamartine. Translated by F. A. Durivage and William S. Chase. In one volume, octavo, with illustrations. Price, in muslin, $2.25.

Same work, in a 12mo. edition, muslin, 75 cents; sheep, 90 cents.

A most graphic history of great events, by one of the principal actors therein.

"The day will come when *Lamartine*, standing by the gate-post of the Hotel de Ville, and subduing by his eloquence the furious passions of the thousands upon thousands of delirious revolutionists, who sought they knew not what at the hands of the self-constituted Provisional Government of 1848, will be commemorated in stone, on canvas, and in song, as the very impersonation of moral sublimity." — *Meth. Quarterly Review.*

"No fitting mete-wand hath To-day
For measuring spirits of thy stature, —
Only the Future can reach up to lay
The laurel on that lofty nature, —
Bard, who with some diviner art
Hast touched the bard's true lyre, a nation's heart."
James Russell Lowell, "To Lamartine."

Hale.

HISTORY OF KANZAS AND NEBRASKA,

With a Map. Compiled with the assistance of the New England Emigrant Aid Society, by Rev. E. E. Hale. Price, in muslin, 75 cents.

This work is the result of labor and research, and will be found invaluable to those who contemplate removing to Kanzas, as well as to those who for other reasons would acquire a knowledge of the geography and capabilities of the territories. The extraordinary scenes which have transpired during their recent rapid settlement are sufficient to attract the public attention strongly to whatever may give authentic information.

Ballou.

THE HISTORY OF CUBA,

Or Notes of a Traveller in the Tropics. By M. M. Ballou. In one volume, 12mo., with illustrations. Price, 75 cents.

In this volume Mr. Ballou has given a well-written, but concise history of Cuba from its discovery to the present time. Following this the author endeavors to place the character and manners of the people and the scenery of the beautiful island directly before the reader's mental vision. Authentic and valuable in matter, attractive in manner, the book combines greater merits than any other similar work.

Craig, D'Aubigne.

HISTORY OF THE PROTESTANT CHURCH IN HUNGARY

From the Beginning of the Reformation to 1850. With reference also to Transylvania. Translated by the Rev. J. Craig, D. D., Hamburg. With an Introduction by J. H. Merle D'Aubigné, D. D., President of the Theological School of Geneva. 550 pages. Price, $1.25.

"This is a translation of a German work, of great reliability and value. The matter it contains has been collated from a large mass of public and private documents, and every pains has apparently been taken to render it what it professes to be, a complete History of Protestantism in Hungary. The hearty indorsement of the work contained in the introductory chapter, by Dr. Merle D'Aubigné, the distinguished author of the 'History of the Great Reformation,' will not fail to secure for the book the confidence of the Christian public, while its attractive style and instructive character entitle it to a place in the library of the clergyman, the Sabbath school, and the private Christian." —*National Era.*

Murray.

PICTORIAL HISTORY OF THE UNITED STATES OF AMERICA,

From the Earliest period to the Close of President Taylor's Administration. With Anecdotes and Sketches of distinguished leading Men. By Hugh Murray, Esq. With Additions and Corrections by Henry C. Watson. Illustrated with numerous Engravings, from original designs by W. Croome. Octavo, muslin, $3 ; library style, $3.50.

Muller and Murray.

A UNIVERSAL HISTORY OF THE WORLD,

From the Creation to the Year 1780. By John von Muller. Revised and brought down to the year 1853, by W. R. Murray, Esq. Illustrated with numerous Engravings, from original designs by S. W. Rowse. Octavo. Embossed morocco, $4.

Altogether the best compendium of the World's History to be found in one volume. The author is generally conceded to be a standard historian, and his work one of great value.

Hume, Smollet.

THE HISTORY OF ENGLAND,

From the Time of the Roman Conquest. Abridged from Hume and Smollet. Continued down to the accession of Victoria. In one volume, 12mo., illustrated. Price, $1.

Those who feel unwilling to devote so much time to English History as to read Hume, Macaulay, and later authors, will find in this careful abridgment all the leading facts important to be remembered, down to a very recent period.

Hildreth.

JAPAN, AS IT WAS AND IS,

By Richard Hildreth, author of History of the United States, &c., &c. In one volume, 12mo. With a Map. Price, $1.25.

This book embraces all that is known of this remote empire, from the earliest discoveries down to the late expedition under Commodore Perry. It will be found attractive to the general reader, as well as indispensable to the man of letters. It contains a full glossary, index, and notes.

BIOGRAPHY.

Carlyle.

THE LIFE OF JOHN STERLING,

By Thomas Carlyle. Second edition. 12mo., muslin. Price, $1.

"A model biography. The noblest tribute from his warmest friend, and the finest thing, we think, Carlyle has ever written." — *London Literary Gazette.*

"Carlyle has shown, in his Life of Sterling, that the interest of a biography is quite independent of the renown of its subject; and that superior intellectual and moral qualities, when hallowed by the sentiment of love, and revealed by appreciative recognition, form the most attractive basis of a memoir." — *H. T. Tuckerman.*

Wayland.

A MEMOIR OF THE LIFE AND LABORS OF THE REV. ADONIRAM JUDSON, D. D.

By Francis Wayland, D. D., President of Brown University. Two volumes, 12mo., with a fine Portrait. Price, in muslin, $2; muslin, gilt, $3; morocco, $3.75; half calf, $3.50; turkey morocco, $6; calf, full gilt, $6.

"It is one of the noblest monuments to true worth that the world has ever produced. Though dead, yet in these printed volumes his spirit will live and speak to this and coming generations in strains of power and eloquence such as his own tongue could never give birth to. It is an occasion of gladness to all the friends of missions that one so well qualified for the task has embalmed all this on the printed page. A sublimer theme could not be furnished any man since the apostles. Let the *Memoir* find its way to every family in the land, and it will not fail to create new sympathies, and enlist fresh zeal in that cause to which Judson gave his all." — *Philadelphia C. Chronicle.*

"To the private Christian we could not commend, next to the Bible, a more serviceable companion than these two volumes." — *American Spectator.*

"This is the union of two great names." — *Rev. Dr. Kip.*

"May it be read by thousands and thousands." — *Dr. Spencer H. Cone.*

"Its style, the deeply-interesting events which it narrates, and the personages whom it brings upon the stage of action, all contribute to make it one of the most attractive biographical sketches in the English language." — *Louisville Presbyterian Herald.*

Emerson, Channing, Clarke.

MEMOIRS OF MARGARET FULLER OSSOLI,

By Ralph W. Emerson, William Henry Channing, and James Freeman Clarke. Two volumes, 12mo., muslin. Price, $2.

"The work before us is devoted to the memory of a remarkable woman, whose life was passed in constant mental activity, whose sympathies were broad and earnest, and whose end was tragical. Genial are the pens that have here traced her brief career. Emerson, Greeley, and W. H. Channing, by whom she was intimately known, each bears interesting and truthful testimony to her gifts. Her friends in Italy also contribute their reminiscences; and her own letters fill up and illustrate the intervals of the narrative. The book is a highly valuable addition to native intellectual biography; it is a glowing and authentic history of a mind and a woman. The development is of deep psychological significance; many of the facts are remarkable; the spirit is beautiful, and the result impressive." — *Home Journal.*

Bancroft.

THE LIFE OF GEORGE WASHINGTON,

By Aaron Bancroft, D. D. In one volume, 12mo. Price, in muslin, $1 ; gilt, $1.50.

A very well written biography of the Father of his Country, from the pen of the father of the eminent historian.

THE LIFE AND CAMPAIGNS OF NAPOLEON BONAPARTE,

Translated from the French of M. A. Arnault and C. L. F. Panckoucke. In one volume, 12mo. Price, in muslin, $1; gilt, $1.50.

A graphic and reliable account of the career of Napoleon, compressed into the brief space of one readable volume.

LIVES OF THE HEROES OF THE AMERICAN REVOLUTION,

In one volume, 12mo. Price, in muslin, $1; gilt, $1.50.

A series of concisely written biographical sketches of the prominent officers in the war of Independence.

Frost.

LIVES OF THE PRESIDENTS OF THE UNITED STATES,

From Washington to Pierce; their Personal and Political History. By John Frost, LL. D. In one volume, 12mo. Price, in muslin, $1; gilt, $1.50.

An indispensable work for the politician, and a valuable work for private libraries.

ESSAYS, REVIEWS, AND LECTURES.

Emerson.

ESSAYS, BY RALPH WALDO EMERSON,

First Series, in one volume, 12mo. Price, $1. Second Series, in one volume, 12mo. Price, $1.

It is too late to present any labored analysis of the writings of Emerson, — too late to set down any eulogy. Whoever loves to deal with first principles, and is not deterred from grappling with abstract truths, will find in these essays a rare pleasure in the exercise of his powers. The popular ridicule which was heaped upon the so-called transcendental literature, at least so far as Emerson is concerned, has passed away; and these volumes are universally admitted to be among the most valuable contributions to the world's stock of ideas which our age has furnished. Every page bears the impress of thought, but it is thought subtilized, and redolent of poetry. Obscurity there is none, save to the incapable or the prejudiced, or to those averse to metaphysical speculations.

NATURE; ADDRESSES AND LECTURES,

By R. W. Emerson. In one volume, 12mo. Price, $1.

REPRESENTATIVE MEN,

Seven Lectures, by R. W. Emerson. In one volume, 12mo. Price, $1.

"It is certainly one of the most fascinating books ever written, whether we consider its subtile verbal felicities, its deep and shrewd observation, its keen criticism, its wit or learning, its wisdom or beauty. For fineness of wit, imagination, observation, satire, and sentiment, the book hardly has its equal in American literature." — *E. P. Whipple.*

"It is a thoughtful book, and better adapted to please the majority of readers than any previous attempt of the writer." — *H. T. Tuckerman.*

"This is not an ordinary book." — *London Athenæum.*

Carlyle.

CRITICAL AND MISCELLANEOUS ESSAYS,

By Thomas Carlyle. In one volume, octavo, with Portrait Price, in muslin, $1.75.

This vigorous and profound writer has been chiefly known to the public at large from the caricatures of his style published by those to whom drapery and ornament are of more consequence than vital force. The faults of Carlyle are sufficiently obvious; they lie upon the very surface; but for nicety of analysis, power, and closeness of logic, manliness of utterance, and genuine enthusiasm for what he deems the good and true. no critic is more justly entitled to admiration

THE LATER ESSAYS OF THOMAS CARLYLE,

(Latter Day Pamphlets.) In one volume, 12mo. Price, in muslin, 60 cents.

Macaulay.

ESSAYS, CRITICAL AND MISCELLANEOUS,

By Thomas Babington Macaulay, author of a History of England. In one volume, octavo, with Portrait. Price, in muslin, $2.

Whoever wishes to gain the most extensive acquaintance with English history and English literature in the briefest space of time, will read the Essays of Macaulay. It is emphatically the book to direct the student in his researches; and at the same time the brilliancy of the author's style, his learning and vast fund of information, and the pertinency of his illustrations, render his writings as fascinating to every thinking mind as the most splendid work of fiction. More scholars and critics of the present day owe their first impulse to self-culture to Macaulay than to any other writer.

"Undoubtedly the prince of the English essayists."

Sydney Smith.

THE WORKS OF REV. SYDNEY SMITH,

(Consisting principally of articles contributed to the Edinburgh Review.) In one volume, octavo, with Portrait. Price, in muslin, $1.25.

The Edinburgh Review, so long known as the leading Quarterly of Great Britain, perhaps owed its existence and its reputation more to Sydney Smith than to either of his illustrious compeers — Brougham, Macaulay, and Jeffrey. The good sense and simplicity of his style, no less than his vigorous logic and bristling wit, have rendered his name known wherever the English language is spoken. The interest in his writings will outlive the occasions which called them forth, and they may now be placed among the British classics.

Jeffrey.

CONTRIBUTIONS TO THE EDINBURGH REVIEW,

By Francis Lord Jeffrey. In one volume, octavo, with Portrait. Price, in muslin, $2.

In these articles of Jeffrey, the curious reader may see a history of English literature for the last fifty years. Now that Scott, Campbell, Wordsworth, Byron, and a few others are immortal beyond cavil or peradventure, with what interest do we look for the first impressions which their works made upon the mind of their contemporary and reviewer! Aside from his learning, vigor, acuteness, and general impartiality, Jeffrey will be read for many years to come for his association with the eminent names which have made the early part of this century so illustrious.

Wilson.

THE RECREATIONS OF CHRISTOPHER NORTH,

(Contributed to Blackwood's Magazine.) By John Wilson. In one volume, octavo, with Portrait of "Christopher in his Shooting Jacket." Price, in muslin, $1.25.

The fame of Wilson, under his chosen pseudonyme, Christopher North, is universal. The wonderful vigor, the wit, satire, fun, poetry, and criticism, all steeped through in his Tory prejudices, with which his contributions to Blackwood overflowed, commanded the attention of all parties, and have left a deep if not a permanent impression in the literature of the age. These articles are full of the author's peculiar traits. Humor and pathos succeed each other like clouds and sunshine in an April day. The character of the Scottish peasantry in some of the Recreations, is depicted with as much power as in the author's famous "Lights and Shadows of Scottish Life."

Mackintosh.

THE MISCELLANEOUS WORKS OF THE RIGHT HON. SIR JAMES MACKINTOSH,

In one volume, octavo, with Portrait. Price, in muslin, $2.

This edition contains all the miscellanies of the author, reprinted from the London edition of his works. The topics are various, from literature to politics. The Revolution of 1688, it is well known, had engaged much of the author's attention, and his articles upon that subject are among the most important and valuable in the language.

Alison.

MISCELLANEOUS ESSAYS,

By Archibald Alison, F. R. S., author of a History of Europe during the French Revolution. In one volume, octavo, with Portrait. Price, in muslin, $1.25.

The distinguished author of the History of Europe, in a series of critical articles, mostly upon modern historical, subjects, has apparently given to the world many of the studies upon which his great work is based. These Essays will be read with profit by every student of European history.

Talfourd, Stephen.

THE CRITICAL AND MISCELLANEOUS WRITINGS OF THOMAS NOON TALFOURD.

Author of "Ion," a Tragedy, &c., with a Portrait, and

THE CRITICAL AND MISCELLANEOUS ESSAYS OF JAMES STEPHEN,

In one volume, octavo. Price, in muslin, $1.25.

The author of "Ion" may surely claim a place among the classic writers of Britain. The essays here collected, though lacking the force and splendor of style that belongs to Macaulay, are among the most elegant and attractive in the language. They refer generally to lighter literary topics, instead of the severe subjects with which Mackintosh, Alison, or Carlyle choose to grapple.

Mr. Stephen, also, has long been known as among the ablest of the great modern essayists.

THE MODERN BRITISH ESSAYISTS,

Comprising the eight volumes octavo preceding. Price, in muslin, $12; in sheep, $16; half calf, or half morocco, $18.

Prescott.

BIOGRAPHICAL AND CRITICAL MISCELLANIES.

By W. H. Prescott. With a finely engraved Portrait. One volume, 8vo. Price, in cloth, $2; in sheep, $2.50; half calf, or half antique, $3; full calf, or antique, $4.

"Mr. Prescott is an elegant writer, and there is nothing that comes from his pen that does not strongly bear the marks of originality. The present volume contains a series of papers on different subjects; biography, belles-lettres, criticism, &c., in which Mr. Prescott has put forward some beautiful ideas on the attributes of mind, the formation of character, and the present condition of various sections of society. It will be read with avidity by the scholar and general inquirer." — *New Orleans Bulletin.*

www.ingramcontent.com/pod-product-compliance
Lightning Source LLC
LaVergne TN
LVHW010146110826
845151LV00002B/438

9781425537753